CRIMINAL LAW AND THE MAN PROBLEM

Men have always dominated the most basic precepts of the criminal legal world – its norms, its priorities and its character. Men have been the regulators and the regulated: the main subjects and objects of criminal law and by far the more dangerous sex. And yet men, as men, are still hardly talked about as the determining force within criminal law or in its exegesis. This book brings men into sharp focus, as the pervasively powerful interest group, whose wants and preoccupations have shaped the discipline. This constitutes the 'man problem' of criminal law.

This new analysis probes the unacknowledged thinking of generations of influential legal men, which includes the psychological and legal techniques that have obscured the operation of bias, even to the legal experts themselves. It explains how men's interests have influenced the most cherished legal norms, especially the rules of human contact, which were designed to protect men from other men, while specifically securing lawful sexual access to at least one woman. The aim is to test the discipline's broadest commitments to civility, and its trajectory towards the final resolution, when men and women were declared to be equal and equivalent legal persons. In the process it exposes the morally and intellectually limiting consequences of male power.

Criminal Law
and the Man Problem

Ngaire Naffine

·HART·

OXFORD · LONDON · NEW YORK · NEW DELHI · SYDNEY

HART PUBLISHING
Bloomsbury Publishing Plc
Kemp House, Chawley Park, Cumnor Hill, Oxford, OX2 9PH, UK

First published in Great Britain 2019
First published in hardback, 2019
Paperback edition, 2020

A catalogue record for this book is available from the British Library.

Library of Congress Cataloging-in-Publication data

Names: Naffine, Ngaire, author.
Title: Criminal law and the man problem / Ngaire Naffine, Bonython Professor of Law,
The University of Adelaide.
Description: Chawley Park, Cumnor Hill, Oxford: Bloomsbury Publishing Plc, 2019. |
Includes bibliographical references and index.
Identifiers: LCCN 2018043568 (print) | LCCN 2018044156 (ebook) |
ISBN 9781509918027 (Epub) | ISBN 9781509918010 (hardback)
Subjects: LCSH: Feminist jurisprudence. | Sex discrimination in criminal justice administration.
Classification: LCC K349 (ebook) | LCC K349.N34 2019 (print) | DDC 345/.001—dc23
LC record available at https://lccn.loc.gov/2018043568

ISBN: HB: 978-1-50991-801-0
PB: 978-1-50994-566-5
ePDF: 978-1-50991-803-4
ePub: 978-1-50991-802-7

Typeset by Compuscript Ltd, Shannon

for Margaret Davies
and Eric Richards

But man, proud man,
Dressed in a little brief authority,
Most ignorant of what he's most assured,
His glassy essence, like an angry ape
Plays such fantastic tricks before high heaven
As makes the angels weep…

William Shakespeare, *Measure for Measure*, Act 2, scene 2, 1

ACKNOWLEDGEMENTS

I have been helped by a number of people in the development and writing of this book. For their thoughtful discussions, suggestions, influence and advice along the way, I thank Frances Butterfield, Cathy Caust, Tricia Dearborn, Michael Ekin Smyth, Laura Grenfell, Paul Leadbeter, Kos Lesses, Callum and Penny McCarthy, Wilfrid Prest, Marian Richards, Allyson Robichaud, Wendy Rogers, James Stewart and Kellie Toole.

For the opportunity to deliver my ideas in a number of forums, I thank Ben Berger and the Law Faculty of Osgoode Hall Law School, Ruth Nichols and the Women's Committee of the Wellington Branch of the New Zealand Law Society, Rick Sarre as past president of the Australian and New Zealand Society of Criminology and convenor of the Society's annual conference, Lindsay Farmer as convenor of the Criminal Law Seminar Series at the University of Glasgow, Arlie Loughnan as convenor of a Criminal Law Workshop at the University of Sydney, Jeremy Gans and Patrick Keyzer as convenors of the Melbourne/Monash Criminal Law Workshop, and Manolis Melissaris and Federico Picinalias as convenors of the criminal law and justice seminar series at LSE.

I thank Gabrielle Appleby for her detailed suggestions when the book was taking shape.

For their comments on Chapter 1 I thank my Honours Research and Writing Class of 2018, and especially Kyriaco Nikias and Gerald Manning.

For his research assistance and suggestions early in the project I thank Richard Sletvold and for his excellent work in helping to get the final manuscript into shape and style, I thank Luke Hannath.

For their supreme generosity in reading and commenting on developing versions of the entire manuscript, I thank five fine scholars: Ian Leader-Elliott for his rich and remarkable understanding of criminal law; Lindsay Farmer for his deep knowledge of the history of criminal law; Niki Lacey for her inspiration as a feminist and legal scholar over many years, and her many thoughtful suggestions for improving the entire argument; Margaret Davies for making sure I got the job done, nobly shepherding the whole thing through, from proposal to final manuscript; and Eric Richards for his perpetual encouragement and for taking the final product and reading it, with a light touch.

TABLE OF CONTENTS

Introduction

Living with this book has been a disconcerting, sometimes harrowing, experience. My subject has frequently slipped from my grasp, but when I have got a firm grip on it, I have not wanted to hold on to it for too long. This is partly because the discipline of criminal law, the criminal legal world of rules and concepts and legal characters, can be fascinating but also gruesome. The cases which are the stuff of criminal jurisprudence are frankly horrible, especially the offences against the person – the crimes of murder, rape and assault – the core stuff of criminal law and the chief concern of this book.

But criminal law scholars and teachers can become inured to the sheer horror of their subject matter. One can get used to treating criminal law as a formal body of rules made up of offences, with particular component parts, all of which need careful identification, interpretation and application. Crime problems, in the class room, the study and the courts, are too easily rendered as the technical application of rules to 'fact situations'. Though this is solid intellectual work, quite consuming in itself, it can prevent one from seeing the actual people involved and their conduct: the killing, the raping, the punching. The teasing out of broader principles from this body of law, the more philosophical strand of criminal law, can also become a remarkably abstract, esoteric, cold-blooded, even a tedious exercise in fine legal scholarship.

What can go missing in all this is the very character of crime and the people who do it. And the most characteristic thing about crime is its overwhelming maleness. Most violent criminals are men. Maleness is also the overwhelming characteristic of the people who have made the criminal legal world – its norms, priorities and characters. Men are both the regulators and the regulated: the main subjects and objects of criminal law. And yet men, as men, are still hardly talked about as the ruling personnel within criminal law and its exegesis. This reality is disconcerting because it seems to be 'the elephant in the room'. And the trained criminal law scholar, even one of feminist persuasion, can easily start doubting the existence of this male 'elephant', which is so rarely referred to or even seen. Try finding the subject 'men' in any textbook of criminal law.

The man problem, which forms the subject of this book, is the problem of men permeating the discipline of criminal law in so thorough and yet natural-seeming a manner, that it is hard to see them at all, and it is also hard to convince that this is so. Men, as men, I will argue, have been so basic to how we think of criminal law, and its very idea of what it is to be human, that it is difficult to demonstrate this simple fact.

The persons of criminal law, in their various guises, are typically portrayed as beings without a sex, as simply human beings. They are also treated as beings whom the law respects equally. The sex of the person is not meant to matter or even count. Blame and protection of the person is not meant to depend on their sex. I will argue that in important ways the persons of criminal law were and are still men and that this has undermined the claims of criminal law and lawyers that theirs is a principled institution concerned equally with the wrongdoing and welfare of all.

My task is to find and display men as the principal, but suppressed, characters of criminal law: they are its makers, its interpreters, explainers and justifiers, and also its subjects. My man problem is therefore, at least, a double problem. There is the problem that men, as men, populate and inhabit the criminal law in virtually every capacity, and therefore criminal law necessarily has a strongly male orientation. This is a problem because criminal law claims to be neutral in its attitude to persons; it claims not to be oriented more towards one sex than the other, and this gender neutrality is indeed vital to its very legitimacy. Then there is the problem that men inhabit criminal law in such a thoroughgoing and comprehensive fashion that, paradoxically, they can barely be seen. It is therefore difficult to discern the male orientation of criminal law: with so many men, and so few women, paradoxically, men become all but invisible. They simply look like the normal case of the person.

My task is to flush out the men of criminal law and see how their maleness, their sex specificity rather than their general humanity, has shaped and formed concepts, theories, norms and also self-understandings of the discipline. And the authors of these self-understandings are the influential male interpreters of criminal law. This is partly why this is such a hard problem to expound and expose.

This book is about criminal law in general, but it makes particular use of an offence which has assumed great moral and intellectual significance for the discipline: the crime of rape. It makes the nature and scope of the offence of rape the acid test of criminal law thinking and its moral claims about its impartial, objective respect for our persons. Along with murder, rape has been treated as the most heinous of crimes requiring absolute condemnation. Such condemnation has been considered an important metric of the civility of society and its central institutions. At the same time the men of law have deployed criminal law, in matters of rape, to override these fundamental duties not to use force, in order to give men lawful access to the persons of certain women, while accepting preclusion from others. A stoutly-defended exemption from the crime of rape was awarded to every man at marriage and persisted to the last decade of the twentieth century. This suggests a profound tension in criminal legal thinking: the simultaneous condemnation and approval of the use of force.

Criminal law is meant to condemn harmful acts and to respect everyone, equally, as persons. But the husband's immunity in rape law had the opposite effect. This clash of principle calls for explanation and so does the fundamental legal reasoning which sustained it.

My aim is to test the discipline's broadest commitments to civility and to neutrality, by tracing the trajectory of this particular law and the scholarly and judicial reasoning that has gone into its justification and defence and its final dissolution. Though I use the husband's rape immunity as a crucial case study, my broader purpose is to take a view of the discipline of criminal law as a whole. I consider its most fundamental suppositions about who we are and the sort of society we should live in.

Over the course of this book I will examine the histories and interests of the influential legal men and their priorities for criminal law. I will examine the writings of mainly English jurists from the seventeenth century to the present day on the uses of criminal law not only to secure sexual access to a woman, but to amplify the legal personhood of men, and I will also consider the various intellectual and psychological devices which they developed to cover over and conceal their interests, including to themselves.

The book proceeds in the following way. In Chapter 1 I get up close to my problem by focusing on a landmark case involving a harrowing serial rape masterminded by the victim's husband. My aim here is to reveal the responses of the discipline to the fact that the husband was excused from the charge of rape as a principal offender, precisely because he was married to his victim. Put simply, this exoneration of the husband barely registered with the legal experts, and when it did register, it tended to be approved as good law. In Chapter 2 I develop a more panoramic view of the criminal law, its persons and its places, which turns out to be an essentially male habitat. Then, in Chapter 3, I commence my examination of the leading men of criminal law who have been responsible for the making of this male world. I trace the development of criminal legal thinking about appropriate male conduct: from Lord Hale and William Blackstone (Chapter 3) to James Fitzjames Stephen and John Stuart Mill (Chapter 4). I then identify the cast of men implicit in this body of legal thought (Chapter 5). I call them the sexual master, the little monarch and the bounded individual. In Chapter 6 I consider the development of male criminal legal thinking in the early- to middle-twentieth century, focusing on Glanville Williams and his contemporaries.

In Chapter 7 I explore the processes of legal modernisation, when the rape immunity was finally dropped, and men and women were declared to be equal and equivalent legal persons. Chapter 8 looks at the current generation of criminal legal scholars and the intellectual and moral tensions generated by their insalubrious legal past. Male right to and control of a woman was important to their predecessors: this sense of male right was manifested in the law of rape, but it was by no means confined to this law. It applied to a number of other laws, perhaps most egregiously to the criminal law of murder so that (until quite recently) male rage with an unfaithful wife could reduce murder to manslaughter. What do the current generation make of this generous legal treatment of angry and sexually controlling men which was sustained for so long? Here I consider how internal tensions in legal thinking have been rationalised and reconciled. In Chapter 9 I characterise the modern individual who has emerged as the central person of modern criminal law: ostensibly of no sex but really more man than woman. In Chapter 10 I review the implications of all this for the modern world. If anything, men as the central characters of criminal law have become even harder to discern, and their past dominance simply forgotten. As I will show, the costs to modern criminal law, as a fair and reflective discipline, and as a civilising mechanism, are considerable.

The argument to be sustained throughout this book is that the common-sense view of the central characters of criminal law, and their basic needs and interests, supposedly reflected in core criminal law, has been developed from a particular stance: that of men of legal influence. The common-sense view has therefore been particular to men, but presented as universal and unproblematic. The men who have forged the character of the criminal legal person and his apparent needs, and the world he is thought to inhabit, have neglected their own role as the makers or forgers of persons, and so they have not considered how persons might otherwise be.

The man problem of criminal law is in large part the problem of powerful men of law, responsible for the making of law, not knowing what it is like to be other than themselves and so, sometimes unwittingly, casting the law in their own image. Women have perhaps been the most alien creatures to criminal law, and their interests have been readily subsumed into those of the powerful sex. The thinking and interests of women, as conscious reflective subjects, as independent legal experts, are remarkably absent from the history of criminal law. This is not mere neglect. As we will see, throughout this book, there is ample evidence of the men of law doing their level best to ensure that women could not stand beside them as figures of authority: as lawyers, as lawmakers, as members of the polity, as legal critics and analysts, as 'persons' legally understood. The result has been a limited and limiting community of lawmakers and interpreters, marked by vested interests and, in the past, by the misuses of law.

This is not to say that the sins of the fathers must be visited on the sons and daughters of the discipline. Rather the point is more, though not exclusively, an intellectual one: that this misogynist narrative, which has formed the criminal legal world and its persons, needs to be actively considered by modern-day thinkers if they are to explain and develop modern criminal legal norms that have purchase and that live and operate in the real world of men and women.

Men of law have been a closed community deeply ignorant of the limitations of their thinking and of their investment in those limitations. The modern criminal lawyer needs to take all of this into account when testing (or asserting) the principled nature of modern core criminal law which has grown out of this male-oriented thinking. The uniform maleness of the legal past should generate concerns of a moral and intellectual nature. And yet the paradoxical effect of this saturation of male interests has been to make men less rather than more visible: to make men harder to discern as characters of interest for criminal law, which is so directly concerned with the conduct, or rather misconduct, of men.

1

The Problem Illustrated: The Landmark Marital Rape Case of *DPP v Morgan* and Its Mixed Significance for the Men of Law

In this first chapter I introduce and illustrate the man problem of criminal law, using a House of Lords decision of the 1970s: *DPP v Morgan*.[1] This is a landmark rape case (the facts of which will be disclosed shortly), still invoked as such today.[2] By close inspection of the legal responses to this famous case, I will 'tweezer out'[3] my principal male characters: the men of criminal law as they give voice to men and their interests. I will begin my task of bringing legal men to the fore, as an enormously powerful interest group, whose wants and preoccupations have shaped the discipline of criminal law, often in silent and obscured ways. This is my 'man problem' of criminal law, which forms the subject of this book.

In *DPP v Morgan* (*Morgan*) the actions and intentions of the main protagonist William Morgan, the husband who raped his wife, were graphic and horrific and not in doubt. Indeed Morgan orchestrated the serial rape of his wife, yet he was not prosecuted as the principal offender. This alone is perhaps a shocking thing. But my interest is in the variety of reactions of legal men of influence to this case (which lets the husband off as principal rapist) and to the marital immunity more generally. Some men of influence take the husband's immunity from prosecution as a given, a background feature of criminal law, perhaps an unsavoury thing, but one that does not need to be gone into. Others treat the immunity as a positive good. Still others proceed as if it does not exist, for it is such a male partisan law, and really their arguments about the general character of criminal law, and especially its claims for civility, depend on the immunity's non-existence.

---

[1] *DPP v Morgan* [1975] UKHL 3, [1976] AC 182.

[2] See, eg Lindsay Farmer, '*DPP v Morgan*' in Henry Mares, Phil Handler and Ian Williams (eds), *Landmark Cases in Criminal Law* (Oxford, Hart, 2017).

[3] Here I am borrowing a term from Grayson Perry in Grayson Perry, 'The Rise and Fall of Default Man: How did the straight, white, middle-class Default Man take control of our society – and how can he be dethroned?' *New Statesman* (London, 8 October 2014) www.newstatesman.com/culture/2014/10/grayson-perry-rise-and-fall-default-man. Perry developed his analysis of this character in Grayson Perry, *The Descent of Man* (Allen Lane, 2016).

I start with the Law Lord who gave one of the majority judgments in *Morgan* and move on to examine the scholarly community and their diverse reactions. Considered together, these views do not cohere and indeed these jurists do not seem to be talking to each other or about the same thing. They seem to be operating at different levels of criminal law and addressing different audiences, and to different ends. What they share is a failure to consider, closely and critically, the immunity from prosecution of men who raped their wives, what it meant for their own sex as responsible citizens and what it meant for criminal law at large. And this is in spite of their intense interest in the crime of rape, treated as a horror crime – judicially, doctrinally, conceptually and philosophically.

There is here a curious mix of attention and inattention. None of these influential men reflects carefully and critically on the non-responsibility of the husband. None reflects on the implications for criminal law as a body of principle. This is odd, for when criminal law is being thought of as a moral force, as a mechanism for civility, the crime of rape is treated as one that is universally wrong and universally condemned. Simply put, this philosophical criminal jurisprudence treats the crime of rape as if the immunity were not there.

I. Introducing the Men of Legal Influence: The Cast of Characters

There is firstly **the judge** in the case of *Morgan* who describes the facts unflinchingly and graphically and then explains in a single sentence, without further comment, that the husband was not prosecuted for rape because of 'an ancient doctrine' that he should be immune from prosecution. He does not look away from the violence of Morgan, but he makes little of the law that does not punish him as a husband. This is put to one side.

Secondly, we have the **textbooks writers** on criminal law, and its organising principles, who must be fully aware of the case, or cases like it, but who persist with a defence of the immunity that is based on a very different understanding of its nature and significance. Implicitly they exceptionalise *Morgan* and do not refer to it. In these accounts of rape and its law, when husbands force sex, it is because the marriage has gone a bit wrong and the bumbling husband is trying to fix things up. He is making a hash of an attempt at rapprochement and asserting his authority as a masterful husband. These legal men are intensely concerned with the interests of the husband but this is the husband benignly understood, as if the theorist were projected into his shoes or pajamas. He is horrified at the very idea of criminal law entering his bedroom.

Thirdly, there are **the doctrinal and conceptual scholars** who examine the case of *Morgan* as an important illustration of a so-called 'core' or serious crime, and the conditions of liability that such a crime should attract. They accept the view of the court that this is a case about the mental element of rape (by a non-husband) and they focus exclusively on what it has to say about subjective criminal responsibility: whether the defendant must realise that his victim is non-consenting; whether an unreasonable belief in consent will excuse. *Morgan* is repeatedly examined by such scholars for its pronouncements on the need for subjective responsibility for serious crimes: the need for the accused to intend the prohibited act in order to be blameworthy. But it is largely invisible to the scholarly community as a marital rape case – or rather as a case where the main rapist was considered legally incapable of rape, as a principal, despite the clear presence of a subjective mental element (he absolutely knew his wife was not consenting), and so was not charged as such.

With these doctrinal scholars there is also something very odd going on because it is the seriousness of the crime that is the reason for the call for subjective responsibility, but the non-application of such serious criminal law to the husband (despite his subjective appreciation that his wife does not want to be forcibly penetrated) is not of note. It is not seen. It is as if they are assuming that such a serious crime, calling for subjective mens rea, were comprehensively criminalised, though the case before them shows that it is not. (There are also the feminists expressing outrage that the unreasonable belief should excuse and who ultimately win the day in England, but not immediately.)

Fourthly, there are the **legal scholars as philosophers** who are trying to make sense of criminal law as a whole, as a body of moral and social norms, and its role in securing a civil society, and who assert, with confidence, that rape *is* a core horror crime which *must* be criminalised and who proceed with their theories of criminal law as if the law did actually comprehensively punish all rapists, husbands included. With this 'as if' built into their theories, they make comprehensive criminalisation and condemnation of rape a major test of the very legitimacy and civility of criminal law. The husband's immunity does not fit into this scheme and it is not referred to.

So my four types of men of legal influence, and their thoughts about men and the crime of rape, its seriousness and its scope and its significance, are The Judge, The Textbook Writer as Husband, the Doctrinal Legal Scholar and The Legal Scholar as Political Philosopher.

II. The View from the Bench and the Man of Law as Judge: Lord Hailsham of St Marylebone and *DPP v Morgan*

Lord Hailsham, who delivered the leading majority judgment in *Morgan* (the one most cited) gives a vivid, memorable, almost novelesque, account of the words and actions of William Morgan which leaves us in no doubt about Morgan's cruelty and his malignant character. He abuses his position of military authority, he abuses his friendships, he incites and enables a serial rape and he rapes his wife after having helped to hold all her limbs apart while his three friends rape her first.

The main legal question for the court, says Lord Hailsham, is one 'of great academic importance in the theory of English criminal law', and it concerns 'the mental element in rape'.[4] The question is 'Whether, in rape, the defendant can properly be convicted notwithstanding that he in fact believed that the woman consented, if such belief was not based on reasonable grounds'.[5] This is cast as a formal question of 'academic importance' but his is no dry legal judgment. It is vivid and visual.

Lord Hailsham describes the facts as given by Daphne Morgan and as accepted by the court graphically, with concision and in ordinary non-legal language. In fact his is an example of lucid and highly visual legal writing, which takes us to the scenes of the crime:

> The question arises in the following way. The appellant Morgan and his three co-defendants, who were all members of the R.A.F., spent the evening of the 15th August, 1973, in one another's company. The appellant Morgan was significantly older than the other three, and considerably senior to them in rank.[6]

We are told that William Morgan and his three friends had spent an evening together in Wolverhampton, drinking. 'Their original intention had been to find some women in the town, but when this failed, Morgan made the surprising suggestion to the others that they should all return to his home and have sexual intercourse with his wife'.[7]

As Hailsham explains, according to the three friends, Morgan had told them that his wife was 'kinky' and that she enjoyed feigning resistance to sex and so they should ignore such resistance.[8] It was on this basis, they said, that they went back to Morgan's home. Hailsham sets the scene in the home and in the bedrooms.

> [William Morgan] was, as I have said, married to the alleged victim, but not, it seems at the time habitually sleeping in the same bed. At this time, Mrs Morgan occupied a single bed in the same room as her younger son aged about eleven years, and by the time the appellants arrived at Morgan's house, Mrs Morgan was already in bed and asleep, until she was awoken by their presence.

> According to the version of the facts which she gave in evidence and which was evidently accepted by the jury, she was aroused from her sleep, frog-marched into another room where there was a double bed, held by each of her limbs, arms and legs apart, by the four appellants, while each of the three young appellants in turn had intercourse with her in the presence of the others, during which time the other two committed various lewd acts upon various parts of her body. When each had finished and had left the room, the appellant Morgan completed the series of incidents by having intercourse with her himself.[9]

---

[4] *DPP v Morgan* [1975] UKHL 3 at 5, [1976] AC 182 at 204.
[5] Ibid 5, 205.
[6] Ibid 6, 205.
[7] Ibid 7, 206.
[8] Ibid.
[9] Ibid 6, 205.

Hailsham gives a stomach-churning account of the rapes, drawing on the evidence of Daphne Morgan which is accepted by the court. He reveals her fear for her life, the seizing of all her limbs, her screaming, the sheer brutality employed.

> According to Mrs Morgan she consented to none of this and made her opposition to what was being done very plain indeed. In her evidence to the Court, she said that her husband was the first to seize her and pull her out of bed. She then 'yelled' to the little boy who was sleeping with her to call the police, and later, when the elder boy came out on the landing, she called to him to get the police and 'screamed'. Her assailants, however, covered her face and pinched her nose, until she begged them to let her breathe. She was held, wrists and feet, 'dragged' to the neighbouring room, put on the bed where the various incidents occurred. At this stage she was overcome with fear of 'being hit'. There was never a time when her body was free from being held. When it was all over she grabbed her coat, ran out of the house, drove straight to the hospital and immediately complained to the staff of having been raped. The last fact was fully borne out by evidence from the hospital.[10]

This is bold, concrete, active writing, which avoids the passive voice. And you can feel the moral outrage of the judge. This is revolting male behaviour, to be condemned utterly.

Morgan's three friends are charged with rape as principal offenders and also with aiding and abetting the principal offences of each other. The fourth defendant, William Morgan, is not charged with rape as a principal offender as the prosecution accepted the common law doctrine that a husband could not rape his wife. I will return to this shortly.

The defence of the three co-defendants of *Morgan* concerned their mental element. They argued that they did not have the necessary guilty mind for the crime of rape because they had believed Morgan – that is, they believed that his wife enjoyed sex in which she was forced but only feigned resistance. Therefore they honestly believed that she was consenting. The three men also maintained that Mrs Morgan was an active participant in the sex (they said that events had not proceeded as she said they had) but that she had enjoyed the various acts of sexual intercourse. Again in Lord Hailsham's graphic language: by their account 'she not merely consented but took an active and enthusiastic part in a sexual orgy which might have excited unfavourable comment in the Courts of Caligula or Nero'.[11] Thus their account was obviously diametrically at odds with the story of Daphne Morgan.

Daphne Morgan's view of the events was accepted, not theirs. And as Lord Hailsham made clear, having accepted Daphne Morgan's account, there really was no room for any argument that the appellants believed that she was consenting. That is to say, if they had done what she said they did and if she had responded as she said she did, they could not have believed she was consenting. It simply was not a credible story. On the facts, the court found the claims of belief in consent

---

[10] Ibid 6, 205–206.
[11] Ibid 7, 206.

preposterous. Whatever the law on the mental element, there was no miscarriage of justice.

Lord Hailsham's primary task, however, as he conceived it (and as it was put to the House of Lords by the Court of Appeal), was to consider the direction that had been made to the jury that the defendants' belief in consent, in order to excuse, had not only to be an honest but also a reasonable one. This was the main point of principle. The appellants maintained that it was a misdirection. Was this good law? According to Lord Hailsham:

> Once one has accepted, what seems to me to be abundantly clear, that the prohibited act in rape is non-consensual sexual intercourse, and that the guilty state of mind is an intention to commit it, it seems to me to follow as a matter of inexorable logic that there is no room either for a 'defence' of honest mistake or belief, or of a defence of honest and reasonable belief or mistake. Either the prosecution proves that the accused had the requisite intent, or it does not. ... Since honest belief clearly negatives intent, the reasonableness or otherwise of that belief can only be evidence for or against the view that the belief and therefore the intent was actually held.[12]

He went on to say:

> A failure to prove this [intention] involves an acquittal because the intent, an essential ingredient, is lacking. It matters not why it is lacking if only it is not there, and in particular it matters not that the intention is lacking only because of a belief not based on reasonable grounds.[13]

This is what the case came to stand for and what attracted controversy and debate. Rape was one of the most serious crimes possible and as a very serious crime, the Court said, the accused should only be blamed if he subjectively understood that thing that made the crime a crime, logically and morally, which in the case of rape was that he did not have consent.

In *Morgan* there was barely a murmur from the highest English court about the spousal immunity. Implicitly it was accepted, with minimal comment, that William Morgan himself, who was understood to have orchestrated all the rapes, and was fully in the picture, could not be held responsible as a principal offender, and thus called to account, even though this best characterised his role. He was the central character in what happened, in fact but not in law.

Lord Hailsham explains, in the most sparing terms, in fact in one sentence, the decision of the prosecution not to proceed against Mr Morgan as a principal offender.

> The appellant Morgan, who also had connexion with his wife allegedly without her consent as part of the same series of events, was not charged with rape, the prosecution evidently accepting and applying the ancient common law doctrine that a husband cannot be guilty of raping his own wife.[14]

---

[12] Ibid 13, 214.
[13] Ibid 14, 215.
[14] Ibid 5, 205.

And this was why Morgan was charged with and convicted of only the offences of aiding and abetting the rapes of the other three. He was charged as an enabler of rape, not as a rapist.

What is striking about Lord Hailsham's brief statement about the immunity from prosecution of the husband is both its brevity and its tone and style. We know that Lord Hailsham is capable of vivid graphic language and of moral outrage. He does not adopt a distant and bloodless judicial stance. His description of the rapes lets us visualise everything, to see and also feel the cruelty and the rough treatment: it has filmic qualities and is almost designed to incite rage against the offenders. The alternative account of what happened, that concocted by the defendants and rejected by the court, is also described by Hailsham in vivid, even florid, prose with its references to Roman despots.

The brief reference to the husband's immunity however – the reason given why William Morgan is not charged with rape as a rapist, only as a helper or enabler – is dry and legalistic. Morgan 'had connexion' and 'allegedly without her consent'. The extreme violence is no longer pictured. Forced penetration is 'connexion'. The 'ancient common law doctrine' is the 'apparent' reason for non-prosecution. Lord Hailsham is deeply exercised by most of the violence and indignities done to Daphne Morgan, the 'various lewd acts upon various parts of her body'. But the husband as rapist is barely considered. There is no reference to any moral or legal wrong in a husband raping his wife and it is simply accepted that legally he cannot.

The facts of Morgan's 'rape' of his wife are also disposed of in a single sentence. To restate it: 'When each had finished and had left the room, the appellant Morgan completed the series of incidents by having intercourse with her himself'.[15] 'Having intercourse' seems a particularly infelicitous term to apply to what actually happened: following a series of brutal rapes, the terrorised wife was then raped (in fact but not in law) by her husband. But this is not said and instead William Morgan is permitted to disappear from legal view, into the bedroom.

Perhaps it could be said, in Lord Hailsham's defence, that his hands were tied by the decision of the prosecution not to proceed against Morgan, as principal offender. After all, it is not up to the judge to decide the charges that will be laid against the accused and brought before the court. And indeed Hailsham does allude to the prosecution's thinking and their evident acceptance of the 'ancient' common law immunity of husbands from rape prosecution. But he could have said a little more than this. If he were unhappy with the state of the law, he could have offered some critical comment on it, no matter how oblique, as judges are wont to do.

---

[15] Ibid 6, 205.

III. The Textbook Writer as Husband

Did marital rape therefore slip under the legal radar when rape was discussed by legal scholars, as it often was? No it did not; on the contrary. So what did contemporary legal experts think of the immunity?

Around the time of *Morgan*, a number of England's and Australia's most influential academic experts in criminal law scrutinised and endorsed the husband's immunity. They even examined the force needed to rape an unwilling wife and tried to figure out which forceful acts were lawful and which were not. They arrived at different views about the degree of force that could be lawfully used.

There was no doubt in their minds, however, that marital rape per se was lawful and rightly so. The differences of agreement were about whether the attendant force would give rise to other offences against the person, such as assault, the rape itself remaining lawful. None expressed deep concern about the immunity or found it of great intellectual or moral interest. Some explained why it made good sense. Later, when it looked like the immunity would be abolished, England's most eminent criminal law scholar actively protested.

The easy acceptance of the immunity, and the assumed good sense of it, was evident in the scholarship emerging from the leading law schools of England and Australia. Twenty years before *Morgan*, in 1954, Norval Morris and AL Turner, then senior lecturers in law at the University of Melbourne, had countenanced and supported the use of force by a husband against a wife in the following terms.

> Intercourse … is a privilege at least and perhaps a right and a duty inherent in the matrimonial state, accepted as such by husband and wife. … There will … be some cases where … the wife may consistently repel her husband's advances. If the wife is adamant in her refusal the husband must choose between letting his wife's will prevail, thus wrecking the marriage, or acting without her consent. It would be intolerable if he were to be conditioned in his course of action by the threat of criminal proceedings for rape.[16]

Norval Morris went on to become Dean of Adelaide Law School and then one of the world's leading criminologists, based in Chicago, and was in other ways a great liberal reformer, concerned about the plight of prisoners. It was in his attitude to women and wife rape that he showed incivility and partiality. I know of no endeavours by Morris to explain, excuse or rescind these views. And yet Morris, with Turner, imagined wife rape as a sort of marital difficulty. If a wife got out of hand, behaved wilfully, if she assumed unnatural authority, the husband might have to take charge, and assert himself in this sexual manner, and he would be wise to do so. This was not a matter for criminal law. This view of the commanding husband, who overcomes the will of a recalcitrant wife, for the sake of the

---

[16] Norval Morris and AL Turner, 'Two Problems in the Law of Rape' (1954) 2 *University of Queensland Law Journal* 247, 259.

marriage, is redolent of the thinking of Soames Forsythe in John Galsworthy's *Forsyte Saga*,[17] after Soames has raped his wife. Soames suppresses his guilt and remorse and comes to see the sense in what he has done.

In 1965 the author of Australia's leading textbook on criminal law, Colin Howard, declared that:

> [A] husband should not walk in the shadow of the law of rape in trying to regulate his sexual relationships with his wife. If a marriage runs into difficulty, the criminal law should not give to either party to the marriage the power to visit more misery upon the other than is unavoidable in the nature of things.[18]

The power that should not be granted was power to the wife, though Howard misleadingly describes it as a grant of power to either party. Howard obviously speaks here for the husband. He also implicitly aligns the interests of the husband and the wife in affording immunity to the husband and so eliminating the rights of the wife. Rape should not form the basis of the breakdown of a marriage. He does not question the compatibility of rape and marriage.

Glanville Williams, England's pre-eminent criminal legal scholar for much of the twentieth century, maintained a consistent position on the domestic power of the husband which he implicitly and explicitly endorsed. In 1947 he adopted a playful attitude to male right in an article on the marital unity principle – the principle that husband and wife are legally one person – published in the *Modern Law Review*. Though the marital unity principle was a 'venerable maxim',[19] he appreciated that 'the spouses' do not 'participate equally in the personality that is thus created for them'.[20] Instead 'it would be closer to the rules of the common law to say, in the words of the wag, that "man and wife are one – but the one is the man"'.[21] He added, waggishly, that 'The wife was not reduced to the position in law of say, a dog'.[22]

In his criminal law textbook, in his exposition of the law of rape Williams suggested that men were masterful beings and women enjoyed mastery. With no contemporary evidence to support it he said 'That some women enjoy fantasies of being raped' and that 'they may, to some extent, welcome a masterful advance while putting up a token resistance'.[23]

Williams was a stalwart defender of the husband's immunity from rape prosecution for a good portion of the twentieth century. As late as 1992, Williams made his husband's viewpoint plain when he persisted with his defence of the immunity and gave a variety of explanations and defences of the misguided husband. He said, with faux modesty, that 'I speak with the handicap of being a male, but a man

---

[17] John Galsworthy, *The Forsyte Saga: The Man of Property* (William Heinemann, 1906).
[18] Colin Howard, *Australian Criminal Law* (Melbourne, The Law Book Company, 1965) 146.
[19] Glanville Williams, 'The Legal Unity of Husband and Wife' (1947) 10 *Modern Law Review* 16, 16.
[20] Ibid 17.
[21] Ibid.
[22] Ibid 18.
[23] Glanville Williams, *Textbook of Criminal Law*, 2nd edn (London, Stevens and Sons, 1983) 238.

can empathise with the female victim of crime, and anyway I take courage from the support of some women (including the woman most important to me), even though they are not the vociferous ones'.[24]

After all, the husband might act 'in pursuance of what he misguidedly thinks of as his rights' or he might be 'suffering from an unbearable sense of the loss of his partner by separation' or 'he may even, stupidly, think that by forcing himself upon her he may regain her affection' or he might be 'distraught by what he regards as the unfaithfulness of his wife'.[25] And anyway 'rape by a cohabitee ... though horrible cannot be so horrible and terrifying as rape by a stranger'.[26] For all of these reasons the foolish husband 'deserves some consideration'.[27]

In 1978 the distinguished English legal scholar Tony Honoré, in a volume dedicated to 'sex law', declared that

> Although the rule about rape survives, it can now only be justified on the basis that it is undesirable for the criminal courts to pry into the exact degree of force or pressure used by a husband in order to have intercourse with his wife. Such matters are best raised, if at all, in matrimonial proceedings under the heading of cruelty or conduct which is not reasonably tolerable'.[28]

It became a different matter once divorce proceedings were commenced. Then

> it would be rational to say that she has thereby withdrawn her consent to intercourse. ... If the spouses separate under a voluntary agreement, the wife can presumably be raped, since, depending on the terms of the agreement, she has no duty to live with her husband and so no duty to submit to sexual intercourse.[29]

Honoré conjured up a forceful man applying pressure to his wife 'to submit' to his strong sexual advances. Honoré spoke for the husband, and again he was a masterful man who should not face the rigours of criminal law.

These scholars openly examined both the intentions and motives of husbands determined to inflict sex on an unwilling wife and declared that if the motive were to assert a husband's right to sex, the intention to proceed without consent did not and should not make the conduct rape. Thus motive (to assert 'marital right') and intention (to proceed in the knowledge that there was no consent) were blended in a manner which was untypical of approved criminal analysis and produced a perverse result. (Motive and intention are treated as separate mental states in criminal law, and only intention is critical to culpability. It is usually said that the motive is irrelevant, whether it is a good or bad motive.)

If a husband's intentions were to 'rape' his wife, that is, deliberately to overcome, by force, her defence of herself, to secure sexual entry without her consent, there should be no criminal wrong here. This intention to proceed with unwanted sex

---

[24] Glanville Williams, 'Rape is Rape' (1992) 142 *New Law Journal* 11, 12.
[25] Ibid 13.
[26] Ibid 12.
[27] Ibid 13.
[28] Tony Honoré, *Sex Law* (London, Duckworth, 1978) 22–23.
[29] Ibid 23.

when it was motivated by an assertion of a husband's right *neutralised* rather than *made* the criminal wrong. Legal men of influence gathered around the husband intent on so-called marital sex[30] without consent, to preserve him from such serious criminal law.

Influential scholars did not flinch in their discussions of the lawful use of sexual force needed to obtain sex with an unwilling wife: in effect the right to apply force to prevent a wife defending herself from attack. To Smith and Hogan, 'the law does not leave the wife defenceless against violence by her husband. In *Miller* Lynskey J held that though the husband had a right to sexual intercourse, he was not entitled to use force or violence in order to exercise that right'.[31] Then quoting *Miller*[32] as authority for the point: 'Thus if he should wound her, he might be charged with wounding or causing bodily harm, or he may be liable to be convicted of common assault'.[33]

Smith and Hogan therefore distinguished the compulsion required to achieve non-consenting sex, and placed it outside the offences against the person. But if the compulsion should lead to injury, then the criminal law had work to do.

To Glanville Williams, in the 1978 edition of his textbook, 'As the law is now interpreted it does not save the courts from investigating the difficult question of the wife's consent because although a husband cannot be prosecuted for rape he can be prosecuted for assault for doing the self-same thing. The law is thus inconsistent with itself'.[34] Here again there is open contemplation of the lawful and unlawful sexual violence within a marriage, but no censure.

In 1977 and again in 1982 Colin Howard implicitly disagreed with Williams' analysis. He delved into the degrees of violence that the criminal law would tolerate from the husband wanting sex from an unwilling wife and explicitly contemplated the idea of justified force to achieve sex with a wife. He surmised that

> Logically, since rape is an aggravated assault by the fact of intercourse, it follows that if V cannot withhold her consent to intercourse she cannot withhold her consent to an assault made for the purpose of accomplishing intercourse; so that the law of assault cannot reach a husband who attacks his wife unless the attack is not for the purpose of overcoming her resistance to sexual relations.[35]

In other words, as long as the husband precisely had the mental element for rape, if his intentions were to assert his marital rights in the absence of consent (the blend of motive and intention), he could not only rape without legal culpability but he could lawfully use the force required to achieve it – to overcome his wife's defence of her person. It was only if the husband employed 'unjustifiable brutality' that he might be convicted of assault 'whatever his object may have been'.[36]

[30] The force, violence and physical pain and probable injury are filleted out with the term 'marital sex'.
[31] JC Smith and Brian Hogan, *Criminal Law* (London, Butterworths, 1965) 292.
[32] *R v Miller* [1954] 2 QB 282.
[33] Smith and Hogan, above n 31 at 292.
[34] Glanville Williams, *Textbook of Criminal Law* (London, Stevens & Sons, 1978) 195–196.
[35] Colin Howard, *Australian Criminal Law*, 4th edn (Law Book Co, 1982) 163.
[36] Ibid.

What is clear is that, to the leading textbook writers around the time of *Morgan*, the most serious crime of rape did not (and should not) include a man's rape of his wife. A husband should receive 'protection' from rape law, as Howard termed it.[37] And indeed the experts openly contemplated and seemingly endorsed a further area of immunity from criminal prosecution: for the assaults the man needed to commit in order to achieve penetration without his wife's consent. Men were entitled to overcome a wife's resistance, to overcome her attempts at self-defence.

It is important to remember that Williams and Howard were not only writing the texts, but they held the levers of law making; they sat on or advised the government committees that provided critical recommendations about the future of law. Thus they provided instrumental advice, in the interests of men and against those of women.[38]

And yet in other ways these legal men were committed to a principled criminal law. Glanville Williams was a liberal progressive thinker who campaigned for abortion and euthanasia rights. Norval Morris campaigned for the rights of prison inmates. It is this progressivism which makes their thinking about male character and the rights of husbands over wives more striking and perhaps more indelible. It suggests an entrenched system of thought and engrained attitudes and a lack of reflection about the problems of consistency with basic criminal law principle.

Singularly missing from the scholarly thoughts about rape of Williams and Howard and Morris and Honoré is the point of view of the wife, as she confronts the husband employing lawful force against her, as he enforces his lawful right to her body and perhaps engages in 'rougher than usual handling', as one South Australian judge put it.[39] What is her view of her assailant? Is he Williams' bumbling and desperate husband, misjudging the situation? Is she Norval Morris's uppity wife? What is her view of the law which supports his actions and denies her the possibility of complaint? Is she a member of the citizenry for whom the law is made? Is she a member of the polis?

IV. Eyes Wide Shut

What these influential scholars are failing to see is wife rape as a crime of inherent violence, one which is likely to induce mortal fear in the person whose 'will' is

[37] Ibid. The husband's 'protection' from rape conviction is the way Howard puts it.

[38] For example, Howard sat on the influential South Australian Mitchell Committee in 1976 which recommended the criminalisation of wife rape, but only after the husband and wife had separated: Criminal Law and Penal Methods Reform Committee of South Australia, 'Special report: rape and other sexual offences' (1976). The government of the day went further and partially criminalised rape in marriage while the husband and wife were still living together.

[39] See Bollen J in *R v David Norman Johns*, Supreme Court of South Australia, No SCCRM/91/452, 26 August 1992. In the words of Bollen J: 'There is, of course, nothing wrong with a husband, faced with his wife's initial refusal to engage in intercourse, in attempting, in an acceptable way, to persuade her to change her mind, and that may involve a measure of rougher than usual handling'.

overcome. They are seeing it from a highly selective male point of view and they are thinking of the rights of the husband, not of the wife. A brutal illustration of wife rape was open to view in *DPP v Morgan*, and Lord Hailsham's description of the rapes is graphic and horrifying. But despite the prominence that *Morgan* comes to assume in legal thinking, this is not the sort of rape that the men of law have in their mind's eye. Rather they are visualising a difficult woman and a bumbling or commanding husband, depending on the scholar.

Nor do these scholarly men turn their minds to the normal, even mundane, foundational concern of criminal law – which is to protect our personal security, our bodies, from unwanted interference. This most basic of rights, to exclude others from our persons, is considered more closely in the next chapter, and there we will see the great weight given to this right – as the very foundation stone of criminal law. Suffice to say, for the moment, that the right to keep others away was not, in these scholars' view, a right which should be held by the wife. The husband envisaged by these scholars is somehow not seen to be engaged in a breach of a fundamental human right. Precisely because the husband's intentions were to 'rape' his wife, that is knowingly to overcome by force the wife's defence of herself, to secure sexual entry without her consent, legal men of influence said there should be no criminal wrong here.

The sentiments of Williams, Howard and Smith and Hogan may now seem dated and unsavoury, but they represented an authoritative male legal view of wife rape up to, at the time of, and even well after the case of *Morgan*, one which held good for decades after the decision. The current author was imbibing their views at law school and then taught criminal law when their texts or their successor texts remained authoritative. Rightly, they said, wife rape, and its associated violence, if it did not lead to intentional injury, fell outside the purview of criminal law and their view held sway. Indeed the legality of the rape of Daphne Morgan by her husband was hardly of note, both at the time of the case (where it was only briefly mentioned) and for the next 40 years. The fact that William Morgan was not prosecuted for rape as a principal, only as an accomplice, almost passed without comment. The immunity was well known and well accepted by some of criminal law's most respected scholars.

V. The Doctrinal Scholar and Selective Attention: *Morgan* as the Focus of Discussion About the Mental State of Serious Crime

Among other members of the scholarly legal community there was also something odd going on in their thinking about rape, the nature of serious crime, and the criminal responsibility of men. Criminal legal scholars spent a good deal of time studying the marital rape case of *Morgan*, fully aware of the brutality of William Morgan, and his pivotal role in setting up all the rapes, but made little of his non-prosecution. This fact hardly registered, and still does not. Their attention was instead directed elsewhere, to other legal principles which were of greater disciplinary concern and thus the case was to become a landmark case.

DPP v Morgan became intensely interesting to criminal legal scholars in quite another way, and it became an important case in the ensuing analysis and teaching of criminal law, for decades.[40] It came to stand for the general criminal law principle that there should *not* be responsibility for very serious crime in the absence of subjective fault. In the case of rape, this meant that the accused must realise that the victim was not consenting. Even a grossly unreasonable belief in consent should be incompatible with responsibility, a principle which engendered strong feminist criticism of the case. Rape and *Morgan* became almost a fixation for the scholar debating the appropriate mental state for truly serious crime and trying to ascertain the principled solution.

The case courted controversy because of its commitment to subjectivism, not because of the husband's immunity from prosecution. Was it right that the unreasonable belief should excuse? In teaching and in scholarship, *Morgan* was the focus of analysis of criminal responsibility and subjective mens rea: the need for a subjectively guilty mind to go with the proscribed act when the offence was a serious stigmatic crime. These, said some but not others, were the necessary conditions of responsibility.

Morgan came to supply the gold standard for the principle that serious wrongs call for a subjective mens rea.[41] This was where the principle was strongly and clearly enunciated. Moreover the case came to assume great analytical interest as a statement of the importance of proof of subjective mens rea, no matter how unreasonable the belief which was at odds with the formation of criminal intention.[42] (And it was here that the case was controversial.) It became the great case on subjectivism. It would be taught to subsequent generations of law students as the case which not only endorsed subjectivism but which contained a warning against departures from this fundamental principle that persons should only be found responsible for serious crime when they understood and intended their wrongful actions.

---

[40] Celia Wells, 'Swatting the Subjectivist Bug' (1982) *Criminal Law Review* 209; Jennifer Temkin, 'The Limits of Reckless Rape' (1983) *Criminal Law Review* 5; Jennifer Temkin, 'Towards a Modern Law of Rape' (1982) 45(4) *Modern Law Review* 399; Jennifer Temkin, *Rape and the Legal Process*, 2nd edn (Oxford, Oxford University Press, 2002); Simon Bronitt, 'Rape and Lack of Consent' (1992) 16 *Criminal Law Journal* 289; Ian Leader-Elliott, 'The "Subjectivist Bug" in Australian Criminal Law, 1937–1965: A History and Epilogue' paper delivered to the University of South Australia (2016); Farmer, above n 2.

[41] This is despite the fact that *Morgan* is also a case which could have gone either way on the requirement of subjective fault. It is also a crime and case which begins to trigger change in criminal law and, some years later, a specific departure from the subjective fault requirement in many jurisdictions. Both the crime of rape and the case of *Morgan* could therefore be described as untypical, especially if a typical true crime is one which is general in its application and stable in its character and its formulation.

[42] Indeed *Morgan* could be said to be a perverse case to represent this principle because it was both implausible and repulsive on the facts, that the men accused could have believed what they said they did.

But there was highly selective attention and inattention. Rarely was the case spoken of as one which invoked the spousal immunity. What drew remarkably little comment was the tolerated legality at the heart of this case. The court itself made little of it, and so too did subsequent commentators on the case.

Morgan could equally be characterised as a case about the refusal to blame when intention is fully present, as long as it is a husband forcing sex and the victim is his wife: the husband was the central character of this case for whom this was all true. The most loathsome person in *Morgan* was Mr Morgan: his intentions were not in doubt. *Morgan* as much severs as establishes the link between subjective fault and blame. This is no mystery to all the lawyers who have examined the case. But it is not the way the case has tended to be understood.

In short, scholarly attention was driven by scholarly interests. There was intense interest in *DPP v Morgan* as setting the conditions of liability and responsibility for serious crime. The case was not ignored. On the contrary; it was studied intensively. But this intense focus was also narrow: it was all about the mental requirements of criminal responsibility; it left unexamined the spousal immunity. The very scholars who were engaged in the discussion of subjective liability in rape law, who required it to be established by the prosecution, because the crime was so serious, at the same time were silent on the matter that the prosecution did not proceed against William Morgan himself as the principal rapist.

VI. The Legal Scholar as Political Philosopher

I turn now to consider the thinking of the (male) criminal law scholar as moral and political philosopher, as someone who is trying to examine criminal law as a central institution within the polity and to depict criminal law as a moral and civilising mechanism, one which fundamentally respects our persons.

Our right not to be touched, without our consent, has been regarded as the foundation right of criminal law. The guiding idea is that we all have a basic right to exclude all others from our bodies, from our persons. Criminal law makes a firm and absolute commitment to this right, which makes it a principled institution and discipline, committed to public and private civility. Thus one can find statements, throughout the criminal law literature, that the most basic function of criminal law and justice is to protect our bodily integrity. The moral and political starting premise of the discipline is that we all, *equally*, have this right to preserve our borders. John Stuart Mill thought of it as our personal sovereignty.[43]

As the most influential legal philosopher of the twentieth century HLA Hart expressed it, because we are not 'giant land crabs with an impenetrable carapace',

---

[43] John Stuart Mill, *On Liberty*, 2nd edn (London, John W Parker and Son, 1859) 22. Mill's statement of our rights over our selves is reproduced and discussed in the next chapter.

which extract nutrients from the air,[44] there must at least be 'rules forbidding the free use of violence'.[45] Hart thought that these were minimal conditions of life if we were to be civilised persons living in developed nations.

To leading criminal law theorists, this criminalisation of unwanted intrusions and the associated use of force – especially the crime of rape – forms the moral centre or 'core' of their discipline which, in turn, is portrayed as a central institution of the civil polity. The view expressed repeatedly is that rape must be condemned outright, and this condemnation is vital to the legitimacy of criminal law.[46] And this is the critical point: the necessary assumption is that it *is* thus condemned. A polity which failed to make criminal such conduct would be failing to respect the personhood of all and so could not call itself civilised. Hence rape as well as murder are often characterised as 'core' or 'central' crimes.[47] They sit at the moral centre of the discipline, supposedly utterly condemned.

The crime of rape has therefore played a vital role in the explanation and justification of criminal law as an institution which sets standards of behaviour for us all. It has been invoked repeatedly as an illustration of a central or core wrong, the worst sort of wrong, a horrific wrong, a true crime. Because of its great symbolic importance to criminal law, there has been ongoing concern to label it precisely, get the wrong right, identify accurately its behavioural and mental elements, and ensure that this wrong is powerfully condemned.[48] No civilised law, it is said, would do otherwise.

Rape has been almost a fixation for criminal law scholars intent on explaining why it is a profound and intrinsic wrong (and how to identify the appropriate physical and mental conditions of liability). Gardner and Shute, for example, have insisted that 'rape is the central case' of the 'sheer use' of a human being,[49] the treatment of the human as a thing, rather than a person.[50] Therefore 'Joel Feinberg is right to place it on the short list of wrongs' criminalised by any civilised polity.[51] Rape has become a talisman or 'stigmata' offence'.[52] If we are to call ourselves civilised, we must have this criminal law. Thus according to Joel Feinberg,

---

[44] HLA Hart, 'Positivism and the Separation of Law from Morals' (1958) 71 *Harvard Law Review* 607, 623.

[45] Ibid.

[46] Such views are to be found in Joel Feinberg, *The Moral Limits of Criminal Law: Volume 1 Harm to Others* (Oxford, Oxford University Press, 1984) 10–11; RA Duff, *Answering for Crime: Responsibility and Liability in the Criminal Law* (Oxford, Hart, 2007) 87; Victor Tadros, *Criminal Responsibility* (Oxford, Oxford University Press, 2005) 2; AP Simester and Andrew Von Hirsch, *Crimes, Harms and Wrongs* (Oxford, Hart, 2011) 7.

[47] Tadros, above n 46 at 2.

[48] On the perceived importance of fair labelling in criminal law see James Chalmers and Fiona Leverick, 'Fair Labelling in Criminal Law' (2008) 71 *Modern Law Review* 217.

[49] John Gardner and Stephen Shute, 'The Wrongness of Rape' in J Horder (ed), *Oxford Essays in Jurisprudence* (Oxford, Oxford University Press, 2000) 205.

[50] John Gardner has sustained this view of the wrong of rape. See John Gardner, 'The Opposite of Rape' (2018) 38 *Oxford Journal of Legal Studies* 48.

[51] Gardner and Shute, above n 49 at 205.

[52] See Robert G Lee and Derek Morgan, 'Regulating Risk Society: Stigmata Cases, Scientific Citizenship and Biomedical Diplomacy' (2001) 23 *Sydney Law Review* 297.

'About the propriety of one class of crimes there can be no controversy. Wilful homicide, forcible rape, [are crimes] ... everywhere in the civilized world, and no reasonable person could advocate their "decriminalisation"'.[53] Such crimes entail 'the direct production of serious harm to individual persons and groups'[54] and hence they are 'the clearest cases of legitimate or proper criminalization'.[55]

To Andrew Ashworth, rape (along with murder) is also one of the 'clear cases' of prohibition of obvious harms and wrongs to persons.[56] Stanton-Ife has characterised rape as a 'horrific crime' and so it is 'the easiest of easy cases for the best known theory of criminalization, based on the harm principle'.[57] It is therefore, in this regard, 'banal from a theoretical point of view'.[58]

To Antony Duff, 'Some wrongs it would be hard to imagine not being criminal in any legal system ... such wrongs as murder and ... rape ... constitute serious violations of any polity's core values ... They are wrongs against which any polity must protect its members'.[59] Duff leaves us in no doubt of the absolute necessity of criminalising rape, comprehensively: 'it is hard to imagine a respect [between members of the polity] that is robust enough to underpin the requisite procedures which would not also preclude murdering, raping or subjecting to other central mala in se those whom I respect'.[60]

The criminality of rape is necessary for our sense of our civility, for our respect for ourselves, and our respect for others, as citizens. Duff continues: 'If we are serious about the values by which we define ourselves as a political community, and about the demand that we show each other appropriate respect and concern as fellow citizens, we will take breaches of such values very seriously'.[61]

Crimes such as rape are thus thought to possess a 'pre-legal wrongfulness: we should refrain from murder, rape and theft ... not because the law prohibits them, but because they are wrongs'.[62] The criminal law 'definitions of central mala in se must thus be understood as declarations, rather than as prohibitions'.[63] The law does not 'make wrong what was not already wrong'.[64] Rather the role of law is

> to declare that these pre-legal wrongs are public wrongs: to declare, that is, not merely that they are wrongs (we do not need criminal law to tell us that), but that they are wrongs that properly concern the whole polity, which should call their perpetrators to account through the criminal courts.[65]

[53] Feinberg, above n 46 at 10–11.
[54] Ibid.
[55] Ibid.
[56] Andrew Ashworth, *Principles of Criminal Law*, 4th edn (Oxford, Oxford University Press, 2003) 1.
[57] John Stanton-Ife, 'Horrific Crime' in RA Duff et al (eds), *The Boundaries of the Criminal Law* (Oxford, Oxford University Press, 2010) 139.
[58] Ibid.
[59] Duff, above n 46 at 143.
[60] Ibid 87.
[61] Ibid 88.
[62] Ibid 86.
[63] Ibid.
[64] Ibid.
[65] Ibid.

As Ian Leader-Elliott has observed, within Duff's analysis of criminal law, '[m]urder and rape ... are taken to be central and exemplary instances of wrongdoing'.[66]

All these criminal law theorists, and especially Duff, are saying that rape is a crime which violates the principles of any civilised polity and so must be comprehensively criminalised. Importantly, their arguments proceed *as if* it were comprehensively criminalised, and that this has been so for a long time, since civilised legal systems demand this condemnation – and by implication, these theorists belong to civilised legal systems. Thoroughgoing condemnation of rape is vital to the logic of their theories of criminal law. These theories only make sense if the core wrong they are describing is actually fully condemned. The message conveyed is that the wrong of rape is so fundamentally wrong that it exists as a wrong before law gets to it. A marital certificate – which is a (post) legal event – should not make a difference to the culpability and immorality of men who rape.

VII. Rape as the Acid Test

Rape is clearly of special significance for the discipline of criminal law, which is why it provides an acid test of criminal law thinking and its moral claims about its impartial, objective respect for our persons. In this first chapter I have begun to test the discipline's broadest commitments to civility, invoking this law. Rape has been treated as an exemplar of a universal, enduring and intrinsic horrific crime, a violation of human beings *as* human beings and *by* human beings. And yet it has been profoundly defined and limited by sex, sexuality and marital status (and jurisdiction).

Marital status, which is a legal status, has been critical to the scope of rape law. Rape has not been comprehensively criminalised. Every husband has been exempted in relation to one woman until the last decade of the twentieth century. Rape as an exemplar of a central serious wrong of criminal law has failed in its respect for persons, but this tends not to be seen or said. Rape has been a crime directed at men but not at all men, or at least not at all men in all their legal statuses, at least not until very recently. All men in their capacity as husbands in the supposedly civilised polity of England were excused from it until the end of the twentieth century; it was a crime only directed at men and only when their victims were women, and those women victims were not married to them. In England, men

---

[66] Ian Leader-Elliott, 'A Critical Reading of RA Duff, *Answering for Crime*' (2010) 31 *Adelaide Law Review* 47, 55. According to Leader-Elliott, Duff implicitly regards the criminal law as 'concentric' in nature, with the offences of murder and rape in the central circle, and the rest of criminal law spreading out from them. Leader-Elliott suggests that criminal law is more accurately viewed as 'polycentric': 'a loose federation rather than a unitary state'.

are still the exclusive targets of rape law, as offenders, but have now been added as potential victims.[67] (In Australia women can now be rapists.[68])

And these criminal law theorists necessarily know this. After all, they are criminal law scholars and this is a mundane fact of criminal law, which is why Lord Hailsham in *Morgan* could dispense with it so quickly and all lawyers reading the case would know why. It is therefore perplexing that these general political theories of criminal law simply do not refer to a vast legal status restriction on liability for rape. Nothing is said about this major exclusion zone in which the crime is blocked from application to most men. Why? Is there something about being a husband which overrides the civility requirements? Do men acquire a different moral and legal character when they marry? Or was this once the case, but has recently changed? What is going on?

VIII. The Developing Argument: Men are Critical to Criminal Law but Very Hard to See

None of these questions are posed or are of evident concern. Instead the criminal law theorists encountered in this chapter convey a common message: that the most vital task of criminal law is to protect 'our persons' from unwanted interference and to respect our right, 'as persons', to have physical relations with others, only of our choosing. This legal protection is said to be offered in an absolute and unqualified way. Criminal law is not about men and women, in this orthodox view, and the orthodox view persists. It is highly influential and difficult to rebut. In this view criminal law is not about men, as men, nor women as women. Rather it is about the vulnerable and threatening *person*, who could be of either sex. Persons, it would seem, are all of us, not just or mainly men.

But in truth, as we will see in the next chapter, criminal law, as a discipline, does in fact engage mainly with men and their antisocial behaviour, and the formulation of its offences has necessarily been in response to male behaviour and male social norms. Men have made the criminal legal world. They have drawn it up, decided on its priorities, and they are also its central characters. It is not just that men are the majority of offenders, and men are the reason why you do not walk alone down dark alleys at night, especially if you are not a man. But it is also that it is the problems of men that have been the problems of criminal law: men's security of 'property' and 'persons'; men's lawful access to some women and their preclusion from others.

---

[67] See Sexual Offences Act 2003 (UK).
[68] See the gender neutral wording of the offence of rape in the Criminal Law Consolidation Act 1935, s 48 (SA).

2

Introducing the Criminal Legal World of Men: The Importance of Personal Border Control

I. The Abstracted World of Criminal Law: 'There's Nobody Here but Us Persons'[1]

If we take a larger view of criminal law, and its remit, we see that it offers us a complete world of persons and places and of the sorts of activities that persons tend to pursue in their various locations. There is a 'public' sphere, where so-called 'persons' or 'individuals' come together for a great variety of purposes: they might be working or playing together; they might be on football fields, in front bars, on work sites or in corporate or government offices. The most basic demand of criminal law is that these imagined 'persons' do not hurt, or even touch, each other if there is no reciprocal desire for touch, if there is a want of consent. If there is unwanted contact, then the offences against the person are potentially engaged, for the basic crime of assault is in essence a touching, or even a threat of touching, without consent.

On the whole, these public persons going about their public lives are not thought of as intimates, in the criminal legal imagination, though they are allowed to become so. Bodily contact is anticipated in some of these public places, but not in others. The rugby scrum demands it and criminal law permits such close and rough treatment and may even endorse it.[2] In the work place, there is no real provision for unwanted contact. In the language of criminal law, the office or factory worker has a right to 'bodily integrity'. Offices are not the places for unwanted touching. Touch another worker when they do not want it and an assault may come into being, though as a practical reality this is unlikely, for a host of other reasons. Much of criminal law operates as unenforced norms.

---

[1] Robert Wolff, 'There's nobody here but us persons' in Carol Gould and Marx Wartofsky (eds), *Women and Philosophy: Toward a Theory of Liberation* (New York, Putnam, 1976).

[2] For example, South Australia's offence of causing harm makes explicit provision for sport. Even the punching of someone to a state of unconsciousness, which is explicitly considered in the offence, may be lawful if done with the right intentions. See the Criminal Law Consolidation Act 1935, s 22 (SA).

There is also a 'private' sphere imagined by criminal law, where marriages still typically occur and where sexual intimacy is considered the norm. In the private part of the criminal legal world, intimacy is expected, and even unwanted contact – including the use of force – has been licensed, sometimes encouraged, and until very recently. Criminal law has taken a specific view of the private and helped to constitute it.

This criminal legal world, just briefly sketched, is not explicitly populated by men and women, though you might ask 'who else is there'? Instead I have talked about 'persons', 'individuals', 'the public' and 'the private', as other criminal lawyers tend to do, and I have also referred to 'touch' and 'bodily integrity'. The criminal legal world is all about men and women and how they may and may not approach each other, especially as embodied creatures.[3] In some ways criminal law is the most personal and intimate of laws, telling us what we are allowed to do with each other's bodies, and even with our own. But whose bodies is it talking about and what forms are they assumed to take? Are they men or are they women? From criminal law theory it is far from clear. But judging from the activities of the police and the courts, and the population of prisons, it is the public and very physical interactions of men which are of particular concern. And yet men, as men, are strangely invisible in criminal legal discourse.[4]

Criminal law is rarely characterised as a man-regulating institution, though it is the violence of men that represents the most serious practical problem for civil society. The vast majority of violent crime is committed by men and men are mainly its objects, though women too can be its objects, mainly in the home, and here the violence can be fatal. In the analysis of criminal law, and in the generation of theory about its very nature, its characters are remarkably abstracted to the point that, often, there are no men or women in sight. 'There is nobody here but us persons', as philosopher Robert Wolff[5] once put it (philosophy can also be a highly abstracted discipline).

The major classifications in criminal legal thought continue to be oddly vague, unsettled and unsettling. Criminal lawyers will acknowledge that the 'public' sphere, which has been the natural domain of criminal law (which is itself a variety of public law), is not a real place but rather a legal concept. And this is also true of the concept of the 'private'. You cannot walk into either place and sit down. You would not find a chair. As theorists are quick to acknowledge, the public and the

---

[3] Of course criminal law is concerned with a broad and increasing array of offences. But my point here is that at its centre, as that centre is understood by some of its most influential theorists, criminal law is most concerned with our physical security and so with the offences against the person, from murder to rape to assault.

[4] And this is also true of criminology, as I have elsewhere observed: see Ngaire Naffine, *Feminism and Criminology* (Polity Press, Cambridge, 1997) and also see Richard Collier, *Masculinities, Crime and Criminology* (London, SAGE, 1998).

[5] Wolff, above n 1.

private are legal ideas, not parcels of land or walls and floors.[6] The private bedroom of criminal law is not a real room with a closed door but rather a legal creation. The door is notionally open for some sexual encounters but closed for others. Those engaged in the notionally private sexual act are also legally and socially classified (as men and women; as heterosexual and homosexual) and so in this sense they are also the creations of public law.

As Katherine O'Donovan has demonstrated in her elegant history of sexual divisions in law, 'The whole fabric of the personal life is imprinted with colours from elsewhere. Not to acknowledge this, and to pretend that the private is free, leads to a false analysis'.[7]

'Persons' and 'individuals', with their so-called 'bodily integrity', are also highly abstracted concepts. What does an integrated body look like? Try to picture it. 'Men' and 'women' seem to be less abstracted beings, though they too have their legal definitions and significances. Men and women certainly have real and different bodies and very different social and legal histories. Whether one was born a man or a woman once made a tremendous difference to one's life's possibilities and trajectory. It still makes a good deal of difference.[8] The terms men and women do seem to force a shift in thinking when used, instead of the terms persons and individuals preferred by criminal law scholars, because they compel some consideration of the distinctive lives of men and women.

Though men's interests, concerns and lives have shaped this criminal legal world, again you would not know it from reading most criminal law texts, of both a theoretical and pedagogical nature. Men have been abstracted out and the continuing use of abstract concepts in criminal law sustains the practice of keeping men under cover and therefore not the subjects of open consideration. Criminal legal theory largely occurs without reference to men and women. This is remarkable when one thinks about it, but most criminal lawyers do not. The places of the criminal law scholar are the public and the private, though sometimes 'the home'; their people are persons and individuals; and even the bodies of the persons they invoke are strangely abstracted – typically lacking a sex and yet somehow imagined as enclosed forms but not thoroughly visualised. Even the artistic criminal lawyer would find it a challenge to draw the body of a person of criminal law. They would probably say that it can not be done and it should not be done. But criminal law is not responsible for this vague and unsettlingly abstract world, in the orthodox view.

---

[6] On the highly conceptual and abstract nature of legal space and place see Kevin Gray, 'Property in Thin Air' (1991) 50 *Cambridge Law Journal* 252 and also Margaret Davies, *Property: Meanings, Histories, Theories* (Oxford, Routledge-Cavendish, 2007) and Margaret Davies, *Law Unlimited: Materialism, Pluralism and Legal Theory* (Oxford, Routledge, 2017).

[7] Katherine O'Donovan, *Sexual Divisions in Law* (London, Weidenfeld & Nicolson, 1986) 15.

[8] As the distinguished classicist and public intellectual Mary Beard has made crystal clear in *Women and Power: A Manifesto* (Profile Books, London, 2017).

II. The Human Comes Ready-made:[9] And the Law is Not Responsible for its Persons

The impression consistently conveyed in the orthodox literature is that criminal law deals in persons for whom it is not responsible, in the sense that persons are thought to have their own natures, before law gets to them. Law is not responsible for the making of its persons; rather law finds its persons already-made. Law then takes its persons and seeks to protect them – all of them. It does not pick and choose its subjects, for protection and admonition, because we are all simply human creatures, in need of law's aid, not social or legal creations. In this view, the remit of criminal law is to treat us as one sort of being – as having similar needs and propensities and as being situated in the world in much the same way: as if the legal and social histories of men and women were not vastly different from one another, and as if they had no bearing on criminal law and its theory. And so the cultural specificity of the world of men, what it is like to be a man in this world, and what it is like to have a male form, as men understand that form, are unconsidered and so unaddressed.

What we have offered up to us instead is a quasi-scientific understanding of the criminal legal project in which the rational criminal law maker and scholar is given his natural criminal legal subject, a natural human, and then works out and explains a law which is suited to him – to his bodily and psychological human needs. HLA Hart famously thought this way. He said that 'rules forbidding the free use of violence' were 'so fundamental that if a legal system did not have them there would be no point in having legal rules at all'.[10] To Hart, it was 'a "natural" necessity' for a society to have rules outlawing violence.[11] Hart was effectively talking about criminal law, and its offences against the person. He was describing what he took to be the *human* capacity and inclination for violence and he was treating it as a human (rather than as a male) predilection or propensity. He was acknowledging what he saw as the vital function of criminal law: to control and channel and prohibit aggression and the means by which one human being can harm another, and will often be moved to do so. But he was not naming it as male behavior, nor was he characterising it as a problem *of* men and a problem *for* men. In short, Hart was thinking like an orthodox criminal lawyer.

In the conventional and influential account, we all have human bodies that have their own solid, innate forms and natures. But they are prior to law, already themselves, and law's role is to regulate them, not to constitute them, not to give them a particular form. Law's purpose is to ensure that the physical 'person' is

---

[9] The 'ready-made' is a term from the art world and is first associated with Marcel Duchamp's appropriation of a urinal to make a work of art – by doing nothing to it but putting it in an art gallery. He called it *Fountain* (1917).

[10] HLA Hart, 'Positivism and the Separation of Law and Morals' (1958) 71(4) *Harvard Law Review* 593, 623.

[11] Ibid.

treated with proper regard, the sort of regard that ensures human dignity. In the liberal legal theory of the body, law's limited role is to dictate the nature of human contact between bodies that already possess their own inherent nature and form and which already demand respect. Law does not dictate the nature of the body itself. The prevailing idea is that law only takes what it finds, in a literal sense.

Duff, for one, refers to the 'pre-legal' wrongs at the middle of criminal law, which are murder and rape, wrongs that in his view exist outside of law and its world of rules, in that they would be wrong whether or not they were criminal offences. Law's job is to make sure that they are labelled as criminal and then punished. The pre-legal nature of the embodied human being, and how it might be violated by the crime of rape, is implicit in Duff's account of the crime.[12] Rape, he says, is a wrong before the law gets to it and makes it criminal: rape law only names it and proscribes it. Duff is advancing the conventional view that violation of the body, by the crime of rape, is something that can be done to any human, and is implicitly the same thing, and that it is the worst violation possible. And so Duff invokes a corporeal human being who exists outside of law, who can be wronged or harmed in a particularly human way.

From this it follows that law and society do not make or manufacture the vulnerabilities or sensitivities or proclivities of the person; rather law responds to the complex demands of our human nature. Criminal law is not about men thinking about men: what is important to a man; what threatens him; what he is capable of doing to others; how his intimate needs are to be met within the framework of criminal law. About this I will disagree.

Because criminal law (and its interpretation) does not treat its subjects as specific legal historical creations, typically it does not make its subjects, its persons, explicit. Usually it does not spell out what we are assumed to be, so that it is not immediately clear how we should visualise the person. Instead it proceeds to make laws about us with often unstated assumptions about our natures; about what we are like. The human imagined here is imagined already embodied in a certain way, but this imaginative process is not discussed, nor probably noticed.

The reason for this slight treatment of their subject by the legal scholars is that our persons, our beings, are thought to be formed in a natural human manner before they enter the world of law and become the subject of regulation. Law then deals with them, and the criminal lawyers and scholars can get on with their various tasks of devising and analysing law. The implicit idea is that law responds to and regulates our human creature needs, and these are unchanging and intrinsic needs and also preferences; not legal creations. Remember Hart's soft-skinned creatures who could nevertheless do harm to other such creatures and indeed had a propensity to violence which criminal law must curtail and regulate. Hart's invocation of the giant land crab, the thing that we are not, places the fleshly human in

---

[12] RA Duff, *Answering for Crime: Responsibility and Liability in the Criminal Law* (Oxford, Hart, 2007).

another sphere of existence though awaiting law for its own protection.[13] These are remarkable thought experiments, but not seen as such.

In common with the liberal theory, from which it derives, criminal law – and its theorists – treats its approach to the body as simply a response to the body's own nature. In other words, implicit in our criminal law, and its justification and explanation, is the idea that law never dictates or determines the nature of the body. It only ever responds to the body's own intrinsic character, which is by nature bounded. (It is not responding to social or legal understandings of the bodies of men and women.)

Though a certain type of physical being, with certain types of preferences for relating to others, indeed a certain type of personality, is conjured up by criminal law and its interpreters, we still get only a rough sense of the nature and character of the person. Surprisingly perhaps, for criminal law theorists, their subject is still not a matter of deep reflection.

III. Introducing Men and the Male Story of Criminal Law and its World

Fascinating insights into the criminal legal world of men, and their persons, have been supplied by a recent history of mainly English criminal law, by one of the leading historians of criminal law, Lindsay Farmer. In this magisterial history of criminal law, Farmer offers a rich account, over time, of the changing character of criminal law, its people and it priorities.[14] This is an important, ambitious and highly informative inquiry into the so-called 'making of criminal law'. What is striking about this historical survey of the changing world of criminal law is that it is very much a male world, peopled on the whole by men, but still it is not designated as such. It is a story of male concerns, predilections, proclivities and rights. It is a male story of criminal law, but not with men as the explicit characters. Implicitly it is about men engaging with men, with women as peripheral characters though strangely necessary to the story. It is told as a story of the persons of criminal law, and how they have changed over time. It is not delimited as a story of criminal legal men.

At the beginning of the historical story, 'the person' of criminal law was understood to be a pugnacious and physically-controlling character, whom the law criminalised but also accommodated. We learn, for instance, that 'there was a high tolerance of violent behaviour in eighteenth century society … It could be seen in popular culture in forms of recreation and sports, such as prize fighting'.[15]

---

[13] Hart, above n 10 at 623.
[14] Lindsay Farmer, *Making the Modern Criminal Law: Criminalization and Civil Order* (Oxford, Oxford University Press, 2016).
[15] Ibid 237.

Legal acceptance of the use of force was also implicit in legal norms permitting 'the "correction" of wives, children and servants'.[16] Farmer further tells us that 'It was widely accepted that disagreements might be resolved by physical means'. Other evidence of the social and legal acceptance of the uses of force was to be found in 'The use of flogging ... in the army and navy'.[17]

From 'about 1750 to 1900', there was then what Farmer calls a 'civilizing offensive', a 'shift in social attitudes towards interpersonal violence'.[18] The upshot was 'the control and policing of violence, particularly in public places'.[19] There was a heightened legal and social expectation 'that individuals control the urge to resort to violence ... Violence ... was to be a last resort for both individuals and the state'.[20] And so there emerged 'civilized modern man': the subject of modern criminal law.[21]

Farmer's account of the changing nature of 'legitimate and illegitimate violence' in the Victorian period entails 'campaigns against public fighting and "wife beating" and other forms of brutal and "uncivilized" conduct'.[22] There were certain areas of life where 'these boundaries were contested'.[23] These were the use of 'consensual fights to settle disputes', which once served to express 'the values of manliness and English national character'.[24] There was drunken violence, with its 'unchecked brutality' and there were new demands for the exercise of self-control.[25] Subsequently, 'ideals of masculinity and femininity' began to change, so that women came to be seen as weak and in need of protection (from men) and the civilized man offered women that protection, not their fist. Thus 'wife beating' became increasingly unacceptable.[26] Nevertheless 'it was clearly recognized that the man [still] had authority, or dominion, over women ... within the domestic sphere and that this extended to the use of physical violence'.[27] So the question was how much force could a good man use? The 'new civic virtues of self-discipline' and of 'control of the passions' did not demand the complete suppression of force.[28]

Though this is presented as an account of the changing nature of 'persons' and 'individuals', and how they come to be civilised by criminal law, the public space envisaged is peopled by men intent on securing a non-violent and regulated and

---

[16] Ibid.

[17] Ibid.

[18] Ibid 235. The 'civilising offensive' in Victorian England has also been documented by Martin J Wiener in *Men of Blood: Violence, Manliness and Criminal Justice in Victorian England* (Cambridge, Cambridge University Press, 2004).

[19] Farmer, above n 14 at 235.

[20] Ibid.

[21] Ibid.

[22] Ibid 244.

[23] Ibid 246.

[24] Ibid.

[25] Ibid 248.

[26] Ibid 249.

[27] Ibid 250.

[28] Ibid 256.

knowable public life, where it is safe to transact business with other men who are perceived as potentially dangerous. By contrast, the private is conceived as a place where husbands exercise domestic authority, without excessive force. In this account of the persons undergoing the civilising process, we move from private blood feuds, implicitly between territorial men, to a more seemly set of relations between men wanting safe and civil relations, with other men, in the market place, and not primitive revenge. Such economic men are themselves made possible, are brought into being, by certain fair and effective institutions that can respond to their perceived needs: for order and safe conditions in which to negotiate between strangers.

The problem of civil order, thus disclosed, is not one of both men and women doing physical violence, and learning to control their violent urges. Rather this is a description of changing standards of *male* civility and the uses of criminal law to establish and enforce them.[29] Men are the subjects of criminal law, we learn about here, the intended subjects of regulation, and it is men's behaviour which represents the changing index, the metric, of civility and national character. Men's treatment of women is one of the measures of that civility. The civility of women, towards men, is not itself the issue (nor is it brought into issue).

Farmer describes well, and in fascinating detail, the changing male nature of criminal law: it has been a vehicle for regulating and responding to men's chang-ing financial and bodily concerns, their shifting interests and priorities, of allaying their fears for their own personal safety, and making it possible to transact with other men, without bloodshed.[30]

Women as threats to men are not part of the story; literally it goes without saying that women do not feature in this way in the story of criminal law. Rather the problem posed by women, as we saw in the last chapter, is one of obtaining lawful access to them, notwithstanding the don't-touch rule. This is a male prob-lem and it is a problem solved by men by permitting lawful access by a particular man to a particular woman, (an overriding of the don't-touch rule) and proscrib-ing access by all others.[31]

---

[29] For a more conscious study of changing standards of male civility over the course of the nineteenth century, especially as reflected in the acceptability of violence towards women, see Martin J Wiener's *Men of Blood: Violence, Manliness and Criminal Justice in Victorian England*, above n 18. However, Wiener is writing more as a social historian, about the changing mores of men, as evinced in the deci-sions of the English criminal courts in homicide and rape cases, rather than as a criminal law theorist concerned about the implications of these mores for the discipline of criminal law and its central prin-ciples – the concern of this book.

[30] More startling evidence of the Victorian crackdown on male violence is to be found in Peter Keatings' collection *Into Unknown England, 1866–1913, Selections from the Social Explorers* (Glasgow, Fontana/Collins, 1976). It includes a description of the legendary man and dog fights.

[31] This is the sexual contract described by Carole Pateman in the book of the same name: *The Sexual Contract* (Stanford, Stanford University Press, 1988).

IV. The Don't-Touch Rule in the Offences against the Person: Who it is For and What it Presumes about its Persons

As Farmer explains, it is in its offences against the person that criminal law openly acknowledges what it takes to be the human capacity and inclination for violence. This it treats as a human, rather than as a male, predilection or propensity. Criminal law seeks to control and channel and prohibit (on the whole male) aggression and the means by which one (male) human being can harm another, and will often be moved to do so.

It is also in its offences against the person that criminal law sets the terms for how humans can intimately engage with one another. These are typically designated 'the sex offences' and so given their own special category in the body of criminal legal doctrine. But really they are a subset of 'the offences against the person'. More explicit here, perhaps, is the understanding that the intimate human of criminal law comes in two sexes and then that the priorities of this intimate human are more obviously the priorities of the intimate man. It is here that the don't-touch rule, which is the defining feature of the offences against the person, has been suspended for husbands. (Securing sexual access to the body of a man is not thought to be a central female concern.) The violent and vulnerable person, outside the sphere of intimacy, is simply cast as human.

It therefore makes sense to go to the offences against the person, within the body of criminal law, to find out more about the personal characteristics of our central (male) characters of criminal law and what they are and are not permitted to do, and why, and what they are thought to be like. As Farmer has shown, the offences against the person are central 'pillars' of criminal law. Through these offences – from murder, to rape, to assault – the boundaries of legitimate and illegitimate violence have been set and adjusted over time.

Perhaps the first and most basic instruction contained within the offences against the person that we all receive is 'don't touch' other persons, unless that other person positively wants to be touched. Criminal law first asserts the autonomy rights of all, especially this right to 'bodily integrity' and security. The important idea is that without an enforceable legal right to exclude others from one's person, one is hardly a person. (And a people who failed to recognise and enforce such a right, could not call themselves civilised.) As Immanuel Kant declared, the basic human respect that man must show man demanded that men 'keep themselves at a distance from one another'.[32]

Keep your hands off others; this is our basic legal duty embedded within criminal law. Again as Farmer has shown, the type of touching that has been found acceptable, in and between men, has changed over time. The don't-touch rule has

---

[32] Immanuel Kant, *The Metaphysics of Morals* (Cambridge, Cambridge University Press, 1996) 198.

changed in response to changing views of men's natures. And yet typically it has been formulated, to this day, as a fixed and absolute rule containing an absolute right and duty. This is how Hart put it, and so does the current generation of legal theorists.

And yet courts have often taken a benign view of violence which is thought to toughen up men and in the right manly way. Thus violence in sport has received, and continues to receive, a high level of legal tolerance, and even positive approval.[33] For it is in the sporting arena that warrior man can confirm and strengthen the boundaries of his body. We are not a long remove from the thinking of East who explained in his *Pleas of the Crown*, 'manly sports and exercises which tend to give strength, activity and skill in the use of arms, and are entered into merely as private recreations among friends, are not unlawful'.[34] Though East was writing early in the nineteenth century, essentially the same reasons are still given for the lawfulness of violent sport today. For example the South Australian offences against the person explicitly accommodate and excuse very violent sports, including boxing, regarding them as social exceptions based on a variety of public interest.[35]

In the last chapter we saw the right to bodily integrity given crucial work in the crime of rape. The clear message was that the ability to exclude others from our bodies is vital for our personhood, hence the horrific nature of the crime of rape, which would seem to be the most intrusive of crimes. The supposed right of each of us to choose, on a moment by moment basis, with whom we connect is said to be part of basic criminal law thinking and, as Hart made plain, flows out of our human natures, because we do not possess the carapace of his imagined giant land crabs. This is why the exceptionalising of the wife, as someone who does not call for this protection, as well as the exceptionalising of the husband, as someone who is not required to keep his hands off, is so jarring and seems to speak of a certain set of interests informing the conceptualisation of the protected person of criminal law.

In the criminal law class room, John Stuart Mill is invoked often for his elegant formulation of the don't-touch rule: our right to ourselves: 'In the part which merely concerns himself', declared Mill, 'his [the individual's] independence is, of right, absolute. Over himself, over his own body and mind, the individual is sovereign'.[36] This tends to be the statement which launches any criminal law course as a declaration of the fundamental intentions and values of the criminal law.

---

[33] The so-called 'gay panic' defence, offered to men who have killed in response to a perceived homosexual advance (as the partial defence to murder of provocation), also contains a judicial message that sometimes the manly man will understandably defend his manhood. For a recent successful application of such a defence see *Lindsay v The Queen* (2015) 255 CLR 272 (High Court of Australia).

[34] Edward Hyde East, *Treatise of the Pleas of the Crown*, vol 1 (London, A Strahan, 1803) ch V, 268 [41]–[42].

[35] See the Criminal Law Consolidation Act 1935, s 22 (SA), which provides that 'A participant in a sporting or recreational activity may ... consent to harm arising from a risk inherent in the nature of the activity (eg a boxer may accept the risk of being knocked unconscious in the course of a boxing match and, hence, consent to that harm if it in fact ensues)'.

[36] John Stuart Mill, *On Liberty*, 2nd edn (London, John W Parker and Son, 1859) 22.

Mill also made clear that '[e]ach is the proper guardian of his own health, whether bodily, or mental or spiritual'.[37] Mill, like Kant, conceived of persons as essentially separate and distinct, as beings whose dignity depended on a respect for the physical integrity of the self and the integrity of others.

As teachers and scholars of criminal law, our starting assumption is that the right to bodily integrity is fundamental and so, we explain, it is unlawful for one person intentionally to touch another without their consent; this is, in essence, the basic crime of assault. The initial point is (a liberal) one of assumed bodily integrity and autonomy. Human separation, human distinctness is what law must protect and preserve. As Goff LJ explained in *Collins v Wilcock*:

> The fundamental principle, plain and incontestable, is that *every person's body* is *inviolate*. It has long been established that any touching of another person, however slight, may amount to a battery.[38] (emphasis added)

In the same judgment, William Blackstone is cited as the basis of the rule. To Blackstone

> the law cannot draw the line between different degrees of violence, and therefore totally prohibits the first and lowest stage of it; *every man's person being sacred* and no other having a *right to meddle with it*, in any the slightest manner.[39] (emphasis added)

Thus the jurist Blackstone took much the same view of the body as the philosopher Kant. A person's integrity depended on a legally enforceable right to police the boundaries of their body and keep others outside of them.

The duty to respect the bodily integrity of others, to contain one's own borders, and to answer for failures to do so,[40] has thus been central to the liberal political tradition and to the moral and legal concept of personhood as it resides within criminal law, especially within the offences against the person. It follows, as we effectively tell our criminal law students, that each of us is also endowed with a clear set of protected borders around our person: a correlative enforceable right to be left alone. The crimes of murder and rape are concerned with these fundamental duties and rights.

The rights to self-sovereignty, to personal security and to bodily integrity, have been treated as the bedrock of liberal philosophy and the liberal polity and as defining of personhood. It is for this reason that the criminal offences of murder, rape and assault have been viewed as the worst wrongs possible. This is the apparent reason why leading criminal law scholars such as Ashworth, Gardner and Duff regard rape as perhaps the most fundamental and horrific affront to the person which law must condemn outright (as we saw in Chapter 1).

Without these rights to our persons recognised, it is said, a polity cannot call itself civilised, as Hart made clear. Without the right not to be touched, and not to

---

[37] Ibid 27.
[38] *Collins v Wilcock* [1984] 3 All ER 374 at 378, [1984] 1 WLR 1172 at 1177.
[39] William Blackstone, *Commentaries on the Laws of England*, vol 3, 17th edn (1830) 120.
[40] As Duff has enunciated repeatedly and elegantly.

be intruded upon, persons are not respected as individuals, as autonomous separate and distinct beings. They are hardly persons. It is hard to underestimate the significance of the claim to civility. To Norbert Elias,

> The concept of 'civilization' refers to a wide variety of facts ... But when one examines what the general function of the concept of civilization really is ... one starts with the very simple discovery: this concept expresses the self-consciousness of the West ... It sums up everything in which Western society of the last two or three centuries believes itself to be superior to earlier societies or 'more primitive' contemporary ones. By this term Western society seeks to describe what constitutes its special character and what it is proud of: the level of its technology, the nature of its manners, the development of its scientific knowledge or view of the world, and much more.[41]

V. The Don't-Touch Person: Men making Men in their Own Image as Self Proprietors

The don't-touch rule, entailed in the offences against the person, necessarily conjures up a don't-touch person. So who is this being? How are we to imagine him? The eighteenth century political theorist John Locke supplied a classic formulation of this rights-bearing other-excluding understanding of the person (the central civil character of the civilised society later imagined by Hart) when he said that 'every Man has a Property in his own Person. This no Body has any Right to but himself'.[42] (Locke talked of 'man' as the owner of his person and it would seem that he really was thinking of men, as we will see below.) Thus Locke conjured up a male understanding of a man posited as simply 'the person'.

The concept of the person as self-proprietor has a secure place within our modern liberal political theory and also within criminal jurisprudence. It has become a convenient way of highlighting the freedoms enjoyed by the modern individual, a sort of legal shorthand, a rhetorical device, which serves to accentuate the fullness of the rights enjoyed by persons in relation to themselves and to others. 'To be a full individual in liberal society', as Katherine O'Donovan observes, 'one must be an appropriator, defined by what one owns, including oneself as a possession, not depending on others, free'.[43]

A number of property theorists have confirmed this view of the liberal person. John Christman, for example, confirms that '[a] powerful way of expressing the

---

[41] Norbert Elias, *The Civilizing Process: Sociogenetic and Psychogenetic Investigations*, trans Edmund Jephcott, revised edn edited by Eric Dunning, Johan Goudsblom and Stephen Mennell (Blackwell, Oxford, 2000) 5.

[42] John Locke, *An Essay Concerning Human Understanding*, John Yolton (ed) (London, JM Dent & Sons, 1991) 287.

[43] Katherine O'Donovan, 'With Sense, Consent, or Just a Con? Legal Subjects in the Discourses of Autonomy' in Ngaire Naffine and Rosemary J Owens (eds), *Sexing the Subject of Law* (North Ryde, Law Book Company, 1997) 46.

principle of individual liberty is to claim that every individual has full "property rights" over her body, skills and labour'.[44] To John Frow the very 'form of the person' in Western liberal legal thought is one of 'self-possession'.[45] Or as Gerald Cohen expresses it, the person 'possesses over himself, as a matter of moral right, all those rights that a slaveholder has over a complete chattel slave as a matter of legal right'.[46]

The appeal which the concept of property-in-self might hold to liberals such as Locke is revealed by a brief inquiry into the etymology of the word 'property'. As Kenneth Minogue explains, '[t]he etymological root of the term (*proprius* – one's own), gives us the sense of the connection between a property and what possesses it',[47] that is between the possessing subject and the object or thing possessed by that subject. Or as Gray and Symes put it, 'semantically, "property" is the condition of being "proper" to (or belonging to) a particular person'.[48] The properties of persons, the attributes they possess, render them distinctive. That which is proper to a person delimits and individuates the person, marking the borders between the person and the rest of the world.[49]

If we examine the modern legal meaning of property, one can see its enduring appeal as a means of asserting the autonomy of the individual. Briefly, property describes a legal relationship *between* persons *in respect* of an object, rather than the relation between a subject and the objects possessed as properties of the person.[50] The invocation of a property right entails the proprietor exercising control over a thing, the object of property, against the rest of the world, which is thereby excluded from use. Property thus defines the limits of one's sphere of influence over the world. It defines the borders of one's control over things and so marks the degree of one's social and legal power. The claim of property in oneself is an assertion of self-possession and self-control, of a fundamental right to exclude others from one's very being. It is a means of individuating the person, of establishing a limit between the one and the other: between mine and thine; between me and you.

The idea of the person, as self-proprietor, demands that there is a zone of non-interference where no one can enter without permission; it extends beyond the

---

[44] John Christman, 'Self-Ownership, Equality and the Structure of Property Rights' (1991) 19 *Political Theory* 28, 28.

[45] John Frow, 'Elvis' Fame: The Commodity Form and the Form of the Person' (1995) 7 *Cardozo Studies in Law and Literature* 131, 149.

[46] Gerald Cohen, 'Self-Ownership, World-Ownership, and Equality' in Frank Lucash (ed), *Justice and Equality Here and Now* (Ithaca, New York, Cornell University Press, 1986) 109.

[47] Kenneth Minogue, 'The Concept of Property and its Contemporary Significance' in J Rowland Pennock and John W Chapman (eds), *Nomos XXII: Property* (New York, New York University Press, 1980) 11.

[48] Kevin Gray and PD Symes, *Real Property and Real People: Principles of Land Law* (London, Butterworths, 1981) 7.

[49] This idea of 'the proper' and its relation to personhood has been explored by Margaret Davies in 'Feminist Appropriations: Law, Property and Personality' (1994) 3 *Social and Legal Studies* 365.

[50] Gray and Symes, above n 48 at 8.

body of the person to encompass a moral and geographical private sphere: the home or the private realm; the realm of intimacy. The strong presumption is that there should be a 'zone in which the citizen has a moral claim to be at liberty, that is, free of legal coercion'.[51]

VI. Questioning the Idea of the Self-Owning and Bordered Man

The concept of the self-owning and self-enclosed person, which has been so amply theorised by the political and legal theorists, and which is central to the perceived wrong of both murder and rape (and the other offences against the person) in modern criminal law theory, has embedded within it a certain understanding of the male form and of male bodily integrity and the integrity of the person. For John Locke, the person with property in self was imagined as a man and this piece of male imagining has been sustained.

As we saw in Farmer's history of the making of criminal law, the changing states of being a man have been almost the total story of criminal law, and this is a story of beings with violent proclivities, whose violence needs channelling (especially through vigorous or violent sport), but who are also vulnerable, and so have a powerful need to ward others off. These self-possessing yet pugnacious persons of criminal law look, in reality, very much like men.

When courts of law have openly considered the degrees and types of violence which are tolerable, even socially approved, they have conjured up men and they have been sympathetic to certain types of men, as men, behaving as men should do, and more condemnatory of others. This selective sympathy for the violent man has been evident in the legal attitudes to deliberate harm inflicted in the course of a rugged sporting activity, especially when the behaviour in question does not stray too far from the rules and the spirit of the manly game.[52]

As Swift J remarked in *Donovan*, 'the case of persons who in perfect friendship engage by mutual consent in contests, such as … wrestling' can be acceptable precisely because 'they are manly diversions … and may fit people for defence, public as well as personal, in time of need'.[53] Here the slide from 'persons' to 'men' is so explicit that it is hard to miss the conflation of the one with the other. For Swift J, the body is the male body which is hard, manly and clearly defined. What is so remarkable about this sustained interpretation of the (male) body in criminal

---

[51] Joel Feinberg, *The Moral Limits of Criminal Law: Volume 1 Harm to Others* (Oxford, Oxford University Press, 1984) 7.

[52] As McInerney J observed in *Pallante v Stadiums Pty Ltd* [1976] VR 331, 339, violence may be acceptable in a sporting contest 'if such violence is inflicted within the spirit and intendment of the rules of the game'.

[53] *R v Donovan* [1934] 2 KB 498 at 508.

law is the faith which is maintained with the idea of the whole complete fully-bordered man, whether it is being pummelled or lacerated (or even engulfed by a woman, as we shall see).[54] These are men policing violent men and setting the limits to approved male violence.

As Lois Bibbings has observed, in her intriguing study of landmark late Victorian cases, which had violent men as their focus,[55] the violence needed the right sort of setting and the right sort of men to receive law's blessing. In other words, the legal view of acceptable male violence had class connotations. Thus the illegal prize fight, outside the official boxing ring, and attracting the wrong sort of men, could invite censure and criminal prosecution, even of the men observing it, if they were thought to be offering encouragement. According to Hawkins J in the now famous bare-knuckle boxing case of *Coney* (discussed by Bibbings): 'The cases in which it has been held that persons may lawfully engage in friendly encounters not calculated to produce real injury to or to rouse angry passions in either', was because 'such encounters are neither breaches of the peace nor are they calculated to be productive thereof'.[56] While to Stephen J in the same decision:

> In cases where life and limb are exposed to no serious danger in the common course of things, I think that consent is a defence to a charge of assault, even when considerable force is used, as, for instance, in cases of wrestling, single-stick, sparring with gloves, football, and the like.[57]

Thus the measure of acceptability of male violence was not so much a matter of degree – it could be very violent and still acceptable – but rather of its mode, and of the class of the persons involved. In his observations on the 'changes in the behaviour of the secular upper classes in the West', Norbert Elias describes the repression of aggression and its channelling into acceptable civilized forms.

> For example, belligerence and aggression find socially permitted expression in sporting contests. And they are expressed especially in 'spectating' (eg at boxing matches), in the imaginary identification with a small number of combatants to whom moderated and precisely regulated scope is granted for the release of such affects. And this living out of affects in spectating or even in merely listening (eg to a radio commentary) is a particularly characteristic feature of civilized society.[58]

And as Richard Collier elucidates: 'far from seeing intra male violence as something disapproved of, it [was] more a matter of location and context, with ideas

---

[54] For an influential discussion of legal attitudes to violence in sport see Paul J McCutcheon, 'Sports Violence, Consent and the Criminal Law' (1994) 45 *Northern Ireland Legal Quarterly* 267.

[55] Lois S Bibbings, *Binding Men: Stories about Violence and Law in Late Victorian England* (Abingdon and New York, Routledge, 2014). And on changing male attitudes to male violence in the Victorian period see also Wiener, above n 18.

[56] *R v Coney* (1882) 8 QBD 534 at 554.

[57] Ibid 549.

[58] Elias, above n 41 at 170.

about what is appropriate mediated by distinctive and class-based ideas of manliness'.[59]

A number of distinguished feminist critics of law, Bibbings[60] and Collier[61] included, have already made my point – that law often has men as its unstated focus and that law is also highly ambivalent about the violence of men. And yet these feminist analyses rarely feature in the mainstream criminal legal literature, though they are rich in information about the character of law's (male) persons, about what it is like to be a legal man. The steadfastly ahistorical approach to the persons of criminal law, in most modern criminal law theory, the easy invocation of the person as simply a member of the human species, has been remarked upon by Nicola Lacey in her recent book on the history of criminal responsibility.[62]

The historical accounts of the changing acceptability of male violence necessarily conjure up different types of men undergoing social change. The improving Victorians increasingly condemned and feared strong violence in a man of the lower classes and actually managed to reduce male violence. As Martin Wiener reports:

> pulled by visions of never-before-attained levels of personal and social security, dignity and betterment, authorities and middle-class publicists went to work to narrow further the boundaries of tolerable interpersonal violence. And as the gospel of self-management spread, impulsive and violent behavior became all the more threatening, by its actual growing rarity, at least in the circles frequented by self-improving persons, and by the increasing contrast it made with the self-improving way of life.[63]

And yet despite the complexity of the story of men's changing codes of conduct for themselves, we can generalise with some confidence and say that men have been the real objects of legal concern, when it has come to the uses of violence, and that this fact has often been lost in general accounts of crime and criminal law.

We can also say that in spite of the known social history of men's violence, with its story of changing male conventions, there has coexisted in criminal law thinking a more enduring, stable and abstract philosophical idea of a male person who is law's subject – a sort of male/human template – someone possessed of inviolate rights to govern the borders of his person. This is the man whom Locke thought of as a proprietor of his person, whom Blackstone declared must not be meddled with and whom Mill said was possessed of an inviolate personal sovereignty.

---

[59] Richard Collier, 'Review of Lois S Bibbings: *Binding Men: Stories About Violence And Law In Late Victorian England*' (2015) 42 *Journal of Law and Society* 664, 666.

[60] See also Lois S Bibbings, *Telling Tales about Men: Conceptions of Conscientious Objectors to Military Service during the First World War* (Manchester, Manchester University Press, 2009).

[61] See Richard Collier's extensive writing on law (especially family law, criminology and also on the legal profession) and masculinity including *Masculinity, Law and the Family* (London, Routledge, 1995) and *Masculinities, Crime and Criminology*, above n 4.

[62] Nicola Lacey, *In Search of Criminal Responsibility* (Oxford, Oxford University Press, 2016) 189–191.

[63] Weiner, above n 18 at 13.

And it is this being who is at the centre of criminal law thinking about the wrongness of rape and murder.

VII. Jennifer Nedelsky and the Bounded Self

The most sustained and critical account of this self-owning, somehow-integrated and bordered legal individual, which has a direct bearing on the current inquiry, has come from Jennifer Nedelsky.[64] Working in the adjacent fields of law and philosophy, Nedelsky has conducted extended character analyses of the liberal legal individual, of 'our self determining, self-making nature'.[65]

In 1989, Nedelsky examined 'The prevailing liberal conception of the self' which she described as 'an autonomous self with rights', with law cast in the role of protecting 'equal, autonomous, rights-bearing selves from harm by each other and by the state'.[66] In 1990 Nedelsky's central concern was the way in which boundary metaphors had been used to characterise the autonomous, rights-bearing individual or self of American constitutional law.[67]

Nedelsky has developed this idea of the 'bounded self' over the course of her writings, applying it to different branches of law, especially constitutional law but also criminal law and property law. In the opening chapter of her major synthesising work, *Law's Relations*, she reaffirms her assessment of the liberal 'self', which, again, she says is best characterised by the idea of boundary.[68] According to Nedelsky, 'the image of protective boundaries as essential to the integrity and autonomy of the self is deep and pervasive in Western culture'.[69] The ability to defend an area of non-interference by others, an area of exclusive private property, has therefore assumed great symbolic importance. The most autonomous individual is the one with the strongest right and ability to secure separation from others: to exclude others from their person and their property. The framers of the US Constitution were preoccupied with property, Nedelsky claims, precisely because of this presumed connection between property rights and personhood.[70]

The bounded individual has come to be so well accepted as an idea of the person, at the centre of much of our liberal law, especially criminal law, as well as human rights law, that it has become a truism. To be a liberal person, it seems, is to have the right to assert separation; to assert personal border control.

---

[64] See 'Reconceiving Autonomy: Sources, Thoughts and Possibilities' (1989) 1 *Yale Journal of Law & Feminism* 7; 'Law, Boundaries and the Bounded Self' (1990) 30 *Representations* 162; *Private Property and the Limits of American Constitutionalism* (Chicago, University of Chicago Press, 1990), culminating in *Law's Relations: A Relational Theory of Self Autonomy and Law* (Oxford, Oxford University Press, 2011).
[65] Nedelsky, 'Reconceiving Autonomy', above n 64 at 8.
[66] Nedelsky, *Law's Relations*, above n 64 at 5.
[67] Nedelsky, 'Law, Boundaries and the Bounded Self', above n 64.
[68] Nedelsky, *Law's Relations*, above n 64.
[69] Ibid 98.
[70] Ibid 94.

This 'bounded' understanding of, and aspiration for, the person, Nedelsky maintains, must lead to frustration and unhappiness, because it is out of reach of most people – men included – for most, if not all of their lives, and can only be achieved by a few people, mainly male, for some of their lives. And then this is only achieved by leaning heavily on others, without acknowledging that debt.[71] (Pateman effectively said this too in *The Sexual Contract*.)

The bounded conception of persons, as bounded proprietors of themselves and of their own personal domains, has unfortunate implications for the development of character, according to Nedelsky, and especially, it would seem, for the male psyche. In her view, it fosters a controlling and possessive nature, as the (male) individual becomes intent on securing dominion over himself and his own. (Blackstone, as we will see, presents a strong endorsement of this character, with his doctrine of coverture, which sets the tone for male thinking about men and control.) To Nedelsky, the result is an impoverished and undesirable model of a male person to build a law around or, more accurately, to instantiate through law, for this 'bounded self' is an artefact of law.

But before we leap too far forward in our story, and start diagnosing the ailments of our criminal legal person, we must consider how this bounded male being came to assume such a prominent position in criminal law thinking. Who were his progenitors? How did he come to seem the natural and normal case of the person? Why and how did criminal law coalesce around him? And where did this leave women?

---

[71] In its place Nedelsky offers a 'relational' conception of autonomy and of the person, one which emphasises the interdependence of us all.

3

Hale, Blackstone and the Character of Men

My historical survey of the men of criminal law, their sense of themselves and their codification of their own conduct, begins in the seventeenth century with the writings of Sir Matthew Hale (1609–1676) on the nature of rape and the husband's immunity from rape prosecution, published 60 years after his death in 1736, and with Sir William Blackstone (1723–1780), and his *Commentaries on the Laws of England*. Hale was a man of the seventeenth century, still revered as the great scholar and judge. He was at the cusp of the medieval and the modern, and with his *Pleas of the Crown* set down a criminal law for England. Blackstone was squarely of the eighteenth century, again the great scholar and judge,[1] who established the scholarly discipline of law.[2]

The reason I look to influential statements on men's relation to women – as husbands – to find out about men themselves, is that men, as men, only come clearly into view when they are defined in relation to women. Logically, it is the other sex, that which men are not, which sets the boundaries and the contours of men's nature. A man's difference from another man will speak only of male variation; it will not tell you what makes a man a man; what makes the male sex distinctive. For man's distinctiveness to be seen, you need a woman (the not-man) to delimit his character, even to provide the setting for his nature.

Blackstone is also helpful in that he created a taxonomy of persons (borrowed in part from the Romans), in which men were implicitly established as the general case of the person, and women were special and inferior versions. Women were sub-people. This only becomes crystal clear when we consider Blackstone's treatment of the husband. Through marriage, which was the general and defining

---

[1] Though this was not necessarily the view of the utilitarian thinker Jeremy Bentham, the great critic of the common law and its supposed basis in natural law. See Jeremy Bentham, *A Comment on the Commentaries and a Fragment on Government* JH Burnsand, HLA Hart and Philip Schofield (eds), (Oxford, Clarendon Press, 1977). And for a thoughtful analysis of the intellectual relationship between Bentham and Blackstone see Mary Sokol, 'Blackstone and Bentham on the Law of Marriage' in Wilfrid Prest (ed), *Blackstone and his Commentaries* (Oxford, Hart, 2014) 91. See also Mary Sokol, *Bentham, Law and Marriage: A Utilitarian Code of Law in Historical Contexts* (London, Bloomsbury, 2013) for an account of Bentham's contrasting utilitarian view of marriage.

[2] See Wilfrid Prest, 'Blackstone, Sir William' in the *Oxford Dictionary of National Biography* (Oxford University Press, 2004; online edn, October 2009), www.oxforddnb.com/view/article/2536.

female experience, each woman according to Blackstone was annexed to a particular man – becoming part of his extended territory. Correlatively, man upon
marriage (equally the expected male rite of passage) extended his person into that
of his wife, enlarging his very legal and social being.

With Hale we have the enduring formulation of the crime of rape, 'the carnal
knowledge of any woman above the age of ten years against her will',[3] and also
of the husband's immunity, which carries through to the end of the twentieth
century as the ancient but persistent legal statement of the crime and its scope.
Hale supplied the first authoritative written declaration of the marital exception,
which travelled through the centuries, unscathed, carrying the force of law into the
last decade of the twentieth century.[4] (The author had it served up to her as a law
student.) Hale stated briefly, but boldly, that rape law could not encroach on the
rights of the husband to the body of his wife, and therefore Hale is highly informative about the legal nature of man and what he found appropriate and acceptable
in himself.

In Blackstone, we have the clearest and perhaps most influential legal communication on the socially-approved behaviour of men, as men, and their codes of
conduct, and this is essentially as husbands in relation to their wives. Blackstone
set the supercilious tone and hubristic attitude for men as they spoke about the
non-status of women and the nature and limits of permissible male conduct to
such non-entities. This in turn helped to mould the entire way of thinking about
what it was to be a rights-bearing man of criminal law.

As we will see in Chapter 4, Hale and Blackstone and their thoughts on the
roles and nature of men carried forward into the Victorian period and were central
to the thinking of 'the great' criminal jurist James Fitzjames Stephen, though such
views were strongly criticised by his contemporary, and staunch liberal, John
Stuart Mill.

I. Sir Matthew Hale (1609–1676)

In 1736 Sir Matthew Hale[5] in his *History of the Pleas of the Crown* provided a brief
statement of the sexual rights of the husband to the wife, thereby ousting the law of
rape. Hale said that 'the husband cannot be guilty of a rape committed by himself

---

[3] Sir Matthew Hale, *Historia Placitorum Coronae*, vol 1 (London, Professional Books, 1971) 627.

[4] For a thoughtful and original historical account of the legacy of Hale within the law of rape, see
Kos Lesses, 'PGA v The Queen: Marital Rape in Australia: The Role of Repetition' (2014) 37 *Melbourne
University Law Review* 786; see also the Report of the Advisory Group on the Law of Rape (London,
HMSO, 1975) 3, which referred to 'the traditional common law definition' of the offence of rape
'derived from the 17th Century writer, and still in use'. In 1977 Barbara Toner observed that 'Matthew
Hale ... is still the most quoted authority on the law of rape': Barbara Toner, *The Facts of Rape* (London,
Hutchinson, 1977) 95. Both are quoted in Gilbert Geis, 'Lord Hale, Witches and Rape' (1978) 5 *British
Journal of Law and Society* 26.

[5] Chief Justice of the Court of King's Bench 1671–1676.

upon his lawful wife, for by their mutual matrimonial consent and contract the wife hath given up herself in this kind unto her husband which she cannot retract'.[6] Here we have man portrayed as husband. He receives the gift of his wife, from the wife herself. In law she is said to hand herself over to him and in a manner that she cannot rescind. She gives herself up 'in this kind': she is now sexually available, all the time. The term gift suggests the passage of property, but the property is the woman herself. This would seem to make the husband the proprietor of her person.

Hale's pronouncement on the immunity of husbands from rape prosecution was written extra-judicially and published posthumously (60 years after his death) but it came to assume the force of law, partly by sheer repetition.[7] As Kos Lesses observes, Hale thus supplied 'the original written source for what is known in English common law as the husband's "immunity" from prosecution of rape committed against his wife' and it persisted, century after century, by dint of the great reputation of Hale and in the absence of any refutation.[8] It is one brief statement, uttered without explanation or justification or reflection, but fully accepted by the men of law.

Hale is still revered as a great jurist and as the enduring authority for the husband's rape immunity. The *Encyclopaedia Britannica* describes him, still, as 'one of the greatest scholars on the history of English common law'.[9] Hale was also Chief Justice of the King's Bench where his work was 'characterized by singular personal integrity and impartiality'.[10] He is still best known for his *History of the Pleas of the Crown* which 'remains one of the principal authorities on the common law of criminal offenses'.[11] According to David Yale, who is responsible for his *Britannica* entry, Hale's 'place is undoubtedly among the principal figures in the history of English common law'.[12] This no doubt is also a reason why his brief statement on the marital immunity has carried so much weight and why it has almost never been questioned (until quite recently).

Hale represents, in the one person, a movement from a period of medieval superstition to a modern liberal sensibility. He combines two mentalities in his own legal thinking. Hale is still the esteemed historian of the common law, an acknowledged great legal thinker. And yet late in his career, in 1662, Hale presided over a trial of two women charged with the crime of witchcraft, provided a condemning summing up to the jury, the jury swiftly convicted, and Hale sentenced these two old women to death and they were hanged. Hale firmly believed in possession by the Devil, and at a time when belief in witches was in retreat. Hale considered the criminal law an appropriate response to women

---

[6] Hale, *Historia Placitorum Coronae*, above n 3 at 629.
[7] See Lesses, above n 4.
[8] Ibid at 787.
[9] David Yale, 'Matthew Hale', *Encyclopaedia Britannica* (online version).
[10] Ibid.
[11] Ibid.
[12] Ibid.

who used their alleged powers to bewitch in order to harm others. This case then formed an important precedent for the Salem trials.[13]

Indeed Hale explicitly connected the crime of rape with the crime of witchcraft, suggesting that both gave rise to special problems of proof:

> [O]f all the difficulties of evidence, there are two sorts of crimes that give the greatest difficulty, namely rapes and witchcraft, wherein many times persons are really guilty, yet such an evidence, as is satisfactory to prove, can hardly be found, and on the other side persons really innocent may be entangled under such presumptions, that carry greater probabilities of guilt.[14]

In his *History of the Pleas of the Crown*,[15] Lord Hale spoke eloquently of women's unreliability when it came to accusations of rape. His analysis of the crime was to become 'the beginning of wisdom'[16] on the subject. In their thinking on rape, leading Australian and English textbook writers continued to bear the mark of Sir Matthew Hale, well into the twenty-first century.

In their 1989 and 2001 editions of the leading Australian text, *Criminal Law*,[17] Brett, Waller and Williams (in the 1989 edition) and then Waller and Williams (in the 2001 edition) cite approvingly and at length the views of Hale.

> It is true rape is a most detestable crime, and therefore ought severely and impartially to be punished with death; but it must be remembered, that it is an accusation easily to be made and hard to be proved, and harder to be defended by the party accused, tho' never so innocent ...
>
> I only mention these instances, that we may be the more cautious upon trials of offences of this nature, wherein the court and jury may with so much ease be imposed upon without great care and vigilance; the heinousness of the offence many times transporting the judge and jury with so much indignation, that they are over-hastily carried to the conviction of the person accused thereof by the confident testimony, sometimes of malicious and false witnesses.[18]

While Brett, Waller and Williams distance themselves from Hale's sentiments on capital punishment, the rest of his pronouncement, they say, 'remains as true now as when it was written'.[19] Despite the great passage of time since Hale's utterance on rape, his good sense is contrasted favourably with the contemporary views of advocates for reform. And yet it is difficult to think of another profession which is so loath to relinquish or question social understandings acquired in the seventeenth century.

---

[13] Gilbert Geis and Ivan Bunn, *A Trial of Witches: A Seventeenth-Century Witchcraft Prosecution* (London and New York, Routledge, 1997).

[14] Hale, above n 3, 290.

[15] Sir Matthew Hale, *The History of the Pleas of the Crown*, vol 1 (1736) 634.

[16] Jennifer Temkin, *Rape and the Legal Process* (London, Sweet and Maxwell, 1987) 134.

[17] P Brett, L Waller and CR Williams, *Criminal Law: Text and Cases*, 6th edn (Sydney, Butterworths, 1989).

[18] Hale, *The History of the Pleas of the Crown*, above n 15 at 634.

[19] Brett et al, above n 17, at 82 (2001 edition at 92).

As Geis and Bunn observe in the course of their extended account of Hale's witch trial, 'In virtually all regards, Hale's warning about rape is singularly inaccurate. Rape is not, and never has been, an easy charge to make and a difficult one to rebut. It certainly was not so in or before Hale's time'.[20] They note, for example, that the historian JM Kaye, in his general survey of the early English criminal law 'could find no trace of an execution during the period between 1285 and 1330', though rape had been declared a capital offence at the start of this period.[21]

Similarly the modern textbook writers provide no supporting evidence for their claim. These are misogynist pronouncements about the unreliability of women, perhaps implicitly addressed to men about the other sex, though female students were also in the classroom and reading the text.

In his 'Letters of Advice to his Grand Children', Hale developed his thoughts on the intellectual and moral defects of young gentlewomen:

> They make it their business to paint or patch their faces, to curl their locks, and to find out the newest and costliest fashions ... The morning is spent between the comb, the glass and the box of patches; though they know not how to make provision for themselves ... Their house is their prison and they are never at rest in it, unless they have gallants and splendid company to entertain.[22]

II.   William Blackstone (1723–1780)

The more complete account of legal man and especially of his right to women comes some 30 years later, from William Blackstone, still celebrated for his *Commentaries on the Laws of England* (first edition 1765). As Mary Sokol explains, 'Blackstone's aims were those of a pioneering expositor and would-be reformer of English law. Writing for an educated public as well as for lawyers, he set out to write a constitution and laws founded on natural law and moulded by history'.[23]

Though Blackstone overstated the case, with his pronouncement on the doctrine of coverture, he thus approved the legal annihilation of women *by men* and their absorption *into* a man, upon marriage. It is hard to imagine a stronger endorsement of the deliberate legal erasure of one person by another, the passing of control over one life to another. The husband was made the master of the very being, the mind, the will and the body, of his wife.

Blackstone studied at Charterhouse School (for affluent middle class boys) and then Oxford and became a fellow of All Souls at 20. He went on to have an interestingly varied career: barrister, 'scholar and man of letters'.[24] He was the first

---

[20] Geis and Bunn, above n 13, at 121.
[21] Ibid.
[22] Quoted by Geis, above n 4 at 30.
[23] Sokol (2014), above n 1 at 92.
[24] Wilfrid Prest, 'Life' in Wilfrid Prest (ed), *Blackstone and His Commentaries* (Hart, Oxford, 2009) 1.

Vinerian Professor of English Law, elected to this new Chair in 1758. His biographer Wilfrid Prest fills in the picture: 'He also served as a busy back-bench MP, [a Tory] pursued an expanded legal practice and angled for professional promotion, while fathering a growing family'.[25] After the publication of the *Commentaries* 'he was at last promoted to the judicial bench and knighted'.[26] He was 'A capable and conscientious judge, albeit increasingly obese and testy'.[27] It goes almost without saying, but not quite, and to complete this briefest of biographies, that had Blackstone been born a woman, he could have done none of these things.

Blackstone enjoyed the enormous privileges of his sex: higher education, a political, legal and scholarly life, an automatic male right to participate fully in public life; and he could be seen to bask in them when he reflected on the position of the husband in law, vis-à-vis the wife. As we will see, Blackstone reeled off the multiple powers and benefits of being a husband, without apology and with evident approval. Little is known about his wife, who bore him nine children. Apparently he adored her.[28]

Blackstone was the immensely powerful, authoritative and assured compiler and defender of the common law. Blackstone's *Commentaries on the Laws of England* started their life as a lecture series, delivered in Oxford, and were to be published in four volumes from 1765 to 1769. They then underwent many editions, eight in his life time, and then under different editors.[29] Blackstone spoke with chilling condescension about the other sex, and yet he is still revered today for his so-called making of the common law. A veritable industry still surrounds his work – preserving it, interpreting it and praising it.

In his *Commentaries*, which ran to four volumes, Blackstone set down an extensive set of organising principles for the common law of England. In Book One, in his account of the law of persons, Blackstone affirmed the utmost importance of the security of the person. The very object of the law of England was to secure the rights of natural persons and the most important, indeed 'absolute', rights were those of personal security, personal liberty and private property. But when he came to what he termed 'private' relations, these rights of persons were qualified and even suspended, for some persons. These private relations were those of 'master and servant', 'husband and wife', 'parent and child', and 'guardian and ward'. Man as master, husband, parent and guardian was to control the person on the other side of these legal relations, diminishing if not destroying their personal security, liberty and rights to property. It is here in his characterisation of the husband that Blackstone most clearly enunciated and laid down a law of man's character and his male rights and how men should relate to women.

---

[25] Ibid.
[26] Ibid.
[27] Ibid.
[28] See Prest, 'Blackstone, Sir William', above n 2.
[29] Kunal Parker, 'Historicising Blackstone's *Commentaries on the Laws of England*: Difference and Sameness in Historical Time' in Angela Fernandez and Markus Dubber (eds), *Law Books in Action: Essays on the Anglo-American Treatise* (Oxford, Hart, 2012).

The implicit idea was that each man would have a wife. Marriage would be the proper setting for his relations with women – for he would not find them as significant participants in the public sphere which was the world of men. Blackstone explained the legal effects of husbands and wives on each other's existence, and offered the pithy defence of these correlative roles and effects in which the husband was master and the wife was his subordinate.

Blackstone's prior edicts on the absolute rights of persons then turn out to be an edict about the absolute rights of his own sex. As he makes plain, marriage profoundly qualifies the rights of women and correlatively amplifies the rights of men. Women once married cease to be persons; and so married men are no longer dealing with persons with absolute rights (which belong to male persons only), but with an inferior specimen. It follows that Blackstone's law of persons is really a law of men.

Here is the central passage of Blackstone's famous statement of the doctrine of coverture.

> By marriage, the husband and wife are one person in law: that is, the very being or legal existence of the woman is suspended during the marriage, or at least is incorporated and consolidated into that of the husband: under whose wing, protection, and cover, she performs everything; and is therefore called in our law-french a *feme-covert* … is said to be … under the protection and influence of her husand, her *baron*, or lord; and her condition during her marriage is called her *coverture*. Upon this principle, of an union of person in husband and wife, depend almost all the legal rights, duties, and disabilities, that either of them acquire by marriage … For this reason, a man cannot grant anything to his wife, or enter into covenant with her, for the grant would be to suppose her separate existence: and to covenant with her would be only to covenant with himself.[30]

Male supremacism, a strong term but a defensible one, assumed its high and classic form in this immensely influential statement about the husband and his absorption of the wife into himself. Tim Stretton describes it as 'one of the most quoted passages' of *The Commentaries*.[31] It may be the most sustained, and least flinching, assertion of male existential imperialism, which goes on to be characterised, one sidedly, as an account of the legal nature of married women (not of men) and in the course of repetition, it perhaps loses its sting.

In truth, Blackstone's statement tells us a great deal about men, as law sees them. It speaks of men's perceived disposition for dominance, for hierarchy. It anticipates a certain male moral education, training in male character, in what men expected to be and become as they mature into controlling and coercive yet somehow civil beings, whose legal and moral task is to take over and assume the will of another. And the general rules governing violence are specifically modified and qualified for the husband's domain in order to permit him to exercise his right.

---

[30] William Blackstone, *Commentaries on the Laws of England*, Book 1: 'The Rights of Persons', 14th edn (London, Cadell and Davies, 1803) 442.

[31] Tim Stretton, 'Coverture and Unity of Person in Blackstone's Commentaries' in Wilfrid Prest (ed), *Blackstone and His Commentaries* (Oxford, Hart, 2009) 111.

In Blackstone's emphatic account, the husband was made the complete controller of the being, the mind, the will and the body of his wife. Blackstone tells us that the wife's 'existence ... is suspended', 'her very being' eclipsed by the act of marriage. And she is 'incorporated' and 'consolidated' into a man. The finishing touch to this account of legal extermination of a person by law, as we will see, is that men are doing it for women: it is in women's interests to disappear, and perhaps reappear as a constituting element of men.

This declaration by Blackstone is typically treated as an account of the incapacities of wives but it is as much a statement about the assumed capacities and powers and legal character of men as husbands. It enunciates and approves their powers over another, including money, body, and in Blackstone's own words, the wife's very 'existence'.[32]

Blackstone's doctrine of coverture has been recited so often that it is hard to hear it afresh, as other than a description of the historical incapacities of married women – as if these were things which inhered in women of the past. Blackstone, with never a backward glance, endorsed the suspension of rights he had considered fundamental to persons only a little earlier in the same volume. He could do this only if he were thinking of persons as men and his doctrine of coverture tells us that this is precisely who he thought persons were.

None of this was the subject of reflection or justification by Blackstone. He gives us no indication of men's stake in women, of men's sexual and economic interests in women's legal inferiority. We are told only of women's natural disadvantages. This is just how it is with the common law. Blackstone presented all this as simple good sense and in the nature of things. And still the doctrine of coverture is generally not seen as a statement of the enlarged existence of each man, as he connected with a woman and acquired rights to her person which would be unconscionable were she another man.

And so Blackstone set both the tone and the cast of the man problem – of securing free access to women while endorsing the absolute rights of persons to personal security. 'Married women' were to be thought of as private non-beings; they were 'unpersons'.[33] Under the enduring influence of Blackstone they would become a standard legal category of inferior persons, along with servants, children and also lunatics. Married men would be persons largely without classification, and so men would not be listed in catalogues of special legal persons and nor would husbands. They would not be indexed separately in legal texts. They would simply be persons.

It is still strangely difficult to keep the focus on men as one reflects on the thinking of Blackstone: on the implications of all the inflated powers of men,

---

[32] Margaret Attwood's female dystopian novel *The Handmaid's Tale* (New York, Anchor Books, 1998) is not far from this and might well have been informed by Blackstone's doctrine.

[33] The term 'unperson' is the invention of George Orwell in his dystopian and increasingly pertinent novel *1984* (London, Arcturus Publishing, 2013). In his invented language of newspeak, the unperson is someone who has been vapourised, erased, made to vanish.

for men, who made them, sustained them, interpreted them, defended them, who lived and breathed them, went to bed with them, who had so many interests in them. They are the tellers of the general legal story and they cast their own characters in a prominent and generally flattering and self-serving light. Blackstone is a fine exemplar of this male enhancement. And yet men, as men, seem to recede into the background. That they are telling the story helps a great deal.

True, the husband bears responsibilities for the wife as a consequence:

> The husband is bound to provide his wife with necessaries by law, as much as himself: and if she contracts debts for them, he is obliged to pay them; ... If the wife be indebted before marriage, the husband is bound afterwards to pay the debt; for he has adopted her and her circumstances together.[34]

Blackstone specified the disabilities of the wife which implicated the husband:[35]

> If the wife be injured in her person or her property, she can bring no action for redress without her husband's concurrence, and in his name, as well as her own: neither can she sue or be sued, without making the husband a defendant ... In criminal prosecutions, it is true, the wife may be indicted and punished separately; for the union is only a civil union.[36]

The personhood of the wife (and so correlatively the husband), therefore, varies according to type and provenance of law. Blackstone is writing about the common law and he tells us that 'In the civil law the husband and the wife are considered two distinct persons; and may have separate estates, contracts, debts, and injuries: and therefore, in our ecclesiastical courts, a woman may sue and be sued without her husband'.[37] The editor's note further explains that a woman may sue and be sued in a court of equity and may even 'by her prochain may sue her own husband'.[38]

We learn more about the character of the husband when Blackstone spells out some associated doctrines concerning the legal effects of marriage. For example under the doctrine of marital 'compulsion' it is assumed that the wife generally acts under the compulsion of her husband: that he compels her acts and decisions to the point that she is no longer responsible for them. (This is a principle that has endured and is now called the doctrine of marital coercion.)[39] Blackstone refers to

> [S]ome instances in which she [the wife] is separately considered; as inferior to him, and acting by his compulsion. And therefore all deeds executed, and acts done, by her, during her coverture, are void ... She cannot by will devise lands to her husband,

---

[34] Blackstone, above n 30 at 442.

[35] See David Rosenberg, 'Coverture in Criminal Law: Ancient Defender of Married Women' (1973) 6 *University of California, Davis Law Review* 83.

[36] Blackstone, above n 30 at 442–443.

[37] Ibid 443.

[38] Ibid.

[39] See for example s 328A of the Criminal Law Consolidation Act 1935 (SA) which abolishes the presumption of marital coercion but then declares that 'it shall be a good defence to prove that [an] offence' other than treason or murder 'was committed in the presence and under the coercion of the husband'.

unless under special circumstances; for at the time of making it she is supposed to be under his coercion. And in some felonies, and other inferior crimes, committed by her, through constraint of her husband, the law excuses her: but this extends not to treason or murder.[40]

Blackstone also examined and explained the principle that a husband might lawfully use force against his wife, if it were to correct her, placing him in the role of disciplinarian. Here he proceeded with greater caution, placing the principle at some distance by referring to 'the old law' and to the practices of people of 'lower rank'. To wit:

The husband also (by the old law) might give his wife moderate correction. For, as he is to answer for her misbehaviour, the law thought it reasonable to intrust him with this power of restraining her, by domestic chastisement, in the same moderation that a man is allowed to correct his apprentices or children; for whom the master or parent is also liable in some cases to answer. But his power of correction was confined within reasonable bounds, and the husband was prohibited from using any violence to his wife.[41]

Blackstone then inserted a division of time and class between the men of his time (and his ilk) and the men of the past.

But, with us in the politer reign of Charles the second, this power of correction began to be doubted: and a wife may now have security of the peace against her husband; or, in return, a husband against his wife. Yet the lower rank of people, who were always fond of the old common law, still claim and exert their ancient privilege: and the courts of law will still permit a husband to restrain a wife of her liberty, in case of any gross misbehaviour.[42]

Blackstone spoke of the married man's 'power of correction' being constrained 'within reasonable bounds', in the old law, and restraint of liberty 'in case of gross misbehaviour' in the contemporary law. This implicit approval of male control, its characterisation as appropriate and reasonable, runs through his entire account of the married man and what he can do to his wife.

What emerges is a coercive and controlling male character, who is to find modern recognition in the English offence of 'controlling and coercive behaviour' of the Serious Crime Act 2015 (UK), s 76, based on the work of Evan Stark.[43] According to Charlotte Bishop:

Research conducted by anti-domestic violence campaigner Evan Stark has shown how coercive control, most often perpetrated by a male against his female partner, can be very hard to recognise. This is because it involves micro-regulation of some of the

---

[40] Blackstone, above n 30 at 443.

[41] Ibid 444.

[42] Ibid.

[43] Evan Stark, *Coercive Control: How Men Entrap Women in Personal Life* (New York, Oxford University Press, 2007).

daily activities already commonly associated with women in their 'traditional' role as home-makers, mothers and sexual partners.[44]

Blackstone's approved male conduct is uncannily similar to the conduct now described in the guidelines to this offence provided by the Home Office.

> Controlling or coercive behaviour does not relate to a single incident, it is a purposeful pattern of behaviour which takes place over time in order for one individual to exert power, control or coercion over another.[45]

And as the Home Office explains, the new object is to retain the focus on the coercing person (though still not designated a man): 'This new offence focuses responsibility and accountability on the perpetrator who has chosen to carry out these behaviours'.[46]

A. 'A Social and Legal Relation not a Natural Thing'

Blackstone gives us a vivid portrait of the reasonable husband as disciplinarian. A powerful and unattractive character emerges. He is a compelling and striking being, in more than one sense. And yet this attention on the man, in Blackstone, is difficult to sustain. Blackstone himself, who cast the law of husband and wife as one concerning the naturally reduced status of women as they formed legal relations with a man, set the tone of future thinking. The ensuing literature portrays 'the unity principle', as it comes to be known, as one concerning married women and their peculiar status; not about the particular or peculiar characteristics of men (who seem implicitly to be cast as the non-particular, generic human type). The abandonment of civil standards, of legal accountability, as men enter marriage, is not how the story goes. As Tim Stretton has observed,

> Blackstone's description of married women's position at common law influenced generations of English and American jurists ... and continues to colour the interpretations of modern historians. For many of the commentators and judges who followed Blackstone the simple logic of unity of person, or marital unity was compelling.[47]

What Stretton calls the 'simple logic' of the principle 'of unity of person' does indeed hold sway. It entails a legal mindset in which our central character, the person – the man – is deemed to be naturally unified with another, who is however absorbed into him. He remains a general human being. We do not see him as

---

[44] Charlotte Bishop, 'Why it's so Hard to Prosecute Cases of Coercive or Controlling Behaviour' (31 October 2016) *The Conversation* theconversation.com/why-its-so-hard-to-prosecute-cases-of-coercive-or-controlling-behaviour-66108.

[45] Home Office, 'Coercive or Controlling Behaviour in an Intimate or Family Relationship: Statutory Guidance Framework' (December 2015).

[46] Ibid.

[47] Stretton, above n 31 at 111.

a member of a sex, one endowed with a nature conditioned by (which takes its nature from) its relation to the other sex, socially and in law.

However, marriage (and sex too) is a social and legal relation not a thing (as EP Thompson once said about class).[48] But this relational nature of the concept keeps disappearing from view. Though marriage is a legal relationship between a woman and a man (until very recently), which can logically only be understood as a set of legal relations between two legal beings, the mutual dependency of each party on that legal relationship for the very definition of each party keeps dropping out. We might say that the legal concept of 'the husband' and the legal concept of 'the wife', and for that matter the legal concept of 'the man' and 'the woman', cease to appear as legal concepts and are treated instead as brute natural facts. The artifice entailed, and those responsible for the artifice, cease to be apparent.[49]

B. 'So Great a Favourite'

We now come to the infamous concluding passage in Blackstone which, following hot on the heels of the account of the husband's right to chastise, now appears particularly provocative.

> These are the chief legal effects of marriage during the coverture; upon which we may observe, that even the disabilities, which the wife lies under, are for the most part intended for her protection and benefit. So great a favourite is the female sex of the laws of England.[50]

Blackstone thus invites us to see the wife as a legally disabled creature but for her own good, given her weaker constitution, a conjunction of ideas to be repeated by James Fitzjames Stephen in the nineteenth century. The correlative legal abilities of the husband – what he can do to her and with her as a consequence of this stripping of rights – and the male character thus created are not brought to our attention. John Stuart Mill, however, will do this some years later.

It is usual for modern critics of Blackstone, and his legal treatment of husbands and wives,[51] to express especial distaste, even disgust, with this last concluding sentence and its hypocrisy, given what has preceded it.[52] Blackstone asserts, archly, that 'So great a favourite is the female sex'. The hypocrisy resides in the fact that Blackstone's chapter on the husband and the wife largely concerns the legal non-existence of the wife and dissects and explains the component parts of her non-status, her non legal being.

---

[48] In EP Thompson, *The Making of the English Working Class* (New York, Vintage Books, 1963).
[49] See Lon L Fuller, *Legal Fictions* (Stanford University Press, 1968).
[50] Blackstone, above n 30 at 444.
[51] See Chapter 15 of Blackstone, above n 30, entitled 'Of Husband and Wife', which enumerates 'the chief effects of marriage' for the wife.
[52] See, for example, Joanne Conaghan, *Law and Gender* (Oxford, Oxford University Press, 2013).

III. Edward Christian and the Footnote

In 1803, Edward Christian, one of Blackstone's posthumous editors (of the 14th and 15th editions)[53] issued a rebuke to Blackstone which is not well known. Edward Christian's extended footnote to Blackstone's now infamous claim that the female sex is hampered by English law only because she is 'so great a favourite' is a bracing and unexpected reply, directly taking on the master. It entails an interesting conversation between men, running beneath the text, between the author, now dead, the so-called 'Learned Commentator', and his editor, about men's understanding of their privileges and powers. It also conjures up an audience of young legal men, law students imbibing the learning of the great Blackstone about their considerable rights as husbands and what they are to make of them.

Here Christian calls Blackstone to account. Perhaps as a scholar and a gentleman he could not stomach the internal contradictions and so asks his readers, who will be men in training for law, to test his logic. Footnote 23 is as follows:

> Nothing, I apprehend, would more conciliate the good-will of the student in favour of the laws of England, than the persuasion that they had shown a partiality to the female sex. But I am not so much in love with my subject as to be inclined to leave it in possession of a glory which it may not justly deserve. In addition to what has been observed in this chapter, by the learned Commentator, I shall here state some of the principal differences in the English law, respecting the two sexes; and I shall leave it to the reader to determine on which side is the balance, and how far this compliment is supported by truth.[54]

Christian then supplies a remarkable denunciation of the inflated status of the husband, who raised to the level of baron becomes kinglike in his powers. For the husband to kill the wife is to kill an ordinary person, in fact it is to kill an inferior being; but for her to kill him is to commit a variety of treason, as she is his subject.

> Husband and wife, in the language of the law, are stiled *baron* and *feme*: the word baron, or lord, *attributes to the husband not a very courteous superiority*. But we might think this merely an unmeaning technical phrase, if we did not recollect, that if the baron kills his feme, it is the same as if he had killed a stranger or any other person; but if the feme kills her baron, it is regarded by the laws as a much more atrocious crime; as she not only breaks through the restraints of humanity and conjugal affection but throws off all subjection to the authority of the husband. And therefore the law denominates her crime a species of treason, and condemns her to the same punishment as if she had killed the king.[55] (emphasis added)

The practical effect of this was breathtaking: 'And for every species of treason ... till the 30 Geo. Ill c. 48 *the sentence of women was to be drawn and burnt alive*'(emphasis added).[56]

---

[53] Edward Christian was a law professor, judge and older brother of Fletcher Christian of the Bounty.
[54] Edward Christian in Blackstone, above n 30 at 443–444, n 23.
[55] Ibid.
[56] Ibid.

Christian continues: 'A woman's personal property, by marriage, becomes absolutely her husband's, which at his death he may leave entirely away from her; but if he dies without will, she is entitled to one-third of his property, if he has children; if not, to one half'.[57]

And the litany of abuse goes on:

> With regard to the property of women there is taxation without representation; for they pay taxes without having the liberty of voting for representatives; and, indeed, there seems at present no substantial reason why women should be denied this privilege.[58]

And so Christian concludes that 'From this impartial statement of the account, I fear there is little reason to pay a compliment to our laws for their respect and favour to the female sex'.[59]

Two thirds of a century later, in *the Subjection of Women* (published in 1869), in the heart of the Victorian period, John Stuart Mill takes up this theme again, to be rebutted by the great legal figure of the Victorian period, James Fitzjames Stephen.

---

[57] Ibid.

[58] Ibid.

[59] For more on Christian see Deirdre Palk, *Gender, Crime and Judicial Discretion 1780–1830* (Woodbridge, Royal Historical Society, 2006) 21. See also Tim Stretton and Krista Kesselring (eds), *Married Women and the Law: Coverture in England and the Common Law World* (London, McGill-Queens University Press, 2013).

4

JS Mill, Stephen and the Victorian Mentality

In Michaelmas Term of 1900 and Hilary Term of 1901, at the Request of the Council of Legal Education, a series of 12 lectures was delivered in the Old Hall, Lincoln's Inn. The speakers were to look back on a century of reform of the law of England and to do so in the last moments of the Victorian age.[1]

The libel scholar, W Blake Odgers QC opened the series. In his lecture on the 'Changes In The Common Law And In The Law Of Persons, In The Legal Profession And In Legal Education', Odgers noted that the nineteenth century only had two months to run and 'must not be allowed to expire without some attempt being made to record and illustrate the changes that have taken place in the law of England during the century'.[2]

Odgers observed that 'Men of other professions have been proclaiming the advance of science, the wonders of invention, the extension of trade, the increase of the population, and of the country's material wealth, during that period'.[3] Now it was time for the men of law to demonstrate their own achievements:

> And it is surely right that here in the Inns of Court, in the School of Law for London, the attention of our students should be expressly directed to the great improvements which have been made, both in our law and in its administration, since the year 1800.[4]

Odgers was particularly struck by the improvements in women's lot. Once it was normal to liken married women to infants and to the insane. He passed over this humiliating convention lightly, with only a wry reference to 'our polite textbook writers' who 'always placed married women' ... 'next to lunatics'.[5] He declared that 'great indeed are the changes that have been made in this branch of our law. In 1800 a married woman had scarcely any rights'.[6]

---

[1] The Council of Legal Education, *A Century of Law Reform: Twelve Lectures on the Changes in the Law of England During the Nineteenth Century Delivered at the Request of the Council of Legal Education* (London, Macmillan and Co, 1901).

[2] William Blake Odgers, 'Changes In The Common Law And In The Law Of Persons, In The Legal Profession And In Legal Education' in ibid at 1.

[3] Ibid.

[4] Ibid.

[5] Ibid 20.

[6] Ibid.

Odgers celebrated the successes of the new law, its 'great improvements'.[7] His mind was turned to the changing status of married women – to their new property rights, their rights to the custody of their children or to seek legal separation if treated cruelly – but he was necessarily also talking about the changing status of men and male conduct. The correlativity of rights and duties is well understood by lawyers: rights are relational and so the non-rights of women in relation to men are necessarily a function of the rights of men.

Odgers described the former rights of his sex to women, and over women, the control and regulation of women in such a manner that they had 'scarcely any rights': only duties to their lawful husbands, to succumb and surrender.[8] The duty to supply sexual access was implied here but not spelled out. Odgers depicted a legally-bloated husband, stuffed with rights to another, but who had been deflated over the course of the nineteenth century. It seemed to be a matter of after-dinner humour.

In the eleventh lecture, Sir Montague Lush reflected at length on 'Changes in the law affecting the rights, status, and liabilities of married women'.[9] 'I do not suppose', he said, 'that there is any branch or department of the law in which the change has been greater or the contrast more violent. It is not that there has been an alteration, but a revolution in the law'.[10] To drive home his point, Lush then engaged in a thought experiment. He conjured up 'a great lawyer of a century ago presenting himself for examination today before the Board of Examiners'.[11] He was to be given a basic exam on the law governing husbands and wives. Lush surmised that 'there is scarcely an answer which he could answer correctly'.[12] He continued in poetic metaphorical language:

> [T]he wife for almost all legal purposes became on her marriage a nonentity. She was the shadow and her husband the substance ... He could put her under lock and key if she didn't please him and could, it used to be said, issue moderate personal correction to her if she did not behave properly.[13]

Lush portrayed the unreformed husband as an arbitrary jailer of his wife, constrained only by his personal pleasure. For the wife was legally 'a nonentity'. And yet again the tone was light-hearted. The husband could say what was proper in a wife. He had the power to employ force to bring her into line. (One must assume that this meant a basic assault.) By the time of this lecture, things had changed dramatically for the husband we are told: his powers drastically reduced; his rights to use force curtailed. The continuing right of forced sexual penetration

[7] Ibid 1.
[8] Ibid 20.
[9] Montague Lush, 'Changes in the law affecting the rights, status, and liabilities of married women' in ibid at 342.
[10] Ibid.
[11] Ibid.
[12] Ibid.
[13] Ibid 343.

of the wife was not discussed, perhaps merely assumed. And yet the talk was still all about the wife: an inquiry into *her* legal status, and her changing disabilities. The husband was pictured, to be sure, but as a benign jailer, whom the law assumed would be measured in his control of his wife, who would be 'moderate' in his 'personal correction' if she failed to behave.

Lush was describing a gradual reining in of the powers of men, especially their uses of physical constraint and force. And yet this was not seen to be a reflection on changing codes of male conduct and their use of force. It was not about men's changing mores for themselves, and their uses of criminal law to set them.

In this room populated by the august men of law, men were both present and absent. We can visualise a sea of men. They were the speakers. They were the audience. Their uses of law to control and punish women were openly acknowledged. Their legal powers were so great that they were thought to be the very stuff of life: the 'substance', rather than the 'shadow'. And yet these men were gentle with themselves. We are given a homily on married women coming out of status, rather than an honest inquiry into the uses of criminal law by their own sex to set the boundaries of acceptable male force. Men were there and they were not there.

Reading these light-hearted lectures, by legal men to legal men, we are made privy to a movement in ideas and attitudes of men of legal influence – of ways of thinking about themselves especially in relation to women – and their uses of criminal law in aid of this thinking. We see them setting standards for their own public and private conduct. They establish and re-establish the limits of their own violence, what is to be acceptable in their own sex. We can observe also a shift in male attitudes to women, from one of easy open condescension and sometimes even jokey contempt for the other sex, whose members are regarded as natural objects of sexual appropriation, to a slightly more measured and liberal stance.

In the time of Blackstone, as these august speakers remind us, male contempt for women was normal and accepted in the most influential circles of men. (Were one to replace the word 'woman' with Jew, or Black, in many of the statements made about women, the bigotry would be immediately obvious, at least to the modern reader.) Respect for women as rational persons and decision makers was not the male cultural norm and men had the power to enforce the male norm, especially by excluding women from education, public office and formal participation in civil society. Accountability to women was beyond contemplation.

William Blackstone set the tone of male hubris and condescension for the other sex, with his wry note that 'so great a favourite' were women to the laws of England that most of their rights were stripped from them upon marriage (to be contrasted with Christian's note of indignation at such hypocrisy). This superior attitude was sustained through the Victorian period as we will see with the thinking of Stephen, and his bristling response to the more egalitarian sentiments of John Stuart Mill, the focus of this chapter. In the words of John Tosh:

> [M]en have seldom advertised the ways in which authority over women has sustained their sense of themselves as men ... One explanation for John Stuart Mill's intense

unpopularity in conservative circles is that he voiced unpalatable truths in precisely this area – like his assertion in *The Subjection of Women* that 'the generality of the male sex cannot yet tolerate the idea of living with an equal'.[14]

I. Baronet James Fitzjames Stephen (1829–1894)

My main character of the Victorian period is Sir James Fitzjames Stephen, prolific legal writer, expounder of the criminal law,[15] senior judge, colonial administrator, journalist and uncle of Virginia Woolf. I take him as an important exemplar of the Victorian legal mentality about the nature of men, the nature of women and the role of criminal law in giving expression to those natures and indeed in counselling the uses of force.

A 'mentality' is a relatively settled collective way of thinking about the world and our place in it. Robert Darnton describes a 'mentalité' as a 'system of meaning', as a 'mental world' and as a 'mental universe', which is amenable to study by the social sciences.[16] A mentality is a shared view of the world held by a particular cultural grouping in a specific place and time, though it is likely to be sustained and then change over a long time.[17] My suggestion is that the collection of ideas that go to make up some of the most influential legal understandings of men and women can be fruitfully studied as mentalities.

Stephen was born in Kensington, London in 1829 and died in 1891, at the age of 65. He was educated at Eton and then King's College London and Cambridge where he became a member of the Cambridge Apostles, an immensely influential intellectual elite: a small exclusive club of clever men. Each of these institutions excluded women. Stephen went on to become a Queen's Counsel, and a legal member of the Council of India in which capacity he drafted the Indian Evidence Act. He wrote extensively as a journalist and also as a legal scholar. His *General View of the Criminal Law of England*, published in 1863, was the first attempt since Blackstone to expound this branch of the law in a literary manner and it was well received. In 1879 he was made a judge of the High Court. He was a man of great

---

[14] John Tosh, 'Essays: What Should Historians do with Masculinity? Reflections on Nineteenth-century Britain (1994) 38 *History Workshop Journal* 179, 184.

[15] See for example James Fitzjames Stephen, *A General View of the Criminal Laws of England* (London, Macmillan and Co, 1863); James Fitzjames Stephen, *Liberty, Equality and Fraternity* (New York, Holt and Williams, 1873); James Fitzjames Stephen, *A History of the Criminal Law of England*, 3 vols (London, Macmillan and Co, 1883); James Fitzjames Stephen, *A Digest of the Criminal Law*, 4th edn (London, Macmillan and Co, 1877).

[16] Robert Darnton, *The Great Cat Massacre and Other Episodes in French Cultural History* (New York, Vintage, 1985) 5, 9, 11. Though I borrow Darnton's term, I am not adopting his historical method of microhistory.

[17] As we will see below, change from one mentality to another is slow.

influence in criminal law of the Victorian period. He expounded it repeatedly and at length. He therefore shaped it and as a judge he also executed it.[18]

Stephen was highly traditional in his view of men and women and their respective natures. But Stephen did not speak for all legal men. In fact it has been said that he was holding on to views of men and women which were already undergoing considerable change.[19] These shifts he tended either to decry or to suppress. In his work most dedicated to the character of men, as men, he engaged in a robust denunciation of John Stuart Mill, and his highly progressive views of the sexes.[20]

Stephen implicitly agreed with Hale and Blackstone. In his writings on women, and why they were ill-suited for public life, and why this should be the exclusive domain of men, he was explicitly responding to his contemporary John Stuart Mill and the provocation posed by his *The Subjection of Women* published in 1869.[21]

II. The Provocateur: John Stuart Mill and the Husband as Critic of Men and Marriage

In *The Subjection of Women* Mill had the temerity to examine the value system endorsed by a law which was unwilling to constrain and regulate men within marriage. Mill perhaps remains unrivalled in his willingness to consider the effects of such domestic power, including the right to use force, on the character of men. To Mill, this amplification of male rights, this discretionary authority, left the husband morally uneducated, even brutal. This so exercised Mill that he devoted a book to the man problem.

The great liberal critic of the common law, Jeremy Bentham, had already characterised the family as 'a little kingdom', with its own particular governance and order, a view which he implicitly defended.[22] In 1869, John Stuart Mill offered a less benign view of the family. *The Subjection of Women* was a blistering critique of this arrangement, of the subjugation of the married woman and its implications for the moral character of the men who thus subjugated. Indeed Mill made much of the extreme brutalisation of men as a consequence. Mill described 'the law of

---

[18] KJM Smith, 'Stephen, Sir James Fitzjames, first baronet (1829–1894)' *Oxford Dictionary of National Biography* online version; see also KJM Smith, *James Fitzjames Smith: Portrait of a Victorian Rationalist* (Cambridge, Cambridge University Press, 1988).

[19] See Kate Gleeson, 'Brutal at his Best, the Problem of Clarence: James Fitzjames Stephen and the Doctrine of Sexual Inequality' (2005) 14 *Nottingham Law Journal* 1.

[20] This was in James Fitzjames Stephen, *Liberty, Equality, Fraternity*, Stuart D Warner (ed) (Indianapolis, Liberty Fund, 1993) discussed below.

[21] John Stuart Mill, *The Subjection of Women* in John Stuart Mill, John Gray (ed), *On Liberty and Other Essays* (Oxford, Oxford University Press, 1991) 500.

[22] Writing specifically in defence of the power of testamentary disposition, Bentham said 'Clothed with the power of making a will ... he [the testator] may be considered as a magistrate set over the little kingdom which is called a family, to preserve it in good order': Jeremy Bentham, 'Principles of the Civil Code' in John Bowring (ed), *The Works of Jeremy Bentham*, vol 1 (Edinburgh, William Tait, 1843) 337.

marriage' as 'a law of despotism',[23] with 'the wife [as] the actual bond-servant of her husband'.

> Above all, a female slave has (in Christian countries) an admitted right, and is considered under a moral obligation, to refuse her master the last familiarity. Not so the wife: however brutal a tyrant she may be unfortunately chained to, though it may be his daily pleasure to torture her, and though she may feel it impossible not to loathe him – he can claim from her and enforce the lowest degradation of a human being, that of being made the instrument of an animal function contrary to her inclinations.[24]

The Subjection entailed an extended analysis of the codes of male conduct implicit in the principle of marital privacy and the legality of wife rape.[25] It was an explosive document, potentially hugely unsettling to the legal community, especially to criminal law scholars. And yet for criminal law scholars, it is Mill's liberal manifesto, *On Liberty*,[26] for which he is most remembered and which supplied the basis of the harm principle of criminal law.

Mill depicted graphically the abuses of married life. He described the uncivilised behaviour which was not only permitted but was indeed countenanced by the state – positively creating men of bad character. Mill did not mince his words. He excoriated his own sex for the powers they had devolved to themselves. He asked:

> [H]ow many are the gradations of animalism and selfishness, often under an outward varnish of civilization and even cultivation, living at peace with the law, maintaining a creditable appearance to all who are not under their power yet sufficient often to make the lives of all who are so, a torment and a burthen to them![27]

Mill was unusual in his reflections on the implications of licensed domestic force for male responsibility and accountability: how it shrivelled the moral personhood of men. He emphasised the size and the scale of the problem of exclusive male rule and the power over women that it gave to every man.

> It would be tiresome to repeat the commonplaces about the unfitness of men in general for power ... were it not that hardly anyone thinks of applying these maxims to the case in which above all others they are applicable, that of power, not placed in the hands of a man here or there, but offered to every adult male, down to the basest and most ferocious.[28]

According to Mill: 'Even the commonest of men reserve the violent, the sulky, the undisguisedly selfish side of their character for those who have no power to

---

[23] Mill, above n 21 at 501.

[24] Ibid 504.

[25] As Stephan Collini observes in the introduction to his edition of Mill's *On Liberty and Other Writings* 'his argument rests upon a sustained analogy between the historical position of women and of slaves': John Stuart Mill, Stephan Collini (ed), *On Liberty and Other Writings* (Cambridge, Cambridge University Press, 1989) xx.

[26] John Stuart Mill, *On Liberty* (London, John W Parker and Son, 1859).

[27] Mill, *The Subjection of Women*, above n 21 at 509.

[28] Ibid 509.

withstand it. The relation of superiors to dependents is the nursery of these vices of character'.[29] Mill described the family 'as respects its chief, [as] a school of wilfilness, overbearingness, unbounded self-indulgence, and a double-dyed and idealized selfishness'.[30] He spoke unflinchingly of the implications of male domestic power for male responsibility, in effect for male personhood: how it detracted from both.[31]

Mill voiced his broader concerns about the inflated powers of men in a number of his works, including *Principles of Political Economy*[32] (1848) and *Representative Government*[33] (1861). As legal historian KJ Smith explains, Mill was an energetic political activist, 'a strenuous platform reformer for the cause [of women] into the early 1870s ... Mill unsuccessfully proposed a women's suffrage amendment to the Second Reform Bill'.[34]

III. Stephen's Dissent from Mill

James Fitzjames Stephen was a towering figure in the criminal law world of England in the last part of the nineteenth century. He wrote extensively on the criminal law in different fora, to different audiences and to different purposes. He was not only a man of considerable influence but he was also versatile. In 1863 he published *A General View of the Criminal Law*, for 'the intelligent layman';[35] in 1873 he published his polemical reply to Mill, *Liberty, Equality and Fraternity*;[36] in 1877 his summary of the criminal law or *Digest of the Criminal Law*;[37] in 1883 he produced a three-volume history of the criminal law,[38] and in 1888 he wrote the leading judgment in the first marital rape case of *Clarence*.[39] His reply to Mill was his most extended account of his views on male right. *Clarence* later supplied the legal clincher, turning the views of the legal commentator into the views of the judge, and so giving them the force of law. The ensuing analysis of Stephen, and his views on the nature and character of men, especially in relation to women, takes soundings from his reply to Mill, from his *Digest*, his history and from his notorious *Clarence* judgment whose influence carried into the twenty-first century.[40]

---

[29] Mill, *The Subjection of Women*, above n 21 at 509.
[30] Ibid, above n 21 at 510.
[31] Mill's *Subjection* precedes the passage of the Married Women's Property Act 1882 (UK).
[32] John Stuart Mill, *Principles of Political Economy*, 2 vols (London, John W Parker, 1848).
[33] John Stuart Mill, *Representative Government* (London, Parker, Son and Bourn, 1861).
[34] Smith (1988), above n 18 at 186.
[35] Stephen, *A General View of the Criminal Laws of England*, above n 15.
[36] Stephen, *Liberty, Equality, Fraternity*, above n 20.
[37] Stephen, *A Digest of the Criminal Law*, above n 15.
[38] Stephen, *A History of the Criminal Law of England*, above n 15.
[39] *R v Clarence* (1888) 22 QBD 23.
[40] See Matthew Weait, *Intimacy and Responsibility* (Oxford, Routledge-Cavendish, 2007) on the legacy of *Clarence*.

Turning first to *Liberty, Equality and Fraternity*, published in 1873, we find Stephen in robust polemical mood, even pugnacious, for this was the book written as a direct riposte to Mill's *On Liberty* and *The Subjection of Women*. Stephen was unqualified in his rejection of Mill.

> There is something unpleasant ... in prolonged and minute discussions about relations between men and women, and the characteristics of women as such. I will therefore pass over what Mr Mill says on this subject with a mere general expression of dissent from nearly every word he says.[41]

Stephen proclaimed the patent superiority of men and affirmed their superior legal powers, which followed as a natural consequence of their superior natures.

> I think that if the rights and duties which laws create are to be generally advantageous, they ought to be adapted to the situation of the persons who enjoy or are subject to them. They ought to recognize both substantial equality and substantial inequality ... Government, in a word, ought to fit society as a man's clothes fit him. To establish by law rights and duties which assume that people are equal when they are not is like trying to make clumsy feet look handsome by the help of tight boots.[42]

The invocation of the clumsy foot and the boot is an odd one given the generally smaller feet of women. His simile does not seem to serve its purpose. For men would not benefit from the tighter (legal) shoes of women but women would benefit, you would think, from the enlarged legal boots of men, though they would hardly look handsome in them. The metaphorical thinking is jumbled. But Stephen is emphatic about the natural supremacy of men.

> I say that there are many such differences ... and of which some are so marked and so important that unless human nature is radically changed, we cannot even imagine their removal; and of these the differences of age and sex are the most important.[43]

Male superiority required no defence, because it was founded in nature.

> Now, if society and government ought to recognize the inequality of age as the foundation of an inequality of rights ... it seems to me equally clear that they ought to recognize the inequality of sex ... if it is a real inequality. Is it one? There are some propositions which it is difficult to prove, because they are so plain, and this is one of them.[44]

So Stephen relied for his argument on strong declarations about what he took to be obvious. Stephen then slid, with relish, into a panegyric to men. (Imagine the following words being applied to the white races rather than to the male sex, and their disturbing qualities are plain.) We are told that

> [t]he physical differences between the two sexes affect every part of the human body, from the hair of the head to the soles of the feet, from the size and density of the bones to the texture of the brain and the character of the nervous system ... men are stronger

---

[41] Stephen, *Liberty, Equality, Fraternity*, above n 20 at 134–135.
[42] Ibid 136.
[43] Ibid 137.
[44] Ibid 138.

than women in every shape. They have greater muscular and nervous force, greater intellectual force, greater vigour of character ... These are the facts, and the question is whether the law and public opinion ought to recognize this difference?[45]

To Stephen, the superiority of the male was manifest and incontrovertible. And yet Mill had pointed out, as a matter of simple measurement, that it was impossible to arrive at a confident conclusion about male superiority because men had systematically been given greater educational, political and economic advantages and he did not know how men would fare without them. (He actually referred to the disadvantages imposed on women, but to keep our eyes trained on men, it is useful to observe the male privileges and benefits.) Stephen was to dismiss this fundamental and irrefutable point. Men did better because they were intrinsically better. It did not matter that women had been positively hampered in their efforts to know, to learn, to acquire and hold on to money. In fact because women were manifestly inferior to men, it was better to keep the power and authority with the superior sex and so keep male legal and economic privilege intact.

The philosopher Janet Radcliffe Richards has explained the logical problem with Stephen's derivation of an 'ought' from an 'is' (the naturalistic fallacy).[46] She states his argument thus: 'Women are at many natural disadvantages to men. Therefore the marriage contract should be one in which the wife is legally and socially subordinate to the husband'.[47] She then points out that: 'The premise makes a claim about what is the case and the conclusion says that something should be the case'.[48] Thus there is a slide from an 'is' (from what is the case) to an 'ought' (to what should be the case), without proper justification as we proceed from the first proposition to the second.

Indeed like Blackstone, Stephen cast the legal disabilities of women, who were already by nature inferior, as a positive benefit to women. After all, the assets of women diminished with age: 'A woman loses the qualities which make her attractive to a man much earlier than men lose those which make them attractive to women'.[49] By contrast, men seemed to improve over time, perhaps like good wine.

Men were defined by their strength, their power and the manner in which they naturally commanded obedience from a woman. 'Strength, in all its forms, is life and manhood. To be less strong is to be less of a man, whatever else you may be'.[50] To Stephen, 'by law and morals' 'the government of the family must be put ... in the hands of the husband, for no one proposes to give it to the wife'.[51] Indeed 'Few ladies would like to be told that they were disobedient wives. Few gentlemen

---

[45] Ibid.

[46] Janette Radcliffe Richards, *Human Nature After Darwin: A Philosophical Introduction* (Oxford, Routledge, 2000). Here she is offering a direct riposte to Stephen and what she regards as his faulty logic.

[47] Ibid 229–230.

[48] Ibid 230.

[49] Stephen, *Liberty, Equality, Fraternity*, above n 20 at 140.

[50] Ibid 143.

[51] Ibid 141.

would feel it otherwise than a reproach to learn that they were not masters in their own homes'.[52]

These views were not confined to the influential men of England. Across the Atlantic, we find very similar opinions expressed about the nature of women, some 20 years earlier, in the writings of Henry James, Senior, (father of William James). James explicitly endorsed what Mill condemned. He was explicit in his contempt for women.

James Senior wrote that: 'by nature [woman is] inferior to man. She is man's inferior in passion, his inferior in intellect and his inferior in physical strength'.[53] These words are strikingly similar to those of Stephen. And on the position of the wife James said that she was rightly thought of as the 'patient and unrepining drudge' of her husband 'his beast of burden, his toilsome ox, his dejected ass, his cook, his tailor, his own cheerful nurse and the sleepless guardian of his children'.[54] Here he echoed the words of Mill, though James was endorsing rather than condemning the subjection and mistreatment of the wife.

For Stephen it followed that marriage could never be a contract of equals. There was always a superior and an inferior person, the man and the woman:

> Follow the matter a step further to the vital point of the whole question – marriage ... whether the law and moral rules which relate to it should regard it as a contract between equals or as a contract between a stronger and a weaker person involving subordination ... I say that a law which proceeded on the former and not on the latter would be founded on a totally false assumption.[55]

Moreover marriage should be a self-regulating institution; or rather it should be regulated by the man of the home.

> Legislation and public opinion ought in all cases whatever scrupulously to protect privacy. To define the province of privacy distinctly is impossible, but it can be described in general terms. All the more intimate and delicate relations of life are of such a nature that to submit them to unsympathetic observation, or to observation which is unsympathetic in the wrong way, inflicts great pain, and may inflict lasting moral injury ... Conduct which can be described as indecent is almost always a violation of privacy.[56]

For Stephen, intimacy between the sexes was rightfully located within a marriage and then it was essentially not a legal matter if the more powerful person, the husband, took charge of the situation and made use of his advantage. Indeed he should. Stephen characterised 'marriage in terms of the ultimate supremacy (or sovereignty) of one party'.[57] For Stephen, then, the criminal law was the wrong sort

---

[52] Ibid 149.
[53] Henry James, 'Woman and the Woman's Movement' (1853) 1 *Putnam's Monthly* 285, as quoted in Louis Menand, *The Metaphysical Club* (London, Flamingo, 2002) 86–87.
[54] Ibid.
[55] Stephen, *Liberty, Equality, Fraternity*, above n 20 at 139.
[56] Ibid 159–160.
[57] Smith, above n 18 at 188.

of law for a marriage. And yet his brother Leslie said of Stephen that he 'loves and honours … women more than he can express, and owes most of the happiness of his life to them'.[58]

In perhaps his most memorable and purple passage, Stephen explained why law must keep out of the marriage. He said: 'To try to regulate the internal affairs of a family, the relations of love or friendship … by law … is like trying to pull an eyelash out of a man's eye with a pair of tongs. They may put out the eye, but they will never get hold of the eyelash'.[59] Stephen overlooked the many ways in which law already regulated the family (as it still does): its definition, the legal meaning and the respective roles of men and women, and the rules of acceptable force.[60]

The dogmatism of Stephen on the particular and inferior nature of women (which was 'so plain') and on sex differences ('we cannot even imagine their removal') was in strong contrast with his concluding comments, at the end of his book. Here he was all doubt and openness to life's other possibilities. Was he having his cake and eating it too? Or was he at his blindest when thinking of the man in his marriage, his little kingdom? On the sexes and marriage he seemed unable to countenance any change or any other point of view – so deep was his belief in the naturalness and immutability of them. But on other matters, even on religion which is often where dogmatism appears, he was open to doubt.

In Chapter 7, his 'Conclusion' to *Liberty Equality and Fraternity*, Stephen entertained these doubts, even counterfactual worlds:

> The firmest of all conclusions and judgments are dependent upon facts which, for aught we know, may have been otherwise in the past, may be otherwise in the future, and may at this moment present a totally different appearance to other intelligent beings from that which they present to ourselves.[61]

He now admitted social complexity and multiple perspectives: 'The facts of life are ambiguous. Different inferences may be drawn from them, and they do not present by any means the same general appearance to people who look at them from different points of view'.[62]

Here Stephen seemed to make an important concession to the limitations of point of view:

> Again, the largest and by far the most important part of all our speculations about mankind is based upon our experience of ourselves, and proceeds upon the supposition that the motives and principles of action of others are substantially the same as our own.[63]

---

[58] Smith, above n 18 at 188 quoting Leslie Stephen's: *Life of Sir James Fitzjames Stephen* (London, Smith, Elder & Co., 1895) 330.

[59] Quoted in Smith, above n 18 at 174; Mill, *Liberty, Equality and Fraternity*, above n 15 at 162.

[60] See Frances Olsen, 'The Family and the Market: A Study of Ideology and Legal Reform' (1983) 96 *Harvard Law Review* 1497, and also Katherine O'Donovan, *Sexual Divisions in Law* (London, Weidenfeld & Nicolson, 1986).

[61] Stephen, *Liberty, Equality, Fraternity*, above n 20 at 208.

[62] Ibid 205.

[63] Ibid.

Stephen here conceded the possibility of error in men's deepest convictions: 'The important thing to remember is the truism that it does not follow that a man is right because he is positive'.[64] This could be another man speaking. Modest specu-lation and reflection replaced absolutism.

A. 1877 The Digest

In his *Digest of the Criminal Law*, Stephen considered briefly, but now explicitly, the rights of the husband to the person of his wife: his right of sexual access. He acknowledged the husband's legal right to use force but said it must be contained. It is revealing to consider his precise words. A vivid picture is given of male control, and coercion to the point of violence: all perfectly lawful, if the 'violence' remained 'decent'.

> Hale's reason [for asserting the husband's immunity] is that the wife's consent at marriage is irrevocable. Surely, however, the consent is confined to the decent and proper use of marital rights. If a man used violence to his wife under circumstances in which decency or her own health or safety required or justified her in refusing her consent, I think he might be convicted of rape, notwithstanding Lord Hale's dictum. He gives no authority for it.[65]

So the husband could lawfully use 'violence', but not when 'decency' or his wife's 'health or safety required or justified her in refusing her consent'. Stephen at this time thought that there were limits to what a husband could do to overcome the resistance of an unwilling wife. Sometimes, he thought, she did have a right to say no.

B. 1883 A History of the Criminal Law of England

In *A History of the Criminal Law of England*, published in 1883, Stephen returned to his more dogmatic mode and now incorporated anger and outrage. The more measured and speculative theorist of the criminal law receded. According to Stephen, it was 'morally right' to hate men who raped and who committed other acts of violence because these were fundamentally immoral wrongs:

> First I will consider the normal case, that in which law and morals are in harmony, and ought to and usually do support each other. This is true of all the gross offences which consist of instances of turbulence, force, or fraud. Whatever may be the nature or extent of the differences which exist as to the nature of morals no one in this country regards murder, rape, arson, robbery, theft or the like, with any feeling but detestation.[66]

---

[64] Ibid 209.
[65] James Fitzjames Stephen, *A Digest of the Criminal Law* (London, Macmillan, 1877) 172, fn 1.
[66] Stephen, *A History of the Criminal Law of England*, vol 2, above n 15 at 80–81.

As a consequence:

> I do not think it admits of any doubt that law and morals powerfully support and gener-
> ally intensify each other in this matter ... the infliction of punishment by law gives
> definite expression and a solemn ratification and justification to the hatred which is
> excited by the commission of the offence ... The criminal law thus proceeds upon the
> principle that it is morally right to hate criminals ... I think it is highly desirable that
> criminals should be hated.[67]

Rape and other acts of violence were absolutely wrong and so the rapist should be
hated and reviled:

> I am also of opinion that this close alliance between criminal law and moral sentiment
> is in all ways healthy and advantageous to the community. I think it highly desirable
> that criminals should be hated, that the punishments inflicted upon them should be so
> contrived as to give expression to that hatred, and to justify it so far as the public provi-
> sion of means for expressing and gratifying a healthy natural sentiment can justify and
> encourage it.[68]

Stephen then made his famous statement, almost poetical in form, on the role of
law in regulating the passions. The passion for justice, he said, was given proper
outlet in criminal punishment. The passion for sex was given proper outlet within
the legal marriage. And within the marriage, as we know from *Liberty Equality
and Fraternity*, it was the man who would give full expression to his passions, in
the role of natural superior: 'The forms in which deliberate anger and righteous
disapprobation are expressed, and the execution of criminal justice is the most
emphatic of such forms, stand to the one set of passions in the same relation in
which marriage stands to the other'.[69]

For Stephen, murder, theft and rape, were what Antony Duff would today call
'pre-legal wrongs'. Thus:

> [S]ubstantive criminal law ... relates to actions which, if there were no criminal law
> at all, would be judged of by the public at large much as they are judged at present. If
> murder, theft and rape were not punished by the law, the words would still be in use,
> and would be applied to the same or nearly the same actions. The same or nearly the
> same distinctions would be recognized between murder and manslaughter, robbery and
> theft, rape and seduction. In short, there is a moral as well as a legal classification of
> crimes, and the merits and defects of legal definitions cannot be understood unless the
> moral view of the subject is understood.[70]

These were immoral acts with which criminal law was rightly in harmony, in
strongly condemning them and punishing them severely. They were wrong
whether or not they were criminalised. People knew them for what they were and,

---

[67] Ibid 81–82.
[68] Ibid 82.
[69] Ibid.
[70] Ibid 75.

to repeat, 'the words would still be in use, and would be applied to the same or nearly the same actions'.[71]

And yet as Lindsay Farmer points out, 'one of the most interesting things [about Stephen] is that although he expresses his strong abhorrence of gross offences, he does not even discuss rape or other sexual offences in the *History*. Instead he dismisses them as intellectually uninteresting'.[72] To wit: 'Their history possesses no special interest and does not illustrate either our political or our social history'.[73] End of story.

To Stephen,

[T]here are in the world a considerable number of extremely wicked people, disposed, when opportunity offers, to get what they want by force or fraud, with complete indifference to the interests of others, and in ways which are inconsistent with the existence of civilised society. Such persons, I think, ought in extreme cases to be destroyed. The view which I take of the subject would involve the increased use of physical pain, by flogging or otherwise, by way of a secondary punishment. It should, I think, be capable of being employed at the discretion of the judge in all cases in which the offence involves cruelty in the way of inflicting pain, or in which the offender's motive is lust.[74]

It is clear that for Stephen a man's rape of his wife and the rape of some other man's wife were at polar ends of the moral spectrum. Outside a marriage, rape was a pre-legal natural wrong and the rapist should be flogged and hanged. Within a marriage the husband was exercising his natural sex right to a woman; he was expressing his passions in a proper manner, one which was sanctioned by law and so law would abstain from censure. He was to be neither hated nor detested. We could say that he was both inside and outside the law, having his cake and eating it too. He was doing the very thing that Mill condemned.

IV. R v Clarence

We learn more about Stephen's thinking about men within marriage from his judgment in the landmark case of *Clarence* in 1888.[75] He had already made clear, extra-judicially, that the family was a private sphere – outside the sphere of criminal regulation (though criminal law should step in for beatings and killing) – and within it there were naturally unequal relations based on the unequal natural abilities of husband and wife. Stephen's conviction that the legal powers of the husband extended to the person of his wife were made explicit in *Clarence* and effectively given the force of case law (though they were embedded in obiter).

---

[71] Ibid 75.
[72] Lindsay Farmer, in email communication with the author, 6 November 2014.
[73] Stephen, *A History of the Criminal Law of England*, vol 3, above n 15 at 118.
[74] Ibid vol 2 at 91.
[75] *R v Clarence* (1888) 22 QBD 23.

In *Clarence* the husband, Charles Clarence, was at trial charged and convicted of inflicting grievous bodily harm to his wife, Selina Clarence, by transmission of gonorrhoea, which he knew he had and which he also knew would cause his wife to refuse sex were she to be told about it.[76] So he said nothing. His conviction was quashed on appeal largely due to the reasoning of Stephen. Stephen insisted that the concealment of the disease did not destroy Selina's consent and also that the transmission of the disease did not constitute grievous bodily harm. Along the way Stephen also indicated that he accepted the rape marital immunity anyway, though this was not essential to the case, and so remained obiter. It was nevertheless what the case came to stand for.

All 13 men of the Queen's Bench were asked to consider whether convictions of inflicting grievous bodily harm and assault occasioning actual bodily harm should stand. On the facts agreed, Selina had consented to the intercourse but in ignorance of the disease. Had she known of it, she would have refused. A majority of the judges, Stephen J included, quashed both convictions. Therefore in transmitting the disease while knowing of the disease and its risks, Charles Clarence had neither inflicted grievous bodily harm nor assaulted Selina causing actual bodily harm.

Lawyers' arguments on both sides were based on the validity of Selina's consent to intercourse, in view of her ignorance of the disease, and both discussed the marital immunity. The Defence supported the immunity. The Prosecution disputed the immunity and the authority of Hale. Though Charles had not been charged with rape, and though on the facts Selina had consented to intercourse, in her ignorance, the framing of the arguments by both sides brought the immunity into question.

Counsel for Charles had specifically raised the marital immunity, arguing that Charles did not intend an unlawful act as the law required. Moreover he specifically invoked and questioned the writings of Stephen, who in his *Digest* had raised doubts about the immunity.

> It is laid down in Hale's Pleas of the Crown that a husband cannot be guilty of rape of his wife, and though this proposition is doubted in Stephen's Digest of the Criminal Law (ed. 1877), p. 172, it would seem to have been always generally accepted ... Here the act of the prisoner was not 'unlawful'.[77]

And on the charge of assault:

> If coition, as between husband and wife, cannot constitute rape it follows that coition cannot as between them constitute an assault by the husband. Consent to coition on the part of the wife is a matrimonial obligation, and consent was also ... expressly given

---

[76] Clarence had been convicted of the offences of 'unlawfully and maliciously inflicting grievous bodily harm' upon his wife and of 'an assault' upon her 'occasioning actual bodily harm' under ss 20 and 47 respectively of The Offences Against the Person Act 1861 (UK) (24 and 25 Vict c 100).

[77] *R v Clarence* (1888) 22 QBD 23, 24–25.

by the prosecutrix … the consent of the woman was both implied by law and actually given.[78]

So the defence lawyer relied on the marital immunity to say that Charles did not intend an 'unlawful act' for the purposes of the charge of grievous bodily harm, as he could not rape his wife – this not being unlawful. And for the purposes of the assault charge, consent was implied by law, and here actually given. As Gleeson explains in her analysis of *Clarence*, this lawyer's address set up the argument for the case.[79]

Counsel for the Prosecution argued that Clarence was 'guilty on both counts'. He said that

> [t]he argument against the conviction proceeds on an erroneous view of the obliga-
> tion of a married woman. The passage cited from Hale's Pleas of the Crown is not
> supported by any other authority. It cannot be doubted that, if the prisoner had effected
> his purpose by force, the prosecutrix knowing his condition and resisting, the prisoner
> would have been guilty of rape. The act of the prisoner was therefore unlawful … the
> prosecutrix did not know her husband's condition and had she known it she would not
> have submitted. The prosecutrix therefore did not consent to the act of the prisoner and
> in the absence of consent by her his act was both an 'unlawful and malicious infliction
> of grievous bodily harm' (s. 20) and an 'assault inflicting actual bodily harm' (s. 47).[80]

There were 13 judgments and even in the majority (made up of nine judges) there were very different reasons given why there should be no conviction.

A. Stephen J

Ultimately, the leading judgment came to be that of Stephen J in the majority, who was referred to approvingly by five other judges. Stephen J did not explicitly base his judgment on Hale and the marital immunity. Rather he considered the effects of deception on consent to sex in general, what types of fraud might destroy consent to sexual intercourse, and concluded that only fraud about the nature of the act and the identity of the person would do so, and here Selina was deceived about neither. He also developed an argument on the distinction between causing grievous bodily harm and assault, both of which he characterised as the use of direct violence, and the transmission of disease, which was by contrast slow and indirect in the harm occasioned.

Stephen J first examined the s 20 offence of unlawful and malicious infliction of grievous bodily harm and considered the defence argument that 'the prisoner did not act "*unlawfully*" because he had by law a right to have intercourse with his wife'.[81] Then he noted the prosecution reply that 'he did act unlawfully because his

---

[78] Ibid 25.
[79] Gleeson, above n 19 at 5.
[80] *R v Clarence* (1888) 22 QBD 23, 26.
[81] Ibid 40.

right ceased when he knew himself to be suffering under the disease'.[82] Stephen decided that the word 'unlawfully' was satisfied because the act constituted cruelty under marriage law.[83] So he declined here to consider whether the husband had a lawful right to intercourse under the criminal law. He did not openly engage with the husband's immunity from rape prosecution, until the end of his judgment, and then as an apparent aside.

Stephen J then considered whether there was infliction of grievous bodily harm and decided that there was not because this required a direct blow, not the slow transmission of disease and so he decided s 20 did not apply and therefore the conviction must be quashed on this basis. He then looked to the s 47 charge of assault occasioning actual bodily harm. 'It is said there is none because the woman *consented* and to this it is replied that fraud vitiates consent, and that the prisoner's silence was a fraud'.[84] He asserted that the act of infection could not be an assault, so on this basis alone the conviction would have to be quashed.[85] 'Apart, however, from this, is the man's concealment of the fact that he was infected such a fraud as vitiated the wife's consent to his exercise of marital rights, and converted the act of connection into an assault?'[86] 'It seems to me that the proposition that fraud vitiates consent in criminal matters is not true ... without qualification'.[87]

Stephen pursued the implications of such a rule and found them to be unacceptable. 'If we apply it in that sense to the present case, it is difficult to say that the prisoner was not guilty of rape, for the definition of rape is having connection with a woman without her consent'. (Again he bypassed discussion of the marital immunity.) He now pursued a floodgates argument. He pinpointed the concerning implications for all men in their sexual activities with women generally. For

> if fraud vitiates consent, every case in which a man infects a woman or commits bigamy, the second wife being ignorant of the first marriage, is also a case of rape. Many seductions would be rapes, and so might acts of prostitution procured by fraud, as for instance by promises not intended to be fulfilled. These illustrations appear to shew clearly that the maxim that fraud vitiates consent is too general to be applied to these matters as if it were absolutely true.[88]

And so he tightly restricted the type of frauds that would destroy consent, concluding that 'the only sorts of fraud which so far destroy the effect of a *woman's* consent as to convert a connection consented to in fact into a rape are frauds as to the nature of the act itself, or as to the identity of the *person* who does the act'[89] (emphasis added). (This ruling would persist in its effects for a century and would

[82] Ibid.
[83] Ibid 41.
[84] Ibid 42.
[85] Ibid.
[86] Ibid 42–43.
[87] Ibid 43.
[88] Ibid.
[89] Ibid 44.

stand as the major authority on this principle.) Stephen noted that other frauds were recognised for the purposes of the law of contract but

> [t]he act of intercourse between a man and a woman cannot in any case be regarded as the performance of a contract. In the case of married people that act is part of a great relation based upon the greatest of all contracts, but standing on a footing peculiar to itself.[90]

Stephen did not explain the peculiarity of this footing, nor the nature of the 'great relation', though we know that it was here consistent with the husband's decision to conceal his gonorrhoea in order to achieve sex with an ostensibly willing wife.

Though he bypassed the immunity for much of his judgment, finding other ways to find that the offences did not apply, Stephen referred to and implicitly endorsed the immunity in the closing words of his judgment, where they argu-ably carried most weight. In direct reply to the comments of the defence lawyer, that Stephen had doubted the immunity in his *Digest* (that he had once contem-plated circumstances in which the husband might be charged with the rape of his wife), Stephen now explained that he had removed these words of doubt from his next edition of this *Digest*. The clear implication was that he now regarded the husband to be immunised from charges of rape, whatever the circumstances of the rape.

By removing this qualification to Hale's 'dictum' of a wife's irrevocable consent to sex with her husband, it must follow that Stephen no longer thought that the husband's immunity was confined to 'the decent and proper use of marital rights' with a non-consenting wife. Even the use of violence which jeopardised the 'health or safety' of the wife would still not turn the act into rape. And so the husband who behaved indecently or improperly was now implicitly countenanced and sanctioned by Stephen.

He added that 'No one can doubt the abominable nature of the prisoner's conduct' but then threw up his hands and said that 'The whole matter is surrounded with difficulties with which the legislature alone is competent to deal' and so he handballed it to parliament.[91]

Only Pollock J (in the majority) was clear that a husband could lawfully exercise force to gain sexual access to a wife; that this use of marital force was a matter of absolute male right. The others hummed and harred. Pollock proclaimed that

> the wife as to the connection itself is in a different position from any other woman, for she has no right or power to refuse her consent. As is said by Lord Hale in his Pleas of the Crown: 'By their mutual matrimonial consent and contract the wife hath given up herself in this kind unto her husband, which she cannot retract'.[92]

---

[90] Ibid.
[91] Ibid 46.
[92] Ibid 64.

Pollock did not flinch from the implications of this statement.

> Such a connection may be accompanied with conduct that amounts to cruelty, as where the condition of the wife is such that she will or may suffer from such connection, or, as here, when the condition of the husband is such that the wife will suffer.[93]

By contrast, Hawkins J, one of the dissenting judges, at first conceded the strength of the marital immunity, but then qualified the extent of male right:

> By the marriage contract a wife no doubt confers upon her husband an irrevocable privilege to have sexual intercourse with her during such time as the ordinary relations created by such contract subsist between them. For this reason it is that a husband cannot be convicted of a rape committed by him upon the person of his wife.[94]

However this was not the end of the matter: for 'this marital privilege does not justify a husband in endangering his wife's health and causing her grievous bodily harm, by exercising his marital privilege when he is suffering from a venereal disorder'.[95]

Hawkins J cited Lord Stowell in *Popkins v Popkins* that 'the husband has a right to the person of his wife, but not if her health is endangered'. Again there were limits to what a man might do in pursuit of his rights.

> So to endanger her health and cause her to suffer from such a loathsome disease contracted through his own infidelity, cannot by the most liberal construction of his matrimonial privilege, be said to fall within it; and although I can cite no direct authority upon the subject, I cannot conceive it possible seriously to doubt that a wife would be justified by resisting in all means in her power, nay, even to the death, if necessary, the sexual embraces of a husband suffering from such a contagious disorder.[96]

Hawkins J granted that

> The wife submits to her husband's embrace because at the time of marriage she gave him an irrevocable right to her person. The intercourse which takes place between husband and wife after marriage is not by virtue of any special consent on her part, but is mere submission to an obligation imposed upon her by law. Consent is immaterial.[97]

Hawkins J then rose fully to the occasion, in defence of women, and against the powers and immunities of his own sex:

> I cannot be party to a judgment which in effect would proclaim to the world that by the law of England in this year 1888 a man may deliberately, knowingly, and maliciously perpetrate upon the body of his wife the abominable outrage charged against the prisoner, and yet not be punishable criminally for such abominable atrocity.[98]

---

[93] Ibid.
[94] Ibid 51.
[95] Ibid.
[96] Ibid.
[97] Ibid 54.
[98] Ibid 55.

But this was not how Stephen saw it. True, he once thought that the wife's presumed consent to marital sex only operated when a man was making 'decent and proper use of [his] marital rights'.[99] He no longer felt this way and in *Clarence* he simply removed this qualification to the marital immunity, almost as an aside. And in what appears to be a measured judgment, which will stand the test of time, he also stated that the concealment of a horrible sexual disease would not turn the act of sex with an unwitting wife into the serious offence of inflicting grievous bodily harm (let alone the crime of rape, for which Clarence had not been charged). The offence of grievous bodily harm was not designed for this sort of behaviour; the wilful transmission of disease was not the same as a direct act of violence (say a punch in the face).[100] In short, Clarence had done nothing legally wrong.

Piecing together Stephen's judicial and extrajudicial writing on men, he appears consistently and openly patriarchal. He cast the legal actor – law's primary rights and duty bearer – as a man and, one might say, in his own image. Women came into legal view primarily as wives, who were under the protection and control of their husbands, their natural superiors. (But from *Clarence* we see that the protection they were afforded was poor; Hawkins J called it 'abominable'.) Each husband was sovereign of his domestic estate. Stephen was dismissive of Mill's concerns – that such unqualified power would eat away at the characters of men. Hawkins J, by contrast, was thoroughly disgusted; surely the law of England could not let this happen. But he did not win the day. Despite the variety of viewpoints expressed in *Clarence*, as Kate Gleeson observes, the case comes to stand for, inter alia, the solidity of the marital immunity.[101] And Stephen J's obliquely-stated view in a case in which the husband was not even charged with rape came to be the dominant and mainstream one, to look like the natural line of (male) authority.

Implicit within this Victorian legal thinking, so dominated by Stephen, was a cast of men, the principal characters of the criminal legal world who were the individuals of legal concern. These men form the subject of the next chapter.

---

[99] Stephen, *A Digest of the Criminal Law Digest of the Criminal Law*, above n 65 at 172, fn 1.

[100] And indeed the so-called wilful transmission of disease was not yet one recognised within the offences against the person.

[101] Gleeson, above n 19 at 7.

5

The Cast of Men: The Bounded Man, the Domestic Monarch and the Sexual Master

I. The Male Body Politic and the Masterful Man

In his history of British portraiture, Simon Schama explained the dilemma once faced by the artist Graham Sutherland when asked to paint a portrait of Churchill. By 1954, the year of the commission, Churchill was an old man, suffering the infirmities of old age, and these were clearly evident to the artist who wanted only to paint what he could see. But there was also before him the personification of Britain, as glorious victor after the War, and Sutherland was also conscious of this other persona.

As Schama points out, this double personification of the state leader was familiar to people of a much earlier time.

> In medieval thought on monarchy a distinction was made between 'the King's two bodies'. The body natural endured all the ills and indignities that time visited upon it; the body politic, on the other hand, for the sake of the state, had to be imagined as immune to infirmity.[1]

It was the glorious leader as body politic that the people of England wanted to see. (Sutherland gave them the man, with all his infirmities.)

In the legal understanding of the men of law, something similar is going on. There are different imaginings of men, for different purposes, and some are more abstract than others, often knowingly so. The physical realisation of our male character is not so much an infirm creature of the flesh, the 'body natural' described by Schama, but more a vigorous, controlling, masterful being, bold even glamorous, with urgent sexual passions.

In Chapter 2 we met one of our cast of male characters and he was only tacitly a man. This was the figure of *the bounded individual*, the liberal person rather abstractly conceived, a being with firm borders who was required to respect the firm borders of other men. The bounded person-respecting individual has been

---

[1] Simon Schama, *The Face of Britain: A History of the Nation Through its Portraits* (New York, Oxford University Press, 2016) 8.

critical to the rhetoric and thinking of central criminal law and remains so. This is the being invoked in general theories of criminal law and the state: the person who requires and must respect personal security, who is clearly individuated.

We have also already met our two other male figures, but they have yet to be formally introduced. In these two other personifications we have explicitly male characters. There is what I will now call *the little king or monarch* of the little kingdom of the family: the male figure of family authority, taking command of his small realm, his domestic regime, and this man is also often imagined quite abstractly as a set of legal powers, and as a collective individual, as a sort of male body politic. But he is definitely a man, as Blackstone made clear with his doctrine of coverture. He incorporates the identities of others. He absorbs the members of his household into himself, to become a collective individual unit. He stands for them and he is a critical figure of authority and decision-making, both within the household and the outside world. He is not so much their representative as their very personification.

Then there is the physical and sensual man, *the sexual master*, the sort of man envisaged by Stephen (and less nobly by Mill) with a muscular male physique and with male genitalia, with sexual needs and sexual passions, who possesses naturally greater physical strength than a woman, who can physically take sexual possession, and who has been given legal permission to do this: to enter the body of a wife, if necessary, forcibly. Implicit in this understanding of the legal man is that he is an embodied creature with male creature needs. He is naturally controlling and dominant; and his sexual satisfaction, his very sense of the erotic, is highly compatible with the use of force. Elsewhere I have characterised him as the sexually possessive man.[2]

Mostly the influential men of law were too squeamish to spell all of this out. Stephen was far less so. He had a lot to say about male musculature, male vigour and energy, and male sexual passions. Here was man made male flesh, with male heterosexual interests which were rightly given legal outlet within marriage and here the use of force was positively countenanced.

This trinity of men – the bounded individual, the little monarch and the sexual master – is still poorly delineated in legal thinking. My point, throughout this book, is that the man problem of criminal law has been poorly formulated and so the man question is still rarely posed. We do not ask: just who are these men who are our very subject matter?

Having been introduced to our three main male characters, we can now take a closer look at them: the classical bounded individual, who was once both explicitly and implicitly male; the little monarch (the body politic) who was explicitly a male head of family, and personification of that group; and the sexually possessive man, an explicitly male character, fully embodied, with his strong controlling personality and pressing erotic needs.

---

[2] Ngaire Naffine, 'Possession: Erotic Love in the Law of Rape' (1994) 57 *Modern Law Review* 10.

The first man, *the bounded individual*, was meant to have firm borders and to respect the borders of others, but really those other bounded beings who demanded respect were other men, because this was public man mainly envisaged in his encounters with others in public life and the public sphere was a male sphere, as we saw in Chapter 2. The borders of women were not so firm and so respectable women, with their inherently poor border defences, were not meant to be out in the public, exposing themselves to the threat of men. Didn't they have a home to go to?

In the Victorian period, and beyond, there were vigorous efforts to ensure that women could not participate in public male life. (The recognition of women as full legal persons came as late as 1929, and after considerable male opposition, which is why it took so long.)[3] The bounded man was bounded in his dealings with other men; and it was vital for this understanding of the bounded man that he was precisely not a woman; that he was not effeminate; that he was a manly man.[4] Great effort went into the policing of the boundaries of this man, ensuring that he acted like a man (and not a woman).

Our second and third male characters were poorly bounded in the sense that they were not expected to keep themselves to themselves. They were more like colonising territories, rather than discrete bounded and individuated selves. We have already examined the man as a bounded individual. Now we consider men in their explicitly extended modes: *the little monarch* and *the sexual master*.

As we will see, the little monarch comprised an extensive set of rights and duties. Coverture was the broadest legal doctrine, which established the rights and duties of this little king. The doctrines of marital correction, marital coercion and marital conspiracy also presupposed and constituted this male body politic. As Lindsay Farmer observes, in his history of criminal law, despite changing standards of masculinity over the Victorian period, and a reining in of the uses of force, 'it was clearly recognised that the man had authority, or dominion, over women ... within the domestic sphere and that this extended to the use of physical violence'.[5]

Hale, Blackstone and Stephen all characterised man in his capacity as sexual master, the physically possessing man who took the body of a woman who offered herself up to him, who virtually became him. Hale imagined this man; Stephen had this character in mind, but so did Williams and Howard. This was the masterful man within the traditional formulation of the law of rape; it was Hale's formulation of rape law and of the marital immunity. But this male character also resided

---

[3] See the discussion of the persons' cases in Joanne Conaghan, *Law and Gender* (Oxford, Oxford University Press, 2013). And for the early classic work on the persons' cases see Albie Sachs and Joan Hoff Wilson, *Sexism and the Law: A Study of Male Beliefs and Judicial Bias* (Oxford, Martin Robertson, 1978).

[4] On the social and legal condemnation of the effeminate man see Richard Davenport-Hines, *Sex, Death and Punishment: Attitudes to Sex and Sexuality in Britain* (London, Collins, 1990).

[5] Lindsay Farmer, *Making the Modern Criminal Law: Criminalization and Civil Order* (Oxford, Oxford University Press, 2016) 250.

within other laws, including family law, which was slow to recognise a husband's cruelty as a ground for divorce.[6]

Each of these male characters depended on women assuming a complementary role and character. For every male right, there was a female duty or at least a non-right.[7]

II. The Woman Problem

For men to fulfil the conditions of their own personhood, men had to be protected from other men, and also told not to go too near to their own sex (unless it was in a manly way). The crime of gross indecency between men contained this clear instruction.[8] Retaining the right distance from other men was the problem of men, for men, and criminal law was brought in aid.

The problem women posed for men, however, was not that they represented a physical threat (which was the problem generally posed by other men). On the contrary: the problem posed by women to men was the very antithesis of the problem posed by other men and it was also more existential. Women posed a fundamental difficulty for men if they too had an unqualified right of freedom from touch or harm. Indeed, it was vital that women, as a general category, did not have the sort of mandated right not to be touched or even to be harmed by men, which men themselves must have if their very persons were to be respected and protected as men, if they were to be persons.

Men must not only be allowed to get close to at least one woman but to penetrate her sexually (if he were to have his sexual satisfaction) and also to have progeny and then ensure control of ensuing progeny (if he were to have paternal rights). But to be civilised, this must all be done in an ordered way. Men needed legally secured access to the physical persons of women in certain state-sanctioned circumstances, and criminal law must not be an impediment. The appropriate sites for male access to a woman (according to criminal and civil law) were marriage and the marital bed. The woman problem (for men) would thus be solved.

The legal institution of marriage, the legally-constituted family, thus supplied this male sexual order and the church gave its imprimatur and indeed provided a

---

[6] On the limitations of family law in dealing effectively with the violent husband, see Michael Freeman, '"But If You Can't Rape Your Wife, Who[m] Can You Rape?": The Marital Rape Exemption Re-examined' (1981) 15 *Family Law Quarterly* 1, 15.

[7] On the complementarity of legal rights and duties see Wesley Newcomb Hohfeld, 'Some Fundamental Legal Conceptions as Applied in Judicial Reasoning' (1913) 23 *Yale Law Journal* 16 and Wesley Newcomb Hohfeld, 'Fundamental Legal Conceptions as Applied in Judicial Reasoning' (1917) 26 *Yale Law Journal* 710.

[8] The crime of 'gross indecency' between men came into being with Labouchere's 1885 amendment to the Criminal Law Act and was not repealed until 1967. In 2017 the Prime Minister finally pardoned the men who had been convicted under this legislation.

complementary set of norms and sanctions.[9] To close the circle of control, women were excluded from higher education and so from professional life;[10] they were excluded from the market place, and they were also excluded from the law of contract within the marriage – from setting its terms and ensuring their equality within the marriage.

Few real choices were given to women. Women could not engage in the lawful sale of their sexual services, perhaps as a last resort in light of their severely constrained options: the criminal laws of prostitution prohibited the 'common prostitute' from 'soliciting' for the purposes of prostitution.[11] Moreover, under the Contagious Diseases Acts, suspected prostitutes could be rounded up, subjected to compulsory intimate inspection for the presence of venereal disease and interned in a 'locked' hospital if the disease were found.[12] Thus they were to be made safe and healthy for their male customers, imagined as soldiers in need of women, and hence representatives of the state with manly needs.

None of this spoke of women's personal sovereignty, the thing considered vital for a man. Rather it spoke of the most intimate forms of the control of women by men. The only proper place for a woman to have sex was within the marriage and here the free provision of sex was considered her female duty. The criminal laws of abortion then effectively required a wife (and all other women) to carry any resulting pregnancy to full term,[13] despite the considerable risks associated with frequent childbirth.[14]

The terms of the relations between men and women within the family (and outwith) were set by the patriarchal state rather than negotiated by each man and woman, in a contractual and market manner, which again would only give women the right to exclude men from their persons – thus reinstating the woman problem.[15] As Matthew Hale explained, the reason that a husband could not be guilty of raping his wife was that: 'by their mutual matrimonial consent and

[9] See Katherine O'Donovan, *Sexual Divisions in Law* (London, Weidenfeld & Nicolson, 1985); Carol Smart, *The Ties that Bind: Law, Marriage and the Reproduction of Patriarchal Relations* (London, Routledge & Kegan Paul, 1984).

[10] See Sachs and Wilson, above n 3.

[11] See Marcia Neave, 'The Failure of Prostitution Law Reform' (1988) 21 *Australian and New Zealand Journal of Criminology* 202; see also 'Report of the Select Committee of the Legislative Assembly upon Prostitution' (New South Wales, 1986); 'Inquiry into Prostitution', Final Report (Victoria, 1985).

[12] See Judith R Walkowitz and Daniel J Walkowitz, '"We Are Not Beasts of the Field": Prostitution and the Poor in Plymouth and Southampton under the Contagious Diseases Acts' (1973) 1 *Feminist Studies* 73; Philippa Levine, *Prostitution, Race and Politics: Policing Venereal Disease in the British Empire* (New York, Routledge, 2003).

[13] It was not until 1967 that the Abortion Act 1967 (UK) 'decriminalised' abortion on therapeutic grounds, or to be more precise it stipulated conditions under which a doctor would not be prosecuted for performing an abortion and nor would the woman. See discussion in Sally Sheldon, *Beyond Control: Medical Power and Abortion Law* (London, Pluto, 1997).

[14] This was no doubt one of the reasons why the first wave of feminists struggled to gain some legal control over the frequency of sexual intercourse and hence of reproduction. See Jill Elaine Hasday, 'Contest and Consent: A Legal History of Marital Rape' (2000) 88 *California Law Review* 1373.

[15] See Frances Olsen, 'The Family and the Market: A Study of Ideology and Legal Reform' (1983) 96 *Harvard Law Review* 1497.

contract the wife hath given up herself in this kind unto her husband, which she cannot retract'.[16] Clearly the woman did not set the terms of this contract and indeed it could hardly be said to be a true contract in that the terms were set by the state and the woman's consent was deemed to be perpetual.[17]

III. The Husband as Little Monarch

While the idea of the bounded man, with firm personal border control, was central to the rhetoric and thinking of central criminal law, and was espoused by its most distinguished thinkers (and still is), this conception of the person poorly described most men. Most adult men were expected to marry, and did indeed marry, and once a man became a husband, he ceased to be bounded. The law was clear about this. Men as husbands not only acquired intimate access to a wife but they were, in a number of other legal ways, made the sovereign, the master and the very personification of another human being. So, most men went through a legal rite (marriage) which enlarged their social and legal personae, and extended their personal borders. Indeed it could be said that men were incited by law not to exercise firm border control: not to keep themselves to themselves.

The legal immunity of husbands from rape prosecution was perhaps the main law which extended the husband's borders and person. The wife 'gave herself up to him' (as Hale put it); she was 'so great a favourite of the law' that she lived under his protection (the message of coverture and Blackstone). Thus the criminal law of rape, which explicitly excluded protection for the wife, maintained a continuous line of male physical authority over another, from the seventeenth century (Hale and Blackstone) to the end of the twentieth century. It was part of the engrained legal thinking of orthodoxy. There was an explicit and solid gender order embedded within criminal law, viewed as utterly right and natural, seen and justified by the influential as neutral and liberal, indeed as an important means of securing and enforcing the liberal social contract.

Within this male order, the personal borders of men – the very bodies of men as understood by criminal law – were extended outwards, annexing and colonising the body of the wife, and then the home and her property. Special criminal legal rules accommodated and approved these expanding and colonising moves. Criminal law ameliorated the wrongfulness of deliberate killing when the man's personal domain was placed under threat (in that a wife's adultery was a classic trigger for the partial murder defence of provocation).[18] And criminal law

---

[16] Sir Matthew Hale, *The History of the Pleas of the Crown*, vol 1 (London, Professional Books, 1971) 629.

[17] As Carole Pateman explained in *The Sexual Contract* (Stanford, Stanford University Press, 1988).

[18] It is only recently that UK law has explicitly excluded the 'provocation' trigger of sexual infidelity, with the enactment of the 'loss of control' defence to murder which has replaced the defence of provocation. See the discussion of this new partial defence in the final chapter. On the male misuses of

excluded the offence of rape from the male province of the marriage. Thus the very character of criminal law's two most serious offences against the person – rape and murder – were transformed and downgraded in significance. These offences were made something other than profound and intrinsic wrongs. Rather they were direct reflections of the prevailing patriarchy.

Concomitantly, the person of the wife contracted, by law, arguably to the point of moral and legal annihilation. As the husband was permitted to retreat into the home and then into the bedroom, to experience his true manhood, with the approval of state law, so the wife found herself with no further place to retreat. No room; no bed; no body to call her own; no place to be at all. Spatially she was cornered in a bedroom and then in a bed.

Contra the official justificatory story of criminal law and responsibility, with its ideal of the individual, who was bound to respect the autonomy of other such individuals, the man who can be pieced together from positive criminal laws (who should not be simply equated with real everyday men, who could be better than this) was more a domain rather a single individual being. (I have called him a 'body politic'.) He was a hybrid of persons (himself and his wife) and place or habitat (the home) and institution (the marriage). His wife and his home became his occupied territory; his realm and his kingdom. Both culturally and legally, the wife was, in many ways, colonised person and occupied space. She was part of his enlarged moral, physical and legal being. She was essential to the rights and duties which made him a moral and legal person. He was precisely not the atomistic sharply bordered sovereign individual typically portrayed by theorists of criminal law, past and present, be they liberal, conservative or critical. His criminal legal rights and duties did not make him thus.

There is already a critical literature on liberal political theory and its treatment of the family (rather than the individual) as a legal and political analytical unit, with the husband/father as head of that unit.[19] My argument goes further; it is that, by force of specific criminal laws, the very person of the husband/father actually extended into the wife and home, subsuming them, and becoming integral to *his* legal and moral being.

The normal wholesome heterosexual man was expected to grow and mature, to leave the life of the singular man, the bachelor, to enlarge himself and so expand into a male territory: to find a wife; to establish a home and family; to create this supposedly natural male habitat; and then to go forth into the world of men where

the provocation defence see Victoria Nourse, 'Passion's Progress' (1997) 106 *Yale Law Journal* 1331. And for recent critical reviews of the defence see David Plater, Lucy Line and Kate Fitz-Gibbon, *The Provoking Operation of Provocation: Stage 1* (South Australian Law Reform Institute, Adelaide, 2017) and David Plater et al, *The Provoking Operation of Provocation: Stage 2* (South Australian Law Reform Institute, Adelaide, 2018).

[19] See for example Susan Moller Okin, *Justice, Gender and the Family* (United States of America, Perseus Books Group, 1989); Carol Smart, *Regulating Womanhood: Historical Essays on Marriage, Motherhood and Sexuality* (London, Routledge, 1992) and Katherine O'Donovan, *Family Law Matters* (London, Pluto Press, 1993).

he would deal with other men as similarly-constituted individuals.[20] Within his own personal domain, his territory, he would operate with a high degree of freedom from the ordinary operation of the offences against the person: those offences which protected person from person and so required clearly separate and distinct persons, to work as intended.

The marital rape immunity, articulated by Hale, explicitly extended the husband into the wife. The male unity principle, articulated by Blackstone, also enlarged the personality of the husband in the sense that he acquired control of, and physical rights to, the physical person of another. Again his physical borders could be said to extend.[21]

But criminal law, in other ways, also made the married man into a blended and bloated legal being. The non-conspiracy (with a wife) rule meant that criminal conspiracy was not recognised between husband and wife, because the husband and wife did not possess separate wills and a conspiracy required at least two persons.[22] With the principle of marital coercion, it was presumed that a crime committed by a wife in the presence of her husband was in response to his coercion. The criminal defence of marital coercion continued to operate in English law until 2014.[23] And the principle of marital correction enumerated by Blackstone meant that the husband could, probably, lawfully employ some force to a wife to bring her into line.[24] In different ways these legal principles combined the woman with the man, enlarging his self, and shrinking hers. Blackstone was mindful of this; other legal writers less so.

Other parts of criminal law therefore helped to give sense to the husband's immunity from rape prosecution, and supplied the richer legal context. The central crime of rape did not sit within the body of criminal law in isolation, as a sort of hard impervious core. Rather its meaning depended in part on its relation to other complementary legal norms with which it interacted. These related and interacting laws operated as a mutually-reinforcing set of ideas.[25]

---

[20] See O'Donovan, *Sexual Divisions in Law*, above n 9.

[21] For an immensely useful guide to the literature on coverture see Claudia Zaher, 'When a Woman's Marital Status Determined her Legal Status: A Research Guide on the Common Law Doctrine of Coverture' (2002) 94 *Law Library Journal* 459.

[22] See Columbia Law Review Association, 'The Effect of Marriage on the Rules of the Criminal Law' (1961) 61 *Columbia Law Review* 73; see also Glanville Williams, 'The Legal Unity of Husband and Wife' (1947) 10 *Modern Law Review* 16.

[23] In 2014 in England and Wales s 47 of the Criminal Justice Act 1925 (UK) (the defence of marital coercion) was abolished by s 177 of the Anti-Social Behaviour, Crime and Policing Act 2014 (UK). In South Australia the presumption has gone, but the defence has been retained. Hence s 328A of the Criminal Law Consolidation Act 1934 (SA), which reads: 'Abolition of presumption of marital coercion. Any presumption of law that an offence committed by a wife in the presence of her husband is committed under the coercion of the husband is abolished; but, on a charge against a wife for any offence other than treason or murder, it shall be a good defence to prove that the offence was committed in the presence, and under the coercion, of the husband'.

[24] See discussion of Blackstone in Chapter 3, noting that Blackstone had his own doubts about the rule.

[25] For an early and highly critical view of the criminal legal treatment of wives, see JS Erwin, 'Husband and Wife in Criminal Law' (1885) vol xvii, 3 *The Criminal Law Magazine and Reporter* 269.

The husband's rape immunity, along with the marital unity principle, which helped to supply its logic, together with the marital coercion presumption and the non-conspiracy rule, disclosed a systematic way of thinking about men and their self-understanding in terms of their relations with women in law. Each of these principles set up relations between husbands and wives within criminal law in a certain manner; they established their status and their rights and duties. But most importantly, for my purposes, they took men to be certain types of beings. A cluster of principles shored up the legal view that the husband and wife were one person, the man, and that the husband, with his extended borders, had remarkable kingly powers which included access to the wife. Indeed the wife was less individual sovereign subject (as Mill understood persons to be) than colonised territory.

Again it is important to keep our eyes on the man, not the woman. These principles are still more typically seen as adjustments to female legal character; as if they do not inform us about him. But the presumption of coercion tells us that the husband's character was presumptively coercive – that his tendency would be to dominate and control. This assumption, and implicit approval, of coercive male character was remarkably antithetical to the liberal idea of the responsible autonomous person-respecting individual. The strange blending of will implicit in the idea that the husband could not conspire with the wife was also antithetical to the liberal model of the person.

Even by the middle of the twentieth century, as we will see in the next chapter, the married woman was still legally and socially understood in terms of her subordinate relations with a man, indeed by merger with her husband, within a notionally private arrangement called the family. Her personal and sexual autonomy – vis-à-vis her husband – were not part of the social or legal deal of marriage. She was still thought to have signed up for merger, not for separation, as a liberal legal individual, and so too had the husband. The crucial difference between the spouses was that the wife was thought to merge into the person of the husband, rather than the husband into the person of the wife.[26]

As domestic monarch, we could even call him dictator, the husband had legally-sanctioned sexual access to his wife and could employ necessary force to secure it.[27] His will was her will and her body was his.[28] There was little legal controversy about this. Her non-rights did not serve (or rather were not thought) to delimit him, which meant that the boundaries of the husband were poorly defined. Both husband and wife had poor border control, but in different ways. It was the husband who had the formal legal power to extend beyond his own

---

[26] See Williams, above n 22. See also Louis Richards 'The Doctrine of Marital Unity in the Modern Criminal Law' (1891) vol xiii, 3 *The Criminal Law Magazine and Reporter* 325.

[27] He could employ at least 'gentle violence': see *G v G* [1924] AC 349, 357.

[28] This view was also reflected in the legal doctrines of marital coercion (which presumed that a crime committed by a wife in the presence of her husband was a response to his coercion) and criminal conspiracy (which was not recognised between husband and wife because they did not possess separate wills).

borders, at will, into the personal territory of another: a highly illiberal act. He was the body politic, into which she was incorporated.[29]

IV. The Sexual Master

A sub-theme running through these man-and-woman joining principles, and their exegesis, is that they were all for the good of everyone. The man was not abusing his domestic powers, he was not behaving like a sexual tyrant (though Mill saw him thus) because it was in the nature of the wife to be mastered and conquered. After all she was a woman. Thus the male solution to the problem of securing sexual access to a woman, without compromising the husband's autonomy (his own physical distinctness) and without destroying the autonomy of the wife (and hence breaching his commitment to her freedom) was to treat the husband as naturally, existentially and physically as a sexual master who was himself unaffected by the act of sex. He always remained master of himself, of his very bodily integrity (a bounded, separate and distinct male being), while she was penetrated and mastered. Stephen made it clear that in marital relations the manly man took control and possession of the wife. But he did not thus strip her of her freedom, he did not breach her integrity, because the wife did not have such integrity, nor autonomy, by nature. Indeed the wife was by nature desirous of submission. The good wife naturally wanted to obey (Stephen said this). The good wife could see that she fulfilled her womanly nature by surrender. What would be annihilation in a man, aided by law, was in a woman a bringing to fruition.

Forced marital sex therefore did not breach liberal principles. It did not compromise liberal man's commitment to the fundamental rights of the individual because it did not infringe woman's freedoms. The wife's naturally subject nature meant that the husband's possession of her was only nature taking its course. 'Erotic love'[30] in the view perpetuated and expressed by our criminal jurists, was the love between a woman and a man, a heterosexual couple, within which there were particular and different roles anticipated for the woman and for the man. Byron, Balzac and Rousseau all described this relation. For woman her love of a man was everything. Her condition was one of constant offering while his was one of perpetual action.[31]

Around the time that Stephen was developing his expansive thoughts about the natures of men and women, the German philosopher Friedrich Nietzsche offered views of the sexes which were remarkably compatible. In *The Gay Science* Nietzsche

---

[29] See Annabel Crabbe, *The Wife Drought* (Sydney, Ebury Press, 2014) for an analysis of the continuing dramatic asymmetry of marital roles in Australia.

[30] This is a term borrowed from a collection of readings on the subject: Robert C Soloman and Kathleen M Higgins (eds), *The Philosophy of (Erotic) Love* (USA, University Press of Kansas, 1991).

[31] An extensive collection of Romantic and modern writing on heterosexual relations is to be found in Soloman and Higgins (eds), ibid.

asked us to suppose 'that there should ... be men to whom the desire for total devotion is not alien'.[32] Such men were to be despised for being too like women, for whom 'love' was servitude. Men who wished to devote themselves, body and soul to another, 'simply – are not men'. In this traditional romantic view, there was no loss of sovereignty for (the real) man when he loved a woman. He remained a free, unitary and whole subject; while she devoted herself utterly to him, he remained utterly himself. As Nietzsche explained, 'Woman wants to be taken and accepted as a possession, wants to be absorbed into the concept of possession, possessed'.[33] She gave herself up to him and he took her and possessed her. Though he received the complete devotion of her body and her soul, the boundaries of his own identity, of his 'body and soul' were not breached. He retained his wholeness, his bodily integrity. It was she who underwent transformation to become his, while his essential person remained unaffected by the having of her.

The ideal man, then, to Nietzsche was a real man who 'loved' a woman through possession and, when he possessed her, he did so completely, both physically and spiritually: body and soul. But in the manner of his 'love', he kept faith with the Western ideal of the bounded rational individual. Man was fundamentally unaffected by the sensual acts of the body, while the woman surrendered both her body and her being to him.

This is an idea of being akin to that advanced by Kant, who wished also to preserve the identity and unity of the rational self.[34] Were it to be otherwise, man could not remain himself in 'love'. He would suffer an unacceptable loss of sovereignty over himself to the point that he would no longer be a man. Nietszche was clear on this. 'A man who loves like a woman becomes a slave'.[35] But by nature a woman was already in servitude to man and so lost nothing in love. Indeed 'a woman who loves like a woman', who devotes herself completely to a man, 'becomes a more perfect woman'.[36] She became more herself because her-self was by nature his. To give in to him was to give in to her own nature. (This could be Stephen speaking.) But the man had to remain himself when she gave herself to him, otherwise her gift of self was to no-one. Thus 'if both partners felt impelled by love to renounce themselves, we should then get – I do not know what; perhaps an empty space?'[37]

Throughout all of the social and legal change I consider, from the seventeenth century to the present, men are treated as legal constants, as liberal individuals, as citizens, as persons, which, to the extent that it is apt, perhaps describes their relations to other men. Illogically, it is only the wife who is undergoing change. Man does not have a delimiting sex which transforms over time. The impression

[32] Friedrich Nietzsche, Walter Kauffman (trs), *The Gay Science* (New York, Random House, 1974) 319.
[33] Ibid.
[34] Immanuel Kant, *The Metaphysics of Morals* (Cambridge, Cambridge University Press, 1991) 95.
[35] Nietzsche, above n 32 at 319.
[36] Ibid.
[37] Ibid.

conveyed is that persons (men) remain the same, as discrete bounded autonomous liberal individuals. They are stable analytical units from which legal analysis can unproblematically proceed.

It is also assumed that men were individuals, even when the marital unity principle was firmly in place. Only the woman had a limiting status which changed, as she gradually emerged out of status and became an individual too. But this is faulty thinking. For as her status was defined against and in relation to his, so he had to inhabit a correlative status category: he took his legal nature from the class to which he belonged, which was defined in relation to the class that he was not. To the extent that she was in status, so was he.[38] But because his legal status was largely defined by privileges and powers, because it did not hamper him, like good health, it was invisible. (We return to consider the full implications of this relational understanding of the person in the final chapter.)

A. Soames Forsyte

In 1908 the English novelist and lawyer John Galsworthy published *The Man of Property*, the opening novel of *The Forsyte Saga*. The protagonist, Soames Forsyte in a now famous passage from the book was given an interior dialogue the morning after he had raped his wife Irene. Was he justified in his actions? After all, his wife had persistently refused his advances. What would the courts make of it? Soames was a middle-class English solicitor, married to the beautiful Irene who repeatedly resisted his sexual advances and who loved another. Galsworthy thus allowed us to enter a male legal mind, as Soames reflected on the rape, not named as such.

As Rebecca Ryan explains in her account of the scene, the rape itself is interestingly absent from the novel, though it represents a powerful climax.

> Neither Galsworthy nor his protagonist use the word rape. Neither the author nor the character describes the incident. The reader learns of its occurrence only as Soames struggles to justify his behaviour, assuaging his self-doubt with an assertion of man's unbridled appetite and the husband's legal authority.[39]

(There are parallels with the court in *Morgan* in which there is graphic description of the rapes by Morgan's friends but nothing about Morgan himself, as principal.) Galsworthy thus created a character, Soames Forsyte, who could take us into the respectable male legal mind, at the beginning of the twentieth century, engaged with the exquisite problem of why it might be proper to rape a wife.

Soames was required to wrestle with, ostensibly, incompatible ideas; in modern psychological parlance, he was experiencing 'cognitive dissonance',[40] which he

---

[38] Status here refers to legal status which defines and limits a person in law.

[39] Rebecca M Ryan, 'The Sex Right: A Legal History of the Marital Rape Exemption' (1995) 20 *Law and Social Inquiry* 941, 951.

[40] We return to a discussion of cognitive dissonance, as a problem for the men of law, in the later chapters of the book.

needed to resolve. Though a legal man, and a respectable man of the city, he had used force to gain sexual access to Irene. But after all, he was her husband. He pondered whether he was right to do so: 'Had he been right to yield to his over-mastering hunger of the night before, and break down resistance which he had suffered now too long from this woman who was his lawful and solemnly consti-tuted helpmate?'[41]

Soames was full of doubt. He remembered 'her terrible smothered sobbing, the like of which he had never heard, and still seemed to hear'. He was 'still haunted by the odd, intolerable feeling of remorse and shame he had felt, as he stood looking at her by the flame of the single candle, before silently slinking away'.[42]

And perhaps he was also struggling with the idea that, as an otherwise civilised man of law, he had found his sexual pleasure, or perhaps release, to be compatible with the use of force. Blackstone and Stephen both understood this and the role of law in giving it lawful expression. To Blackstone it was 'that natural impulse' that 'must be confined and regulated'.[43] To Stephen, marriage was the proper and lawful outlet for men's passions.[44]

Soames is a combination of the little domestic monarch and, ultimately, briefly, the masterful sexual man. Within his little kingdom, which was still secure at the beginning of the twentieth century, he was expected to be a firm but fair master in his own home, to take control and bring it order. And there was no clearer way to do it than to take sexual control of his recalcitrant wife. Soames reflected on the law and what it would tell him about the morality and even civility of his conduct. He considered what a divorce court would make of his behaviour and concluded that it would condone it; that he had behaved in a proper manly and lawful way: 'in the cool judgment of right thinking men, of men of the world, of such as he recollected often received praise in the Divorce Court, he had but done his best to sustain the sanctity of marriage, to prevent her from abandoning her duty ... No he did not regret it'.[45]

He had 'asserted his rights and acted like a man'.[46] We can almost hear James Fitzjames Stephen whispering in his ear, though Soames is in other ways a milder-mannered figure of a legal man. As thoughts of Irene's sobbing recurred on the London underground, on his way to his legal practice (in his 'first-class apartment filled with City men'), he tried to smother them with the 'the rich crackle' of *The Times* but then read the 'long list of offences' which included a 'surprisingly high number' of rapes.[47] (Here the word does occur.) He was soon immersed in the 'ordinary affairs' of his busy legal practice and the moral drama ends.

---

[41] John Galsworthy, *The Man of Property* (London, William Heinemann, 1953) 292.
[42] Ibid.
[43] William Blackstone, *Commentaries on the Laws of England*, Book 1: 'The Rights of Persons', 14th edn (London, Cadell and Davies, 1803) para 422.
[44] James Fitzjames Stephen, *A History of the Criminal Law of England*, 3 vols (London, Macmillan and Co, 1883).
[45] Galsworthy, above n 41 at 293.
[46] Ibid 292.
[47] Ibid 293–294.

V. The Nursery of the Vices

Our men of criminal law, now traced up to the beginnings of the twentieth century, were less independent and self-contained than they thought. They were existentially dependent on another (they needed the wife to assume a complementary and subordinate role) and hence they were insecure. If these men were to be put on the psychoanalyst's couch they might appear as self-important, hubristic, control freaks, coercive, outraged at challenges to their authority, deeply sceptical of the motives and reliability of those unlike themselves (women), who assumed the right to control the mind and body of these other types (women), who were dead to their needs and responses, and who used law to assert their own rights and to strip the female other of their power. This has disturbing practical implications. Frustrated access to a wife can lead to the use of legally justified or excused force and rape, as it did with Soames Forsyte.

Fury at a woman's rejection can also lead to homicidal rage.[48] The official gloss offered by Blackstone and Stephen was that the man was a protecting guardian, placing woman under his wing. In truth the men they described were *least* liberal, were least responsible, in their legal relations with a wife. This is when they were most feudal, when they were most reliant on the benefits of legal status and its enhanced rights for men. And this is why Mill regarded the man's marriage as a nursery of his vices. The personality of men therefore departed dramatically from the prevailing idea – of the responsible legal individual whose borders stopped with himself.

Marriage completed the man, with a woman, thus giving him access to sex, reproduction, property and companionship. The unity principle did this job in law and other legal principles supported this change to man's status and nature as he joined with a woman. But the impression conveyed was that women were the incomplete ones – in need of a guardian; woman was gathered into him. The official story was that men were already whole; they were already individuals. It was the dependent woman who was the needy one. She tucked herself into him because she was needy, not because he needed her. (There was no question of the formation of a contractual marital relation between equal individuals.) This was the legal and moral infrastructure of male being as imagined by the Victorians and their legal predecessors. And, as we have also seen, it was supplemented by a range of other laws – from prostitution law to abortion law[49] to contagious diseases legislation – which further undermined the legal bodily integrity and autonomy of man's other half and enhanced his own.

So in truth the husband was not a bounded liberal legal individual and nor was his wife. It was the wife whose adjusted legal status was made explicit; not so

[48] And this was a principal reason for changes to the provocation defence to murder: either the full removal of the defence or its heavy qualification, depending on the jurisdiction. The idea behind these reforms was that men should no longer be able to use anger with an unfaithful wife as even a partial excuse for killing.
[49] Incidentally both of which are still in operation in different ways in different jurisdictions.

the husband, who remained invisible as an extended illiberal person. A range of laws physically bloated and morally withered men's legal personality. These laws diminished or withered men in a moral sense in that they removed from men legal duties or responsibilities regarded as defining of Kantian moral and liberal legal personhood: the duty to respect the autonomy of others and not to breach their personal security.

This moral diminution of the personality of the husband, as a consequence of his reduced responsibility to (female) others, has received little scholarly attention. And yet it represents a serious significant adjustment to the liberal idea of the individual. We are accustomed to thinking of this adjustment as one which pertains to women. But equally, and perhaps more damagingly, it pertains to men. After all, the wife was not making an incursion into her husband. She was not taking his rights away from him in her interests. She was not coercing and controlling him with the aid of law. The legal relation ran in the other direction.

The variety of laws which countenanced and enforced the subjugation of women by men positively undermined the liberal credentials of criminal law and its interpreters and advocates. The dark illiberal figures of the husband and the wife were the direct effects of these social and legal understandings. Not only was the husband not a bounded individual, because his boundaries were legally extended. He was also mistakenly thought of as a self-choosing and regulating individual. He did not freely choose to be himself, or to assume the available cast of male characters, because he too was a creation of social and legal institutions. These institutions manufactured his rights and his duties; they constituted his moral and legal nature.

True, he helped to engineer these very male rights, which formed these male legal characters, and he derived positive benefits from the acquisition of these rights. But then he too was the product of his legal labours, from which he could not easily escape. He made these characters and yet they made him. To different degrees, he remained in the grip of them, in all their unlovely manifestations, right up to the end of the twentieth century, as we will see in the next chapter. And as we will see in the final chapter, their legacy is with us still.

6

From Male Supremacy to Sexual Euphemism: Good Men Trapped in their Own Assumptions

In 1924 the House of Lords made it crystal clear that the self-respecting husband was the sexual master of his wife. In G v G, the husband had sought a decree of nullity of the marriage on the basis of his wife's alleged inability to consummate the marriage. Applications for such a decree had been dismissed in the courts below. Undeterred, Mr G pursued his appeals to the highest court and the five Law Lords agreed that the decree should be granted. They found the wife to be the victim of 'an invincible repugnance to the physical act [so] as to paralyse her willpower to carry out what she had promised'.[1] It was not a matter of mere wilful refusal, which would not have provided the necessary ground for such a decree.

To the Law Lords, the husband had displayed a regrettable degree of sexual 'forbearance'. The couple had married in 1913 and the evidence of non-consummation examined by the court spanned nine years. Both sympathy and frustration were expressed by the Lords for and with the unfortunate husband. Unwisely (thought the Court) he had agreed at the outset of the marriage not to insist on his 'conjugal' or 'marital rights' for at least a year, despite his express wishes for their fulfilment. His wife's refusal to 'fulfil her duty',[2] however, persisted well after this period had elapsed and so did his forbearance. As Lord Dunedin, who gave the leading judgment, put it:

> Unfortunately, as I think, for the happiness of all concerned she chanced on a man who gave a promise which not one in a hundred man would have given, and which, if given, not one in a hundred would have kept.[3]

This passage bears reading more than once, for what it says about men, to men, and by men of the highest legal authority, about what is fitting sexual conduct in a man. Not even one man in a hundred, we are told, in other words *no* man, would or should put up with his wife's refusal to 'submit' to intercourse over such a period. Lord Shaw of Dunfermline called it 'the unfortunate and stupid bargain of abstention'.[4]

---

[1] G v G [1924] AC 349 at 364 (Lord Dunedin).
[2] Ibid 365 (Lord Dunedin).
[3] Ibid (Lord Dunedin).
[4] Ibid 368 (Lord Shaw of Dunfermline).

So what was the Court saying? That the husband should employ force? Though seemingly reluctant openly to counsel the use of violence, the Court did just this. Lord Dunedin put it most plainly in his judgment and the four other judges concurred. Lord Dunedin first reflected on the concerns of the judges in the court below, that perhaps Mr G had failed to display 'sufficient virility' in his attempts to win over his wife. He countered these slights to Mr G's manhood by observing that his attempts to assert his marital right 'were animated by such excitement of desire ... as to entail on occasion ejaculatio ante portam'.[5] The man was desperate. And thus, 'It is indeed permissible to wish that some gentle violence had been employed; if there had been it would either have resulted in success or would have precipitated a crisis so decided as to have made our task a comparatively easy one'.[6]

Lord Dunedin leaves us in no doubt that the simple and obvious do-it-yourself remedy was for Mr G to rape his wife, though the word rape is not used, for it is not rape in a legal sense. He tries to understand and excuse the husband's reluctance to use 'even mild and gentle force', though repeatedly 'baulked' and 'thwarted'.[7] Such forbearance 'may have been mistaken' because if Mr G had only done what all other men would have done, this would have forced the issue. (Lord Shaw spoke in a similar vein about the husband's 'excessive patience' and 'avoidance of force'.)[8]

Lord Dunedin puzzles about the nature of this curious marriage and this curious man who 'did not use a little more force than he did'.[9] But ultimately he decides that the wife was incapable of performing her 'duties' (it wasn't simply a matter of Mr G's failure to overcome her resistance) and so the remarkable but misguided Mr G was entitled to his decree of nullity.

Galsworthy's reflections about the divorce courts, and their thinking on the use of 'marital' force, when a man is denied 'the ordinary privileges which accrue to the husband'[10] (thoughts he puts into the mind of Soames Forsyte), are prescient. They are not overstated.

And the legal approval of male mastery continued into the middle and late twentieth century. The husband's little kingdom persisted and so did the sexual master within it, as well as legal sympathy for the man of the house.

In the 1951 English Court of Appeal decision of *Kaslefsky v Kaslefsky*,[11] the most distinguished Lord Denning showed his concerns for the welfare of the husband, refused sex, and found the husband's anger to be understandable and natural:

> This wife refused her husband sexual intercourse. If there were any ground for inferring that this was with an intention to inflict misery on him it would, I think, be cruelty. The wilful and unjustifiable refusal of sexual intercourse is destructive of marriage, more

---

[5] Ibid 357 (Lord Dunedin).
[6] Ibid (Lord Dunedin).
[7] Ibid 364 (Lord Dunedin).
[8] Ibid 368 (Lord Shaw).
[9] Ibid 358 (Lord Dunedin).
[10] Ibid 370 (Lord Phillimore).
[11] *Kaslefsky v Kaslefsky* [1950] 2 All ER 398, [1951] P 38.

destructive, perhaps, than anything else. Just as normal sexual intercourse is the natural bond of marriage, so the wilful refusal of it causes a marriage to disintegrate. It gives rise to irritability and discord, to nervousness and manifestations of temper.[12]

I. The Men of Law Recede from View: The Resort to Euphemism

Returning now to the influential scholars of criminal law of the 1950s, 60s and 70s (encountered in the first chapter), we find many of the same attitudes expressed. These new legal men of the universities and the law schools, who came to be major names, accepted that the province of criminal law, on the whole, should not extend into the home. Certainly they did not endorse murder or violence for violence's sake. But they did say that criminal law should not interfere with a husband who felt the need to use force for sexual purposes. They endorsed the sex privileges and exemptions which criminal law granted to their own sex, without perceiving any conflict of interests. They made little, if anything, of the fact that they were themselves virtually all men and that it was men who formed the main objects of their analysis and understanding of criminal regulation. Moreover, they communicated this approval of male authority, and of the use of force, to their colleagues and to their students who, in the early and middle parts of the twentieth century, would all have been men. And these thoughts about male right emanated from the most influential men of criminal law – they were both background assumptions and sometimes explicitly asserted, forming the backdrop of their thinking about the very nature of criminal law.

Domestic privacy and supposed domestic harmony, and the need to preserve both, were the common themes. There was a greater use of euphemism. The sexes were generally described as equal but different, as complementary, as belonging to different domains. Men were still for the public world; women for the hearth as homemakers. Man was no longer the absolute master of his home: the one person; the body politic. And yet the husband's authority was taken as a given, including his right to demand and obtain sexual intercourse, a poor term for something which was hardly an activity between two persons. The husband was to retain control of his domestic sexual life, without the interference of criminal law. And again it was in women's interests that this be so. (For a splendid visual evocation of this idea see John Brack's 1953 painting 'The New House'.)

The legal men of the middle of the twentieth century tended to retreat in their assertions of explicit male right to domestic authority, and cast the relations between husbands and wives in a more benign manner which endeavoured to harmonise their interests. (But then Stephen did this too.) The misleading and

---

[12] Ibid 403, 47.

criticised idea of different but equal roles emerged, in men's relation to women as wives, though the role of the wife remained vastly more constrained than that of the husband.[13]

In some ways, men began to lose their identity as men in criminal legal thought. No longer explicitly and self-consciously the superior and dominating sex, described by Stephen, no longer the single consuming male personalities of the principle of coverture, men were less visible and so retreated from view as men: as regulators and as the regulated. They were now less conspicuous as a social group with a particular character or characters, with norms of male behaviour, with certain priorities and interests, which found their way into criminal law (without being called male norms).[14] The prevailing legal mentality of the powerful entailed a new sort of blindness to their own man problem, the problem of who they were as a grouping of male thinkers and how their own particular demographic might influence and limit their thought. This moral and intellectual problem, of one sex speaking for two, was almost never mentioned.

An implicit 'man of law' continued to steer and inform legal thinking and, as Richard Collier has observed, it was 'a particular kind of masculinity, one broadly culturally associated with white, middle and upper-middle class, and able-bodied men'.[15] For this was the group of men who 'historically dominated – and continued to dominate – the upper echelons of law, government, and business'.[16] And to those we may add the universities.

II. Glanville Williams (1911–1997)

The long intellectual life of the great criminal law scholar Glanville Williams is revealing of these changing male preoccupations and emphases of legal men, mirroring changes in the century. Williams not only had a remarkably long career but he exerted considerable influence on the discipline. In many ways he organised and shaped it. He helped to identify and develop what came to be known as the general part of criminal law,[17] with its idea of a centre or core of principles and a special part (particular offences) which were meant to reflect these principles, especially the offences against the person.[18] Thus a centre and organisation and logic

---

[13] See Bell J's account of this period in *PGA v The Queen* [2012] HCA 21, 245 CLR 355.

[14] On the dominance of heterosexual norms see Richard Davenport-Hines, *Sex, Death and Punishment: Attitudes to Sex and Sexuality in Britain* (London, Collins, 1990).

[15] Richard Collier, 'Masculinities, Law and Personal Life: Towards a New Framework for Understanding Men, Law, and Gender' (2010) 33 *Harvard Journal of Law and Gender* 431, 439.

[16] Ibid.

[17] See his *Criminal Law: The General Part* (London, Stevens, 1953).

[18] See Stephen Shute and Andrew Simester (eds), *Criminal Law Theory: Doctrines of the General Part* (Oxford, Oxford University Press, 2002). See also Nicola Lacey, 'General Principles of Criminal Law: A Feminist Perspective' in Donald Nicolson and Lois Bibbings (eds), *Feminist Perspectives on Criminal Law* (London, Routledge-Cavendish, 2000) 87.

were established for criminal law. Williams' criminal law textbook was important for setting the liberal orthodoxy of criminal law and its analytical framework.[19]

Over the course of nearly half a century as a scholar, Williams moved from a slightly amused and relaxed attitude to coverture, as a male principle on the wane, once conferring great legal power on men, but one which had served its time; to a firmer but eventually less assured position on the husband's rape immunity, in defence of male right. This he found to be in the interests of marriage and (somehow) of both husbands and wives. The male supremacist, implicit in coverture, acquired a fresh livery and reappeared as a concerned but still controlling husband, a figure of benign authority within a more companionate marriage, though he too could be masterful when the occasion demanded. (Had Mr G only been such a man, all his marital problems might have been solved. For example, Soames Forsyte seized his moment.[20])

Williams was a mixed legal character: liberal on abortion and euthanasia[21] and sensitive to the plight of women harmed by orthodox rape law. In his obituary, he was said to be 'a kind man' and 'a quiet-spoken, modest, gentle, serious-minded Welshman'.[22] Unlike Stephen, he believed

> that law should be humane. He was a convinced utilitarian, who held that punishment was an evil to be avoided unless there was a good reason for imposing it, and for whom 'good reasons' meant the well-being of society, not the tenets of religious belief.[23]

He could also be highly effective. As his obituary explains:

> He took a major part in the campaign to liberalise the law on abortion, which largely succeeded with the Abortion Act of 1967. He was also very active in the campaign to legalise voluntary euthanasia, which has so far largely failed. He was both president of the Abortion Law Reform Association, and a vice-president of the Voluntary Euthanasia Society.[24]

But to the very end, Williams could not see the non-alignment of male and female interests for the purpose of marital rape law. (This was not said in his obituary.) For Williams, the private and the intimate were generally inappropriate subjects of criminal law. This was a point of blindness in his world view, harking back to an earlier time. It suggests entrenched and systemic thinking, particularly since Williams was in most other ways a strong critic of illiberal and inegalitarian laws.

Williams wrote in support of male domestic authority from the 1940s to the 1990s and with some influence for much of this time. Importantly, he helped to

---

[19] See Lindsay Farmer, 'The Modest Ambition of Glanville Williams' in M Dubber (ed), *Foundational Texts in Modern Criminal Law* (Oxford, Oxford University Press, 2014).

[20] Though this was not with the happiest of consequences.

[21] His book of 1958 *The Sanctity of Life and the Criminal Law* (London, Faber & Faber, 1958) bravely and critically examined laws against contraception, sterilisation, artificial insemination, abortion, suicide and euthanasia.

[22] JR Spencer, 'Glanville Williams Obituary' (1997) 56 *Cambridge Law Journal* 437, 439.

[23] Ibid 438.

[24] Ibid 439.

establish the Criminal Law Revision Committee, which as late as 1984 recommended against abolition of the immunity. Towards the end of his scholarly life, his views appeared outdated and unacceptable as feminist thinking gained purchase. In the 1940s he could make light of the idea that man and woman were one person, the man; in the 1990s he was bridling at the feminists.

A. The Younger Glanville Williams on the Unity of Husband and Wife, 1947

Glanville Williams maintained a consistent position on the domestic power of the husband which he implicitly and explicitly endorsed. This said, he was mindful of its changing and diminishing nature. As we saw in the first chapter, in 1947 he adopted a confident and light-hearted attitude to men's great legal power over women in the form of the marital unity principle. Recall that Williams regarded the principle as a 'venerable maxim', though admittedly one in which 'the spouses' did not 'participate equally in the personality that is thus created for them'.[25] Instead 'it would be closer to the rules of the common law to say, in the words of the wag, that "man and wife are one – but the one is the man"'.[26] This was interesting to Williams, enough to stimulate the writing of a scholarly survey article on this principle. It was not a cause of regret or real concern about the near annihilation of women by law.

What is interesting and especially revealing about this early writing on the marital unity principle, which gave an unvarnished exposition of the cluster of principles which attach the wife to the husband in criminal law, is its patriarchal attitude to the wife. This did not change fundamentally over the course of his career (though it becomes defensive in tone and new rationales are employed), even though in other ways Williams was a liberal and a progressive thinker. He was a model citizen, a good man, trapped in his own assumptions and passing on those beliefs to the rest of the scholarly community.

Then in his middle thirties, Williams expounded a male point of view – that of the husband around whom these rules were tailored and for whom they made sense. He did this in one of the most reputable law journals, the *Modern Law Review*, where it necessarily carried considerable authority. Having noted that women were not quite reduced to the status of dogs by the common law (his moment of levity), and that the unity principle was imperfectly applied, he affirmed the view of Pollock and Maitland that 'the main idea which governs the law of husband and wife ... is not that of "unity of person" but that of the ... profitable guardianship, which the husband has over his wife and over her property'.[27]

---

[25] Glanville Williams, 'The Legal Unity of Husband and Wife' (1947) 10 *Modern Law Review* 16, 17.
[26] Ibid 17, 18.
[27] Ibid 18.

This did not inspire the indignation, even rage, that John Stuart Mill had felt as he documented these legal values. At the end of this piece Williams concluded that 'in almost all' of the contexts in which the unity principle had been applied it 'subserved public policy, or at least humanitarianism' and so was 'not lightly to be cast aside'.[28] (We will return shortly to Williams' more mature work, after a brief inquiry into what his contemporaries were thinking about the rights of husbands.)

III. Norval Morris (1923–2004)

In 1954, the distinguished criminal law scholar and criminologist Norval Morris also pointed to the good sense of a law which empowered men as husbands. Recall from the first chapter that Morris and his colleague Turner characterised 'intercourse' as 'a privilege at least and perhaps a right and a duty inherent in the matrimonial state, accepted as such by husband and wife'.[29] No evidence was supplied for this strong empirical assertion of mutual acceptance. Morris and Turner conceded that there would 'be some cases where … the wife may consistently repel her husband's advances'[30] (which hardly sounds like acceptance). Here we are reminded of Soames Forsyte and Mr G. And like the House of Lords, these legal scholars were of the view that 'If the wife is adamant in her refusal the husband must choose between letting his wife's will prevail, thus wrecking the marriage, or acting without her consent'.[31] Criminal law must stand by the husband. 'It would be intolerable if he were to be conditioned in his course of action by the threat of criminal proceedings for rape'.[32]

Morris did not adopt this approach to other vulnerable groups. Morris combined in himself a mix of liberalism, reformism, positive advocacy for some underdog groups (such as prison inmates) and blindness to the legal plight and subordination of wives by men. He was selectively attentive and inattentive; impartial and partial. Again a good man was trapped in his own assumptions.

IV. Rollin M Perkins (1889–1993)

American criminal law textbook writer Rollin M Perkins subscribed to similar views about male right in marriage and communicated them, in explicit terms, to

---

[28] Ibid 31.
[29] Norval Morris and G Turner, 'Two Problems in the Law of Rape' (1954) 2 *University of Queensland Law Journal* 247, 259.
[30] Ibid.
[31] Ibid.
[32] Ibid.

generations of students.[33] Like Williams, Perkins had a long career, teaching for six decades, and in some of the most prestigious American universities. His own life started in the last part of the Victorian period and ended in the final decade of the twentieth century, so he had a good deal of time to spread his influence.

In her legal history of the marital exemption as it applied in the United States, Rebecca M Ryan notes Perkins' sustained support for the husband's immunity and over a span of years, ensuring a considerable exposure of these ideas to law students and then to the legal community: 'In a number of works published between 1957 and 1972, he defended the marital rape exemption, emphasizing the moral/legal distinction between marital and extramarital sex'.[34]

Perkins, like Williams, was mindful that coverture had gone, that 'almost no bride promises to obey her husband'[35] and that the rape immunity too was bound to disappear. And yet in a late version of his text, he was still declaring that sexual assault by a husband was not rape because 'unlawfulness' was 'an essential element of the crime'.[36] As Mary Irene Coombes observes, in her sustained analysis of Perkins' criminal text of 1982, the term 'rape' to describe the husband's rape of his wife was considered 'not necessary and seems undesirable'.[37] Assault was the appropriate charge here. Thus mixed messages to men and women were again delivered from the authoritative law texts.[38] Consistently the law of assault and other non-sexual offences against the person were considered fully applicable to the husband using force on a wife. Only the more serious crime of rape was not a fitting response to his violence.

V. Colin Howard (1928–2011)

In 1965 Australia's scholarly equivalent of Williams and Perkins, Colin Howard, also spoke up for the husband. As we saw in the first chapter, Howard declared, in purplish prose, that: '[A] husband should not walk in the shadow of the law of rape in trying to regulate his sexual relationships with his wife'.[39] Howard conjured up a solitary male figure walking in the gloom cast by law, which was an odd way of currying sympathy for the husband. Without the law, the husband was operating his household in the light? It was the husband's efforts

---

[33] See Rollin M Perkins, *Perkins on Criminal Law* (Brooklyn, Foundation Press, 1957) discussed in Rebecca M Ryan, 'The Sex Right: A Legal History of the Marital Rape Exemption' (1995) 20 *Law and Social Inquiry* 941, 941.

[34] Ibid 954.

[35] Rollin M Perkins, *Cases and Material on Criminal Law*, 2nd edn (Brooklyn, Foundation Press, 1959), discussed in Ryan, above n 33 at 955.

[36] Quoted in Ryan, above n 33 at 955.

[37] Internal quotes from Rollin M Perkins and Ronald N Boyce, *Criminal Law*, 3rd edn (Mineola, Foundation Press, 1982) and as quoted in Mary Irene Coombs, 'Crime in the Stacks, or a Tale of a Text: A Feminist Response to a Criminal Law Textbook' (1988) 38 *Journal of Legal Education* 117, 125.

[38] On Perkins, see also Coombs, ibid.

[39] Colin Howard, *Australian Criminal Law* (Sydney, Law Book Co, 1965) 146.

'to regulate his sexual relationships', free from too much legal interference, which were important to Howard. Again a leading criminal law scholar spoke openly, though not self-consciously, on behalf of the husband and against the interests of the wife, and he took as a given that the husband was in charge: he was regulating 'his sexual relationships'. Howard expressed these views for decades. Even as his text was being updated by a younger colleague, Brent Fisse, this male partisanship remained the same.

Howard explicitly contemplated the use of justified force to achieve sex with a wife in his influential text book *Criminal Law*.[40] Here he was unusual in pursuing and accepting the logic of the immunity. Howard could see that to force sex was to commit an assault. If forced sex was permissible at law, then so too was assault, when its purpose was to achieve rape. As Howard expressed it: 'If a husband cannot be guilty of rape upon his wife, it follows that he is entitled to overcome her resistance to intercourse'.[41]

As late as 1990, Brent Fisse, who went on to update Howard's text, ensured that this book was still exerting its influence and in a manner which continued to speak for the husband. Fisse thus echoed the views of Williams, in his exposition of the crime of rape, when he examined what he called 'the realities of sexual courtship'.[42] We are told that 'Outward reluctance to consent may be no more than a concession to modesty or a deliberate incitement to D (the defendant) to persuade a little harder. The approach to and consummation of sexual intercourse is not usually made an occasion for detached self-analysis'.[43] In this view, the masterful man exerted an erotic power and women derived erotic pleasure from having their will overborne. For Howard/Fisse sex was an inarticulate activity comprised of 'masterful advances' from the man accompanied by a show of 'outward reluctance' from the woman.

VI. Tony Honoré (1921–)

In the 1970s, a scholarly defence of the rights of the husband came from an unusual quarter. Tony Honoré, writing in 1978, was a complex academic. Honoré was the liberal scholar (of his time) pressing for an enlightened view of marriage, sex crimes, and homosexuals, but he was still a man of his time, now cognisant of the beginnings of second-wave feminism. He was concerned about the responsibilities of the husband to support the wife and saw this as a burden avoided by homosexuals, whom he portrayed as dissenters (rather than as unnatural deviants, hence a progressive move).

---

[40] Colin Howard, *Criminal Law*, 3rd edn (Sydney, Law Book Co, 1977) 62–63.
[41] Ibid.
[42] Brent Fisse, *Howard's Criminal Law*, 5th edn (Sydney, Law Book Co, 1990) 178.
[43] Ibid.

Sex Law[44] (discussed briefly in Chapter 1) is an unusual book by a distinguished scholar[45] who in his middle fifties wrote a work which endeavoured to go beyond the confines of formal scholarship and its narrow scholarly audience to reach a broader public. It was an endeavour to approach the body of law governing sex in an open and liberal manner. It consciously moved across different parts of law. It purported to set the law in its social context. It was written with an awareness of the newly-developing women's liberation movement. It had a strong English focus. It revealed a man of his times who also admitted that he could only write from the man's point of view, which was an interesting concession, stated once. And yet Honoré openly defended the immunity of the husband from criminal prosecution for rape, implicitly adopting the position of the husband and neglecting that of the wife.

From the outset Honoré described the sexual relation within marriage as a 'mutual duty' which he said was 'not recognised a hundred years ago'. Thus

> [a]ccording to Victorian standards, a wife was simply expected to 'submit to her husband's embraces' [no reference supplied] and was not thought to have any rights in matters of sex except perhaps the right to have children if she wished. This consent could not be withdrawn and so a husband, apart from exceptions, could not (and still cannot) be guilty of raping his wife, however unsuitable the time and place in which he forces her to submit. According to a decision which must mark the summit of the English disregard for logic he can, however, be found guilty of indecently assaulting his wife.[46]

But there appears to be little sense indicated here of the gravity or cruelty of the behaviour described, and no sense of how it would appear to the wife. Honoré was unconcerned about the role of criminal law in justifying force; his concern was with its inconsistency. He went on to seek a justification for the immunity in modern times and found it in what he saw as the appropriate type of law to apply to the behaviour, implicitly affirming the idea of domestic privacy. The matter was best dealt with by marriage law ... if at all. He objected to the prying eyes of the criminal law – eyes which could be on the husband and the force he was using against the wife. Again a good and influential man of law was trapped in his own assumptions.

---

[44] Tony Honoré, *Sex Law* (London, Duckworth, 1978).

[45] As Regius Professor of Civil Law in the University of Oxford. The Chair was founded by Henry VIII in the 1540s. The Chair is an appointment of the Crown, hence Regius. The offer of appointment is still in a letter from the Prime Minister, though actually decided and accepted beforehand (Richard Evans has written about the new Regius Chairs in 'On Her Majesty's Scholarly Service' *Times Higher Education* (7 February 2013)). Honoré is a legal theorist known for his work on ownership, causation (he wrote with Hart on causation) and responsibility, who held the post from 1971–1988.

[46] Honoré, above n 44 at 22.

VII. The Mature Glanville Williams *Textbook of Criminal Law*

Returning to Glanville Williams, who from the 1970s to the 1980s was including his thoughts on the character of rape in his criminal law textbook, we encounter the eminent scholar, organising the principles of criminal law and dissecting the offences, and the broad social commentator on men and the socio-sexual world, which he believed informed these offences.

In the 1978 edition of his textbook, Williams as technical scholar attended to the internal inconsistency of the offences against the person in relation to the 'rape' of a wife: what he called 'the difficult question of the wife's consent'.[47] The legal and analytical difficulty was that the rape was lawful, but the associated assaults were criminal and hence 'the law is thus inconsistent with itself'.[48] This was obviously an awkward thing for the men of law, who sought to be consistent and principled. Williams was aware of the analytical and social difficulty. But then women themselves were party to the problem, because they did not always want principled behaviour from a manly man. Williams went on to suggest that men were masterful sexual beings and women enjoyed mastery which posed a difficulty for lawmaking, which in turn complicated the law and the demands placed upon it.[49]

Though in other ways an important liberal with reforming tendencies, Williams was an unconstructed Victorian male in the area of rape law generally and this is well illustrated in the 1983 edition of *Textbook of Criminal Law* in which he drew on a literature on heterosexual relations of the 1950s. In his analysis of the law of rape, Williams devoted much of his time to the female complainant and her unreliability.[50] To Williams, 'The facts of life make consent to sexual intercourse a hazy concept' and so 'pose grave problems of proof and justice'.[51] Williams was himself vague about what he meant by 'the facts of life', though his ensuing discussion threw some light on the matter. He suggested that in sexual relations, men might not be in a position to know what women really want, that women were given to changing their minds, and that they often did so after the event. All of this made heterosexual men particularly vulnerable to women.[52]

Williams developed the theme of women's mendacity at some length. He explained 'That some women enjoy fantasises of being raped' and that 'they may, to some extent, welcome a masterful advance while putting up a token resistance'. He found the verse of Byron illuminating:

A little still she strove, and much repented,

And whispering 'I will ne'er consent' – consented.[53]

---

[47] Glanville Williams, *Textbook of Criminal Law*, 1st edn (London, Stevens and Sons, 1978) 195.
[48] Ibid 196.
[49] Glanville Williams, *Textbook of Criminal Law*, 2nd edn (Stevens and Sons, London, 1983) 238.
[50] Ibid.
[51] Ibid 238.
[52] Ibid.
[53] Ibid.

According to Williams, young girls lied about rape to placate their parents. Or they lied out of shame that they had engaged in sexual relations and may even have convinced themselves that the lie was true. Women who were jilted might lie out of spite. Or women might lie 'for obscure psychological reasons'.[54] To Williams, women were dissimulators who could neither be trusted nor understood.

Williams offered supporting footnotes for these propositions, but from some eccentric sources. For example, he offered us the wisdom of Lilian Wyles from her 1952 publication, *A Woman at Scotland Yard*.[55] 'Taken as a whole', said Wyles, 'there are not a large number of cases of genuine rape, though there are many spurious and doubtful complaints alleging that offence'.[56] Williams then qualified, but did not contradict, this statement with the observation that 'this opinion was expressed before the present explosion of violence'.[57] We are left to make of this what we will. On rape and seduction fantasies in women he cited a 1945 publication entitled the *Psychology of Women*.[58] And yet no equivalent volume was cited on rape and seduction fantasies by men – despite the proliferation of a pictorial literature which suggested that they may well have been common.[59]

Williams held to a Victorian view of relations between men and women in which the man naturally assumed the position of sexual master and the woman was his natural and willing subordinate. In Williams' view, some criminal principles should apply within the marriage sphere – assault, homicide, accessory to wife rape – but not forced sexual penetration by the husband himself. As Michael Freeman observed in his startlingly titled article, 'If you can't rape your wife, who[m] can you rape?', it is hard to find a criminal lawyer who opposed the application of the law of assault to marriage.[60] But many, like Williams, opposed the application of rape law.

Williams was precisely the scholar who could parse these different actions and offences occurring in the one incident of sexual violence within a marriage and indeed he wrote of it. There could be no 'excuse' of wilful blindness. He could certainly see how the law would operate. He was the leading expert on it. As a liberal, he thought that criminal law most importantly protected the personal security and bodily integrity of the person and saw murder, rape and the other offences against the person as directed at this purpose and principle. As a husband, he did not see these purposes and principles applying to the wife in relation to the

---

[54] Ibid.

[55] Lilian Wyles, *A Woman at Scotland Yard* (London, Faber & Faber, 1952).

[56] Ibid 121.

[57] Williams, *Textbook of Criminal Law*, 2nd edn, above n 49 at 238.

[58] H Deutsch, *The Pyschology of Women*, 2 vols (New York, Grune & Stratton, 1944–1945).

[59] As Jennifer Temkin observes: 'It seems strange ... that Professor Williams fails to mention male rape fantasies or to suggest that these might be considered in assessing whether the defendant was prepared to override the victim's wishes'. *Rape and the Legal Process* (London, Street & Maxwell, 1987) 83.

[60] Michael Freeman, '"But If You Can't Rape Your Wife, Who[m] Can You Rape?": The Marital Rape Exemption Re-examined' (1981) 15 *Family Law Quarterly* 1.

husband. By the 1990s he was saying that rape by a husband, a known person, was something less severe than a stranger rape.[61]

VIII. Disdain for Women

What is characteristic of the legal writing for the entire period documented in this chapter is a male disdain for women and an assumption of the rightness of male power over these weaker beings. The men of law did not operate in a vacuum. Male intellectuals more generally supported these views and gave vent to them.

In his study of *The Intellectuals and the Masses: Pride and Prejudice Among the Literary Intelligentsia, 1880–1939*, John Carey introduces us to the anti-female sentiments of the literati coupled with their class prejudice. For example, he quotes Louis McNiece, when 'surveying West End Theatre audiences in 1938', characterising them as

> mainly women – who use the theatre as an uncritical escape from their daily lives. Suburb-dwellers, spinsters, schoolteachers, women secretaries, proprietesses of teashops, all these, whether bored with jobs or idleness, go to the theatre for their regular dream-hour off. The same instinct leads them which makes many hospital nurses spend all their savings on cosmetics, cigarettes and expensive underclothes.[62]

For Carey, 'MacNeice's snobbish outburst, like his airy familiarity with nurses' underclothes, does not seem to be grounded in any very rigorous research. But it reflects a prejudice against female suburbia that was shared by other intellectuals'.[63]

Carey observes of the artist Clive Bell, in his *Civilization*[64] that 'Bell accords with general intellectual consensus in recognizing that civilizing women presents special difficulties. It is impossible, he decides, for a housewife to be civilized, for home and children blunt her intelligence and sensibility'.[65] According to Carey, HG Wells also found women to be an inferior people:

> Though Wells was highly susceptible to feminine allure, his considered view of women's influence on civilization was not favourable ... The evidence suggests that Wells thought of women as by nature extravagant, and addicted to clothes, chatter and shopping ... When Wells's women divulge to their menfolk the true nature of femininity, it is not a flattering picture. Women, Clementina tells William Clissold, [in *The World of William*

---

[61] This is a view which will be reversed in the legal literature then in the law. Rape by a husband will come to be seen as a great betrayal of trust. This will be the view of the Law Commission discussed in the next chapter (Law Commission, 'Criminal Law: Rape Within Marriage', Law Com No 205 (London, HMSO, 1992)).

[62] John Carey, *The Intellectuals and the Masses: Pride and Prejudice Among the Literary Intelligentsia, 1880–1939* (Academy, Chicago, 1992) 52. Inset quote from A Heuser (ed), *Selected Literary Criticism of Louis MacNeice* (Oxford, Oxford University Press) 1987.

[63] Carey, ibid 53.

[64] Clive Bell, *Civilization* (London, Chatto and Windus, 1928).

[65] Carey, above n 62 at 81.

Clissold] are ungenerous, parasitic, fearful, vain, easily muddled, tired by brain-work and untruthful. They are also less individualized than men ... and the vast industry of fashion, perfumery and cosmetics has come into existence solely to bestow on them the individuality they lack. Marjorie, in *Marriage*, is similarly frank. 'What are women' she demands. 'Half savages, half pets, unemployed things of greed and desire'.[66]

These views were repeated by senior civil servants, and at the highest levels, and they persisted through the middle of the twentieth century. In 1963, the Australian Civil Service issued a Minute Paper on whether women should be trade commissioners. The minute came to the point expeditiously and answered the question in the negative. 'Even after some deliberation, it is difficult to find reasons to support the appointment of women Trade Commissioners'.[67] It was conceded that

> [i]n countries where publicity media is well developed, such as North America and England and where there are no other major drawbacks, such as the Islamic attitude towards women, a relatively young attractive woman could operate with some effectiveness, in a subordinate capacity. As she would probably be the only woman Assistant Trade Commissioner in the whole area, as other countries employ women in this capacity hardly at all, she could attract a measure of interest and publicity.[68]

Indeed, 'If we had an important trade in women's clothing and accessories, a woman might promote this more effectively than a man'. However 'Even conceding these points, such an appointee would not stay young and attractive for ever and later on could well become a problem'.[69]

Such was still the easy attitude of male dominance, at the centre of power, considered normal and natural in the mid-1960s. There are echoes of Stephen and his understanding of the limited and temporary sexual assets of women, as opposed to the enduring assets of men. As the memo reminded the Director: 'A spinster lady can, and often does, turn into something of a battleaxe with the passing years. A man usually mellows'.[70] Humour may be intended here but it is humour borne of quiet confidence in male right.

Really, women were better out of public life in this view. 'It [was] difficult to visualise them as Trade Commissioners': 'they could not mix freely with businessmen'; most men's clubs didn't let them in; and it was 'extremely doubtful' that they could 'stand the fairly severe strains and stresses, mentally and physically'.[71] Men were the natural holders of power. The public person was a man. And the nature of public power, and who should exercise it, was still something for men to discuss and decide among themselves.

---

[66] Ibid 122.

[67] AR Taysom, Acting Director of the Trade Commissioner Service, internal memo to the Director, entitled 'Women Trade Commissioners?' under the letterhead of the Commonwealth of Australia (see Australian Archives).

[68] Ibid.

[69] Ibid.

[70] Ibid.

[71] Ibid.

IX. The Attitudes of Ordinary Men and Women of the Time

Williams, Howard and even Honoré were men of their times. They implicitly accepted that criminal law was one of a number of regulatory systems and that it relied heavily on other regulatory systems, other social institutions, other supporting social practices which were overlapping and mutually reinforcing. Most importantly, it relied on the regulatory system of the family, with the patriarch as authority figure. This was a system which was formally and informally recognised by criminal and other law and indeed formally imposed.

Where the family was a strong regulatory mechanism, it took up the slack of criminal law and provided a complementary order. And these scholars saw the family and family law as the more appropriate mechanisms for dealing with wife rape.[72] The family provided a powerful system of norms which claimed a moral basis, which sought to guide behaviour, which assumed and commanded habits of obedience.

Our legal scholars made strong and confident empirical claims about the nature of sexual relations within the family in the middle of the century. But according to David Kynaston, in his study of the British form of the family, from 1951–57,

> [s]ex was the subject of only one systematic survey during the 1950s – Eustace Chesser's *The Sexual, Marital and Family Relationships of the English Woman* (1956), based on questionnaires completed in 1954 by more than 6,000 female informants, located via GPs and with a middle class bias … overwhelmingly it was felt by wives that men wanted sex more frequently than women did.[73]

Simon Szreter and Kate Fisher's groundbreaking study of the sex lives of the British, pointedly titled *Sex Before the Sexual Revolution: Intimate Life in England 1918-1963*,[74] gives us a rare view of the sexual thinking of both women and men from within the 'ordinary' marriage of the middle of the twentieth century. As the authors explain:

> It presents evidence from an oral history study which solicited first-hand accounts from eighty-nine men and women, drawn from both the middle and the working classes, whose adolescence, marriage and childrearing occurred during the interwar and immediately post-war decades … The interviewees were asked how they had learned about sex in childhood and youth, how they had approached sex in adolescence and courtship, what sex had meant to them as adults and what part it played in their marriage relationships.[75]

---

[72] Michael Freeman makes just this point in 'But If You Can't Rape Your Wife, Who[m] Can You Rape?', above n 60.

[73] David Kynaston, *Family Britain 1951–57* (London, Bloomsbury, 2009) 592.

[74] Simon Szreter and Kate Fisher, *Sex Before the Sexual Revolution: Intimate Life in England 1918-1963* (Cambridge, Cambridge University Press, 2010).

[75] Ibid 1–2.

Perhaps the strongest and most consistent finding of this study was the strong ethos of privacy shared by both men and women. Sex was not something to be talked about: it was assumed and accepted. For women it was sometimes a pleasurable intimacy, sometimes a duty.

According to Szreter and Fisher 'many respondents presented sex as a marital duty. Many women accepted that the provision of sex was both a husband's right and a wifely responsibility from which they could not completely disengage'.[76]

> The conviction that a wife had an obligation to provide regular sexual access for her husband was relatively uncontested among the majority of interviewees. Although most women argued that sex should be a consensual act and that men should not press sex upon wives who were not in the mood, at the same time most women supported the notion that is was their duty to be sexually available some of the time, and recognised that this entailed consenting at moments when they did not want it for themselves. For some interviewees, then, sex was an unpleasant obligation.[77]

In effect these interviewees were echoing the law and they were echoing the views of the legal scholars, but only in part. Our men of law did not give voice to women who found themselves within a marriage required to fulfil their sexual obligations. More conspicuous in the legal writing were masterful husbands whose mastery would be sexually appreciated once the wives were made to see the good sense of it.

X. Reflections on the Men of Law and the Shifting Ground

The influential men of criminal law examined in this chapter did not regard themselves as illiberal, and a number were, in other respects, on other laws, bold liberal reformers. They campaigned for the rights of the vulnerable: the pregnant woman, the dying person, the prisoner. The *Cambridge Law Journal* obituary of Williams described him as 'a hugely effective law reformer – a kind of legal Asterix, whose boundless energy and unquenchable optimism led him into endless battles against unjust laws, many of which he won despite the overwhelming odds against him'.[78]

These men of law also accepted that coverture had gone, and rightly so: that men no longer absorbed the identity of their wives into their very persons. Such overt and explicit male supremacy was a thing of the past. But with this despatch of the views of their less enlightened forebears also went an awareness that men as a sex represented the primary persons of concern of criminal law and that they were still talking about men, but no longer as men, and also usually talking to men. The old guard knew that they were talking about and to men.

---

[76] Ibid 326.
[77] Ibid 327.
[78] Spencer, above n 22.

The new guard endeavoured to be more fair-minded. And yet they were reluctant to relinquish the idea of male control of the marriage, marital privacy and the ousting of criminal law from the home, including the most serious offences against the person. They remained committed to domestic privacy and its underlying idea of the harmonious self (male) regulating home. They believed in the special nature of the institution of marriage and as an institution naturally still run by the husband, which should be cordoned off from criminal law, out of respect for domestic privacy – but only in some respects.

These leading scholars of the criminal law had mixed beliefs and convictions. They knew perfectly well that criminal law entered the home for some purposes but not for others. After all they were criminal lawyers who knew the various applications of criminal law to the public and private sphere. Criminal law, they thought, *should* be permitted to intrude and apply to the violent husband for the purposes of the law of assault and the other offences against the person, including manslaughter and murder. But rape law, they thought, should not apply to the husband, even though these men of law were also of the view that rape was one of the worst crimes possible and so should be fully condemned. This was an uneasy intellectual and moral position to sustain. It combined close attention to some parts of the criminal law, and their technical elements and applications, and a vaguer more sociological, even moralistic approach to others.

Our men of legal influence were in the grip of incompatible ideas. Rape, they insisted, was the worst wrong possible, close to murder. This was how they conceived of the crime in their general accounts of criminal law. And yet a man's rape of his wife was either not wrong or it was much less serious. The accepted view was that it was not really rape.

In some ways, these scholars knew exactly what they were saying and doing. Their legal training required them to examine closely the different specific acts and offences which could be committed when a man employed sexual violence, say the choking and the force. And sometimes they did parse the offences occurring in a given set of violent acts within a marriage; there was the criminal assault, the criminal harm, even the accessorial responsibility for the rape of the wife by another and then the husband's lawful rape.

The licence given to men within the crime of murder posed a similar set of problems of principle and internal consistency for criminal law. The provoked husband, the man homicidally outraged at the infidelity of his wife, could have murder downgraded to manslaughter, as the scholars well knew. So what was it about the husband's position that made sense of this partial excuse for intentional killing? And what did the husband's partial excuse to murder do to the general character of the crime of murder, which was meant to be so utterly wrong? Surely these man-assisting rules within the law of murder also had implications for the general principles of criminal law. And perhaps the crimes of rape and murder might be considered together. Perhaps one 'defence' shored up the other. Perhaps the husband's partial excuse for a murder, when angered by an unfaithful wife, had some bearing on the husband's complete exemption from the crime of rape.

These are all intriguing and fundamental questions which go to the heart of criminal law and its understanding of the most serious offences against the person. And yet leading scholars did not pose them. They did not inquire into the way that the mores of their own sex served to delimit and modify the principles of central criminal law. They could not see the man problem. And so some of the most concerning dimensions of criminal jurisprudence went uninspected.

It seems likely that Williams and his contemporaries reconciled their ideas, to themselves, and so avoided these awkward questions of legal principle. (The problem of cognitive dissonance, and how our scholars dealt with it, will be considered in Chapter 8.) And of course they were not alone in their thinking. These men of law had ideological bents about the nature of men, women and marriage which were supported by the broader culture, ways of thinking which were probably more subtle and less bright than clear propositions.[79] They subscribed to general ideologies about the nature of sex roles within a marriage, as generally benign. They held loosely formulated ideas, often poorly articulated and not supported by robust empirical evidence. In fact for Williams and for Howard, their family and sexual ideologies were precisely not held, nor inspected, in a manner in which they conducted their other scholarly work. Their bold assertions about the nature of male and female sexuality were poorly supported. Adamant opinions about the sexual interests and preferences of women were based on slender and antiquated evidence, a general state of affairs which could be said to continue to this day.[80]

Williams maintained views that now seem difficult to square with one another. He expounded the position of the husband, from the point of view of the husband, and that being was an extended rather than bounded person, potentially extending into the person of the wife. At the same time, Williams was advancing a strong liberal idea of the nature of criminal law and the individual, with its defining rights of personal security and bodily integrity and inviolability and the correlative duty to respect it in others – or face the full force of criminal law. One way to reconcile these positions is to surmise that Williams genuinely did not see women, in their capacity as wives, as legal individuals or legal subjects, possessing an independent point of view. Though not articulated as such, his subject of criminal law was still a particular sort of (extended) man who was not subject to certain criminal laws within the sphere of his marital responsibility.

Another related way to reconcile the views of Williams with one other is to say that Williams believed that marriage was regulated, and appropriately so, by another set of principles, the family with its implicit patriarchy. Williams made this second attitude explicit in his writings. For him, marriage naturally ousted some of the most serious criminal law because it was a benign self (husband)-regulating

---

[79] I am indebted to the philosopher Allyson Robichaud for these observations.

[80] On the continuing appalling medical ignorance of female genitalia, their component parts, their scale and their function, and what makes women tick, as active sexual beings, see *The Woman Down Under: A User's Guide to the Vagina* (Great Britain, Yellow Kite, 2018) by Danish medical doctors Nina Brochmann and Elen Stokken Dahl.

system with formal criminal legal principles still unifying husband and wife. But for Williams, the worst that a husband could be in this husband-regulating sphere was a cad or a bounder. He did not depict the harm of marital rape which the point of view of the wife might reveal and about which Mill was explicit. There was also perhaps a class bias in his thinking. By the 1990s he was invoking his own wife and his friends' wives. He did not think of husbands as brutal – at worst as frustrated by sexually recalcitrant wives. He was not thinking of William Morgan, even though *DPP v Morgan* was one of the most analysed rape cases of the twentieth century.

As we saw in the opening chapter, Williams was a stalwart defender of the husband's immunity from rape prosecution for a good portion of the twentieth century. As late as 1992, he was still defending the man of the house, persisting with his defence of the immunity and giving a variety of explanations and excuses for the 'misguided' husband. He spoke of his 'handicap of being a male', but then insisted that 'a man can empathise with the female victim of crime, and anyway I take courage from the support of some women (including the woman most important to me), even though they are not the vociferous ones'.[81]

Williams conceded that husbands might 'misguidedly' think they retained conjugal rights. The husband might 'even, stupidly, think that by forcing himself upon [his wife] he may regain her affection'.[82] This seemed to be the view of the House of Lords in *G v G* much earlier in the century: forced sex would either save or destroy a marriage; the wise husband would force the issue. For the House of Lords, the foolish husband was the one who failed to employ 'some gentle violence' when faced with his wife's repeated refusals of sexual intercourse. By the last decade of the twentieth century, these views were no longer palatable. But Williams was hanging on to them, though now obliged to consider that such actions might perhaps amount to rape. Recall that Williams believed that 'rape by a cohabitee ... though horrible cannot be so horrible and terrifying as rape by a stranger'.[83] Thus the misguided husband deserved 'some consideration'.[84]

Williams was also the scholar perhaps best placed to take a larger view of criminal law, to see how its different parts fitted together, and whether they told a coherent story. Williams was a hugely influential definer and organiser of the principles of criminal law. Like other criminal law scholars, Williams of course utterly condemned murder and rape, which he helped to characterise, as the most important harms or wrongs one could do to another. However the substantial qualifications to these two most heinous of crimes, qualifications which were in the interests of men, did not get him thinking about the consistency and coherence of central criminal law, as a whole: as a single body of principles. It did not prompt him to consider its fairness and impartiality, and what it really stood for.

---

[81] Glanville Williams, 'Rape is Rape' (1992) 142 *New Law Journal* 11, 12.
[82] Ibid 13.
[83] Ibid 12.
[84] Ibid 13.

Williams knew that murder was effectively qualified by the defence of prov-ocation, in a manner that could favour the enraged and dishonoured husband confronted with his wife's adultery.[85] After all this was a classic use of the defence.[86] Williams knew also that rape was qualified by the husband's immunity and he openly sought to retain that great limitation to the defence. Considered together, what did these two qualifications to the most serious offences against the person say about criminal law's actual condemnation of male violence? Williams was just the man to ask this question, but he did not. Why were there circumstances in which the infliction of harm by a man was lawful, or not as bad as it might be, because it was inflicted within the context of a marriage and was concerned with the retention of male authority? How was the nature of men shaping central criminal law? Again Williams did not pose these fundamental questions about the general defining commitments of criminal law, questions which would have gone to the heart of the man problem.

My claim is that from the Victorian period, up to about the mid-1970s and beyond, men were neither seen nor delimited as men by influential legal men. This claim might seem counterintuitive given that the most serious and concerning behaviour regulated by criminal law was (and is still) that of men: in particular their sexual and non-sexual violence. However as both the agents and objects of criminal law making, the influential men of criminal law seemed to encounter a serious perceptual problem – a sort of blindness to a central feature of their work.

Men, as specific sexed men, crept into much of their legal analysis, and they were still making assumptions about the nature of men. And because of these understandings about men's nature, the most serious offences against the person, rape and murder, were qualified or limited. But men, as men, were all but invisible. Men were not delimited as a class of persons in criminal analysis, even though men as a class of persons delimited the law. The men of law believed that their theories of criminal law and its organisation were theories for all; they entailed general principles for general humanity. This was to have a bearing on how legal modernisation was achieved and characterised, as we will see in the next chapter, which considers the abolition of the husband's rape immunity.

---

[85] Indeed Williams observes, in his 1978 textbook, that provocation by adultery was one of 'The two standard situations of provocation': Williams, above n 47 at 482. And Williams envisages a situation in which 'a man, suspecting his wife of infidelity' might arm himself and kill 'the wife or her lover when he catches them out' (though, as he notes, here the defence might be precluded because of premedita-tion): Williams, above n 47 at 483. And yet, oddly, Williams also asserts, without supporting evidence, that 'Many mammals will attack another that makes advance to its mate, but will never on that account attack the mate. A woman, on the other hand, who finds her husband unfaithful seems to be more ready to kill the husband than her rival': Williams, above n 47 at 483. This is a statistical statement that calls for empirical support.

[86] As a recent Australian report concisely summarised the long-term problematic uses of the prov-ocation defence: 'the defence operated in practice to ameliorate the criminal responsibility of men when their sense of male dignity or honour was deeply compromised. Provocation was often invoked in cases where a jealous husband killed his wife in response to actual or suspected sexual infidelity'. David Plater, Lucy Line and Kate Fitz-Gibbon, *The Provoking Operation of Provocation: Stage 1* (South Australian Law Reform Institute, Adelaide, 2017) 10.

7

The Modernisation of Men, Or Men Assuming Responsibility without Taking Responsibility

In January of 1972, English journalist and broadcaster Jill Tweedie surmised in *The Guardian* that there were 'thousands of households across the country where rape will be committed tonight, carefully camouflaged by the sacraments of marriage'.[1] And so Tweedie conveyed the gravity, the pervasiveness and the ordinariness of 'domestic' rape. Rape at home was the quotidian, the mundane. It was violence disguised or shrouded by the sacrament of marriage: almost a religious rite. Though Tweedie called rape at home 'rape', in 1972 this was not legally true. Rape was lawful if the man were married to the woman.

Almost two decades later, the most senior judges of Scotland, England and Australia wobbled on this matter. Asked to say whether wife rape was now criminal rape, they said that now it was. Why it was now criminal, when it had become criminal, how it had become criminal, were not matters of deep contemplation. There was no close inquiry into the sexual perquisites of the husband up to that point, and what they meant for fundamental criminal law and for men. And there was little reflection on the implications for their own sex,[2] for their very masculinity, of this substantial renunciation of power: from enhanced and then diminished male rights.

In the highest courts of law, reform occurred in a perfunctory and piecemeal way, with little in the way of social, political or even legal analysis. There was virtually no inquiry into the implications of such a large-scale legal change for men and for the principles of criminal law proper. In the change recorded, men were generally missing from the analysis. Men were missing as a double legal status category undergoing change: as 'men' and as 'husbands'.

---

[1] Quoted in Mary Abbott, *Family Affairs: A History of the Family in Twentieth Century England* (London, Routledge, 2003) 140.

[2] All of these judges were men. In the landmark UK abolition case of *R v R* [1992] 1 AC 599, [1991] 2 WLR 1065, the all-male cast of judges were Lord Keith of Kinkel, Lord Brandon of Oakbrook, Lord Griffiths, Lord Ackner and Lord Lowry. In the landmark Australian abolition case of *R v L* [1991] HCA 48, (1991) 174 CLR 379, the Bench was made up of Mason CJ, Brennan, Deane, Dawson and Toohey JJ, all men. The Australian High Court Chief Justice is now a woman (Kiefel CJ) and she is the first female chief justice.

My task here is to work out how such change was explained, justified, philoso-
phised and understood; whether legal change was willing or grudging; explicit
or oblique or euphemistic. I examine the responses and justifications; the denials
and the resistance. And perhaps most importantly, I consider what the men of law
thought of this transformed law for men, who were now formally relinquishing
their right of sexual access to at least one woman after centuries of legal control.
What bearing did they think it had on criminal law proper? None? A little? A lot?

I. The Committees that Modernised Men
in the Law of Rape

South Australia was the first state of Australia to modify the legal right of the
husband to force sex on his wife and the first jurisdiction to do so in the common
law world. The recommendation for legal change was contained in the report of a
three-member law reform commission established in 1975 by the state Attorney
General and chaired by South Australia's first female judge, Roma Mitchell.[3] In
the first instance, the Mitchell Committee was of the opinion that the immunity
should be abolished, wholesale.

> The view that the consent to sexual intercourse given upon marriage cannot be revoked
> during the subsistence of the marriage is not in accord with modern thinking. In this
> community today it is anachronistic to suggest that a wife is bound to submit to inter-
> course with her husband whenever he wishes it irrespective of her own wishes.[4]

But then the Committee introduced a major qualification, and in making sense of
the qualification, it did so from the point of view of the husband worrying about
what a 'vindictive wife' might do, once armed with a right to complain of rape. The
application of criminal law was too strong a response: it was better to rely on the
remedies of family law until the woman was safely out of the home.

> Nevertheless it is only in exceptional circumstances that the criminal law should invade
> the bedroom. To allow a prosecution for rape by a husband upon his wife with whom
> he is cohabiting might put a dangerous weapon into the hands of the vindictive wife and
> an additional strain upon the matrimonial relationship.[5]

So what should a wife do?

> The wife who is subjected to force in the husband's pursuit of sexual intercourse needs,
> in the first instance, the protection of the family law to enable her to leave her husband
> and live in peace apart from him, and not the protection of the criminal law. If she has
> already left him and is living apart from him and not under the same roof when he

---

[3] Criminal Law and Penal Methods Reform Committee of South Australia, *Special Report on Rape
and other Sexual Offences* (Mitchell Committee Report) (South Australian Government Printer, 1976).
   [4] Ibid 14.
   [5] Ibid.

forces her to have sexual intercourse with him without her consent, then we can see no reason why he should not be liable to prosecution for rape.[6]

The South Australian Government of the day rejected the advice of the Committee, that the immunity should be abolished only after separation. First it moved to abolish the immunity completely but then in order to get the proposed amendment through both houses of parliament, it agreed to limit the scope of the reform in a gruesome manner. Rape by a husband would be a highly constrained offence. To qualify as rape, there must also be actual bodily harm, or threat of it, or acts of gross indecency or an act intended to humiliate. When South Australia thus became the first jurisdiction in the Anglophone common law world to criminalise wife rape, it both proscribed wife rape and licensed it.[7]

This supposedly reforming legislation entertained the idea of a husband who raped lawfully when he did so in a manner not calculated to humiliate. It is difficult to imagine such an act.[8] The man who inflicted something less than actual bodily harm, in the course of the rape, also committed no offence: this was now spelled out in legislation. So too the man who was not grossly indecent, only ordinarily so, while raping his wife committed no crime. We are returned to the idea of 'gentle violence', as something acceptable in a man.

The men retained within this rape law had affirmed, in the middle 1970s, their rights to force sex on a woman in the right manner. There are echoes of Fitzjames Stephen here who, before he affirmed the right of the husband to force sex in *Clarence*, expressed the more qualified view that 'surely' the irrevocable consent of the wife 'is confined to the decent and proper use of marital rights. If a man used violence to his wife under circumstances in which decency or her own health or safety required or justified her in refusing her consent, I think he might be convicted of rape, notwithstanding Lord Hale's dictum'.[9]

---

[6] Ibid. Colin Howard, the textbook scholar we encountered in the last chapter, also sat on this committee and these words echo his general views of the immunity.

[7] A 1976 amendment to South Australia's criminal law act (the Criminal Law Consolidation Act) first removed the presumption of a wife's consent to intercourse with her husband:

'Section 73 ... (3) No person shall, by reason only of the fact that he is married to some other person, be presumed to have consented to sexual intercourse with that other person. (4) No person shall, by reason only of the fact that he is married to some other person, be presumed to have consented to an indecent assault by that other person.'

Then the qualifications were introduced. More was needed than rape *simpliciter* (whatever that might look like) to make wife rape the crime of rape.

'(5) Notwithstanding the foregoing provisions of this section, a person shall not be convicted of rape ... upon his spouse ... unless the alleged offence consisted of, was preceded or accompanied by, or was associated with ... (a) assault occasioning actual bodily harm, or threat of such an assault, upon the spouse; (b) an act of gross indecency, or threat of such an act, against the spouse; (c) an act calculated seriously and substantially to humiliate the spouse, or threat of such an act; or (d) threat of the commission of a criminal act against any person.'

[8] Indeed, the sheer confusion of ideas drew critical comment at the time. See Jocelynne A Scutt, 'Consent in Rape: The Problem of the Marriage Contract' (1977) 3 *Monash University Law Review* 255.

[9] James Fitzjames Stephen, *A Digest of the Criminal Law* (London, Macmillan, 1877) 172, fn 1.

The reforming rape law of South Australia entailed a strikingly explicit legal statement about the acceptability of the controlling and forceful man and one housed within a new modern criminal law ostensibly designed to make wife rape a crime. The modernisation of the husband was taken only so far.

At about the time that the Mitchell Committee was formed in South Australia, a committee was established in England to report on the state of English rape law and to make recommendations for reform. Its Chairperson was Mrs Justice Heilbron.[10] Notwithstanding extensive discussion of *Morgan*, of the facts of the case, and of the pronouncements of the court on the mental element for rape (see Chapter 1), there was no discussion of the marital immunity which was at the centre of the case and was simply taken as a given.[11] As Tweedie had observed three years before *Morgan* and this committee, wife rape was probably occurring across England with little legal fuss, in an ordinary and sanctioned manner.

Notwithstanding the qualified removal of the immunity in a backwater of Empire (South Australia), the English remained steadfast in their endorsement of lawful wife rape. In the appropriately Orwellian year of 1984,[12] the Criminal Law Revision Committee of England and Wales published its 15th report on 'Sexual Offences' in which it openly considered the question: should a man be permitted to rape his wife lawfully?[13] The Criminal Law Revision Committee had been established under the urgings of Glanville Williams, who was also a member of the committee from its inception in 1959 to 1980.[14]

All but one of the 17-member Committee responsible for the report on sexual offences were men, and it could be said that the sex imbalance showed. This was a remarkably anecdotal report on the law, with almost no supporting footnotes and hence little supporting evidence for its bold empirical claims. It was essentially presented from the viewpoint of the husband. The committee members seemed oblivious to this fact.

However this was also an internally divided committee. There was disagreement about whether the husband's immunity should go completely. A narrow majority was against full abolition. The minority wanted it. (Eight years later another government inquiry would recommend full abolition.) Notwithstanding this division of opinion, the Committee's report dedicated less than eight pages to its reasoning on why 'marital rape' (the subject heading of this part of the report) should remain lawful.[15] There was reliance on bald assertion: 'The circumstances of rape may be peculiarly grave', but not so when the parties were married.

---

[10] Great Britain Home Office, 'Report of the Advisory Group on the Law of Rape' (Cmnd No 6352, 1975).

[11] Of greater interest was the use of sexual history evidence.

[12] Indeed by 1984 other jurisdictions around the world had also proceeded against the immunity: for example Canada abolished it in 1982.

[13] Criminal Law Revision Committee, 15th Report, 'Sexual Offences' (London, HMSO, 1984).

[14] JR Spencer, 'Glanville Williams Obituary' (1997) 56 *Cambridge Law Journal* 437, 438–439.

[15] This division of opinion among the commissioners did not lead to a searching inquiry nor to an open-minded evaluation of the competing views.

This feature [rape's peculiar gravity] is not present in the case of a husband and wife cohabiting with each other when an act of sexual intercourse occurs without a wife's consent. Should he ... force her to have intercourse without her consent this ... is far from being the 'unique' and 'grave' offence described earlier ... Where the husband goes so far as to cause injury ... the gravamen of the husband's conduct is the injury he has caused not the sexual intercourse he has forced.[16]

Earlier the Committee had declared that 'We approach this part of our Report [on rape] on the basis that rape should continue to be regarded as a unique and grave offence, and in the knowledge that anything which appears to diminish its gravity will be viewed with suspicion by Parliament and the public'.[17] But soon we are told that wife rape is 'far from being' this sort of offence. This was a bold claim. What was its basis? Why was the 'forcible' nature of the sexual intercourse not 'the gravamen' of the husband's conduct, but rather the injury caused and how were the two to be distinguished clearly?

That a man's rape of his wife lacked the seriousness of a man's rape of any other woman was simply a starting premise of this inquiry, even though an object and purpose of the inquiry was to determine just how heinous was the conduct of the man who 'raped' his wife. If wife rape were serious enough, it should become the crime of rape. But because wife rape, from the outset, was taken to lack 'the gravamen' of other rapes, wife rape was not true rape. And so the Committee employed a type of syllogism. Rape was one of the most serious of crimes that a man could commit. But the husband who raped his wife did not commit a crime of that gravamen. A man's rape of his wife was therefore not the true, serious crime of rape. The law should not change.

Because of the Committee's first premise, and also its conclusion, which was that the husband's use of forced sex lacked the 'gravamen' of the serious crime of true rape, it followed that the legal recognition of wife rape would water down the crime which came into being when men raped women they were not married to; it would diminish the seriousness of the true crime. This premise/conclusion was repeated throughout. 'For rape between cohabiting spouses ... imprisonment might not be appropriate; where no physical injury was caused to the wife, imprisonment would be most unlikely'. Thus 'A category of rape that was dealt with leniently might lead to all rape cases being treated less seriously'. After all, 'in those cases where imprisonment would be called for', which must be those causing injury, 'there exist already offences against the person to protect the wife'.[18]

In short the wife had enough rights to personal security supplied by the criminal law. She did not need the additional right to complain of rape. This was one right too many. It was too great an incursion on male right.

Indeed the wife was not the right type of right holder for such a serious crime with all its consequences for men. She could not be relied upon to maintain a

---

[16] Criminal Law Revision Committee, above n 13, 19–20, para 2.64.
[17] Ibid 4, para 2.3.
[18] Ibid 20, para 2.65.

consistent position: she might well change her mind. 'Violence occurs in some marriages but the wives do not always wish the marital tie to be severed, *whatever their initial reaction* to the violence'[19] (emphasis added). No evidence was supplied by the commissioners for this proposition. No study of the thinking of 'wives' – a survey perhaps? – was offered in support.

Furthermore an ill-considered rape complaint might end a marriage, in an untimely manner. The police would come in and 'she [the wife] may not be able to stop the investigative process if she wanted to'. And rather chillingly: 'The effect of the intervention of the police might be well to drive couples further apart in cases where a reconciliation might have occurred'.[20] It seems that rape and its prosecution should not be permitted to destroy what was thought to be an otherwise healthy relationship.

The Committee continued, again in anecdotal vein (not a study in sight):

> There are also other considerations that weigh with some of us who do not wish to see the offence extended to all marriages. There are apprehensions, gained from experience of when the granting of a divorce depended upon proof of a matrimonial offence, that an allegation of the serious and emotive offence of a rape might be used by a wife as a bargaining counter in negotiations for maintenance or custody, or as the basis of a charge of unreasonable behaviour in a divorce petition.[21]

No supporting evidence was supplied of the experience gained from the divorce courts of the trickery of wives. Instead there were knowing references to divorce proceedings. There was no mistaking the side of the divorce court on which the commissioners were placing themselves. They were not with the wife.

> Moreover, a prosecution for rape might necessitate a complicated and unedifying investigation of the marital history ... before issues such as the wife's consent and the husband's belief could be assessed. Some of us consider that the criminal law should keep out of marital relationships between cohabiting partners – especially the marriage bed – except where injury arises, when there are other offences which can be charged.[22]

Thus the commissioners steered attention away from the criminal law and the serious crimes of male violence, to the civil sphere, of marital conflict and the divorce courts. And there were conjured up unseemly divorce proceedings, domestic lives which were better left uninspected, and certainly not exposed to criminal investigation. At no stage did the Committee members spell out that it was the husband's, not the wife's, rights under serious criminal law which were in issue: that the woman's right not to be raped was being balanced against the husband's right to rape her.

Only six years later in 1990 the English Law Commission issued a working paper which recommended full criminalisation of wife rape. It endorsed this

[19] Ibid 20, para 2.66.
[20] Ibid.
[21] Ibid 21, para 2.69.
[22] Ibid.

recommendation in its final report in 1992.[23] In a direct reversal of the thinking of Glanville Williams and of the majority of the 1984 Criminal Law Reform Commission (CLRC), the Law Commission declared that wife rape was not a lesser form of rape. On the contrary, it was a breach of the wife's trust in the marriage and so might be 'particularly offensive in that it was an abuse of an act which has been or should have been his means of expressing love for his wife'.[24]

Both the working paper and the final report of the Law Commission disclosed evidence of careful and scholarly research and responded to the wide-ranging submissions solicited, received and examined. The constitution of the 1990 Commission was interesting; it included the first openly feminist law commissioner, who was also a distinguished law professor (and so a scholar in her own right), and Queen's Counsel,[25] who would become the President of the Supreme Court of the United Kingdom.

The Law Commission considered closely each of the arguments of the CLRC against abolition, and whether they were supported by the available evidence, and found them to be unsustained. The Law Commission made the further point that the remedies supplied by marriage law (and which were preferred by the CLRC) simply did not serve the basic function of criminal law, which was to label and proscribe unacceptable conduct and so set standards of civil behaviour.

The remarkable timing of these reports, the first immediately postdating the judicial abolition of the immunity in Scotland, the second immediately postdating the judicial abolition of the immunity in England and Wales, meant that their more sustained critical commentary on the law, supported by extensive evidence, functioned almost like a Greek chorus (as the law had already changed). Thus the work of the Law Commission came too late to have its full scholarly and moral effect. As we will see, at around the same time, Scotland and then England were despatching the immunity judicially, and in a far less considered fashion.

II. The Judiciary on (Male) Modernisation: Cherchez la Femme

In the 1990s the spousal rape immunity simply fell over. The judicial men of law at last declared that husbands could now be held responsible for rape, though, as we will see, this was not how they tended to describe the change. There was an apparent domino effect in Scotland, England and Australia, within the span of a few years. What is significant about these reform cases is not just the slight treatment of what was strictly speaking a major change in law, one that had a direct bearing on central criminal law and its serious offences against the person. (After all it greatly expanded the scope of the crime of rape.) It is not just that the judges did

---

[23] Law Comission, 'Criminal Law: Rape Within Marriage', Law Com No 205 (London, HMSO, 1992).
[24] Ibid 9, para 3.12.
[25] Then Professor Brenda Hoggett QC, now Lady Brenda Hale.

their best to diminish the scale of the change; that they failed to take stock of the fact that a husband's rape of his wife had probably been lawful up to then and at the insistence of many of the men of law; or that they fobbed off the past or dissociated themselves from it. What is significant is that their focus of attention was essentially on women and women's emergence from a subordinate status category, as if women had gone though some sort of social and legal metamorphosis, all on their own – and that the men of law had had very little to do with the legal making of women.

In short, when the most senior judges proceeded to remove the husband's immunity from rape prosecution, they did not say that they were redefining the lives of *both* men and women, within a fundamental institution, sanctified by the state. Most of the talk was of the modernisation of women and their changing status, as if that status could change unilaterally. And as if the changes were not about the changing status of men. *Cherchez la femme* was, in a sense, the judicial message. The correlative change in men, and the changing models of masculinity which were necessarily implicit in all of this, were hardly mentioned.

The judges couched their decisions amid stories about the changing nature of women and their lives, which eventually warranted a new female right to complain of rape by a husband. Little was said about the shifting nature of men's lives and their emerging civic responsibilities, especially their new duty not to rape, though the crime of rape was (and remains in England) a crime exclusively aimed at men. The direction of attention was nearly all towards women and away from men, as it was for the men of law, such as Odgers and Lush, who contemplated changes in women's legal lives at the start of the century (Chapter 4).

In 1989, the Scottish High Court of Judiciary relied on the idea of 'female modernisation' in *S v HM Advocate* when it recognised the right of the married woman to complain of rape. The message conveyed was that the law was bound to change because married women had emerged out of their limiting legal status. 'By the second half of the 20th century … the status of women, and the status of a married woman, in our law have changed quite dramatically'.[26] Again little was said about the reining in of male power and the correlative social and legal change in the male sex, ushering in new models of masculinity.

In 1991 in *R v R* the English Court of Appeal and then the House of Lords decided to recognise wife rape as the crime of rape. Again, as the court effected this major change to the criminal law directed explicitly at men, attention was directed towards the changing status of women and away from the changing lives and responsibilities of men. According to the Court of Appeal:

> It seems to us that where the common law rule no longer even remotely represents what is the true position of a wife in present day society, the duty of the court is to take steps to alter the rule if it can legitimately do so in the light of any relevant Parliamentary enactment.[27]

---

[26] *S v HM Advocate* [1989] SLT 469 at 473.
[27] *R v R* [1991] 2 WLR 1065 at 1073, [1992] 1 AC 599 at 610 (Lord Lane CJ).

There was admittedly a short bracing statement about appropriate codes of conduct for men.

> We take the view that the time has now arrived when the law should declare that a rapist remains a rapist subject to the criminal law, irrespective of his relationship with his victim.[28]

Indeed the Court went further saying that 'it [the immunity] is repugnant and illogical in that it permits a husband to be punished for treating his wife with violence in the course of rape but not for the rape itself which is an aggravated and vicious form of violence'.[29] The Court was obviously troubled by the law and what it said about acceptable male behaviour. And so it reversed the view expressed by the Criminal Law Revision Committee only a few years earlier, that the criminal law should concern itself with the force used by the husband but not the rape.

The House of Lords employed similar reasoning when it spoke of the modernisation of the status of the wife. It approved the statement of Lord Lane that it was time for: 'the removal of a common law fiction which has become anachronistic and offensive and we consider that it is our duty having reached that conclusion to act upon it'.[30] The unfortunate implication, conveyed by both courts, was that it was not offensive before. Lord Keith of Kinkel, speaking for the rest of the Law Lords, observed:

> It may be taken that [Hale's dictum] was generally regarded as an accurate statement of the common law of England. The common law is, however, capable of evolving in the light of changing social, economic and cultural developments. Hale's proposition reflected the state of affairs in these respects at the time it was enunciated. Since then the status of women, and particularly of married women, has changed out of all recognition in various ways which are very familiar and upon which it is unnecessary to go into detail.[31]

Again the analysis was mainly of a social and legal transformation in women as a legal category. The immunity was 'to be understood against the background of the status of women and the position of a married woman'. The Court did not set the decision against the background of the status of men and the position of a married man, which it could equally have done. In the past 'no doubt, a married woman could be said to have subjected herself to her husband's dominion in all things'.[32] But now women had entered the modern world and had become full and free liberal individuals, choosing subjects (much like men had always been). And so the Court concluded that 'in modern times the supposed marital exemption in rape forms no part of the law of England'.[33]

[28] Ibid 1074, 611.
[29] Ibid 1072, 609.
[30] Ibid 1074, 611 (Lord Lane CJ, Sir Stephen Brown P, Watkins, Neill and Russell LJJ).
[31] Ibid 616.
[32] Ibid 617.
[33] Ibid 623.

R v R proceeded to the European Court of Human Rights, on an argument of retrospective law making, which the Court rejected.[34] Nevertheless the European Court did accept that 'It is unfair to expect citizens to live their lives according to laws which are unclear or are not even in existence when decisions or actions have to be taken by individuals'.[35] The startling meaning of this statement, in the context of this law, is that it would be unfair to permit men to decide to rape, rightly believing rape to be lawful, and then punish them for it. For the rule against retrospectivity essentially addresses the potential offender at the point of decision making. The decision is, should he proceed with the given act? Is he sufficiently apprised of the fact that it is unlawful? And concomitantly, if the act is lawful, how can he be fairly and justly punished for doing what the law fails to prohibit?[36]

With its single-minded focus on the incapacities of women, *R v R* implicitly treated men as liberal subjects all along, their status as men essentially unchanged by these amendments to the law of rape (though they would no longer have the same freedoms). This of course made no sense in law, given the necessary interdependence of rights and duties – the male right to a woman necessarily corresponded to the female duty to 'submit', placing the man in the role of sexual master and little monarch.

In 1991, the Australian High Court in *R v L* also declared that by that year, and maybe even before, the husband had lost his immunity.[37] According to the Court it was never entirely clear when this had occurred and how: perhaps by spontaneous combustion? Mason CJ, Deane and Toohey JJ described the change in the briefest of terms.

> Without endeavouring to resolve the development of the common law in this regard, it is appropriate for this Court to reject the existence of such a rule as now part of the common law of Australia ... The notion is out of keeping also with recent changes in the criminal law of this country made by statute, which draw no distinction between a wife and other women in defining the offence of rape ... It is unnecessary for the Court to do more than to say that, if it was ever the common law that by marriage a wife gave irrevocable consent to sexual intercourse by her husband, it is no longer the common law.[38]

Again it was the woman who was alone transformed by marriage, from a free person into a perpetual consenter, but who was finally permitted to say 'no'. The man was missing from this account of the law. In 1992, South Australia fully criminalised wife rape by statute, also with little ado.

[34] *SW and CR v UK* (1996) 21 EHRR 363.
[35] *R v R* [1992] 1 AC 599 at 623.
[36] The use of the male pronoun here seems perfectly appropriate in this context.
[37] *R v L* [1991] HCA 48, (1991) 174 CLR 379.
[38] Ibid paras 18–19, 390.

III. Assuming Responsibility

Equally missing from these legal decisions is a sense of legal and moral responsibility by the men of law for the making of 'the status of women', which was frankly an existential disaster, as Blackstone made plain. Nor did these judges hold their legal forebears to account for the enhanced status of men as husbands. These impaired (female) and augmented (male) legal statuses, respectively, were necessarily created and sustained by lawmakers. They were not natural things residing in the world; they were not spontaneous human formations.

We might contrast this anodyne mode of reform with the mode adopted in other countries, when laws were found to be odious and so openly condemned. For example, it was made abundantly clear when the law of apartheid in South Africa was critically examined and abolished that law was man-made and by the interested, and in their own interests.[39] The wrongness of former laws was made abundantly clear, too, when Nazi laws of human status were evaluated as law. But this was not so here. The reference to 'recent changes in the criminal law' has a far off sound and appears to be something happening on its own in the judicial imagination, not by dint of positive legal decisions by lawmakers. There is a moral distancing. There is almost no assumption or inspection of responsibility for these laws – made by men – and their sustained operation, for men.

On the whole the tone of these cases is flat; the emotion dulled. Certainly in the Australian decision, there was little sense that the subject of discussion was lawful highly intrusive violence and that the decision being made was whether that violence should remain lawful. There was little sense of whose interests the laws under consideration had necessarily reflected to date. As the violence in question was explicitly directed by a man and against a woman, it could hardly reflect women's interests. There was no inspection of vested interests, or even of the possibility of them, and the effects of those interests not only on the laws themselves but also on the quality of reasoning and judgement about those laws, as those doing the reasoning were also the beneficiaries of the law.

IV. Historical Revisionism and Denial of the Past

In 2012, the Australian High Court in the case of *PGA* went further still in denying the uses of male power and male interest in shaping the law of rape.[40] Stated simply, the majority judges denied the lawfulness of wife rape, and effectively rewrote the past. The dissenting judges recognised the exclusion of husbands from criminal responsibility, though they did not fully condemn their predecessors.

---

[39] See Richard L Abel, *Politics by Other Means: Law in the Struggle Against Apartheid, 1980–1994* (New York, Routledge, 1995).

[40] *PGA v The Queen* [2012] HCA 21, 245 CLR 355.

For these men of law spoke for the men of different times, so they could be excused for their thinking.

The facts of *PGA* can be stated simply. In 2009, criminal proceedings were commenced against P,GA (Mr P) for the rape of his wife in 1963 in South Australia, when the two were cohabiting. This was not the first time that the alleged offence had come to the notice of the authorities. There is evidence that 'on numerous occasions during the 1960s' Mrs P had contacted the police, complaining of brutal violence, but that the police had declined to act, regarding it as a private matter.[41]

In 2010, Mr P was charged with the rape of his wife in 1963. The charges were laid under South Australian law: s 48 of the Criminal Law Consolidation Act 1935. As it stood in 1963, the section stated that 'any person convicted of rape shall be guilty of felony, and liable to be imprisoned for life, and may be whipped'. The section merely classified the crime and specified the punishment. The identification of the elements of the crime of rape was left to the common law.

P's trial before the South Australian District Court was stayed so that the South Australian Court of Criminal Appeal could answer the question 'Was the offence of rape by one lawful spouse of another … an offence known to the law of SA as at 1963?'. Doyle CJ, who gave the judgment for the majority of the Court of Criminal Appeal, declared that it was, and the matter went on appeal to the High Court of Australia.[42]

In 2012, the Australian High Court declared that wife rape had not only been a crime in 1963 but that it had been a crime at the time of the passage of the critical South Australian rape provision in 1935 and possibly before then. How did it arrive at and justify this surprising and seemingly retrospective determination? It is helpful to examine the manner in which legal counsel for the defence and the prosecution steered the thinking of the High Court.

Counsel for the appellant, Mr Bennett, submitted that the common law position in 1963 was that, upon marriage, a wife was deemed to have consented to sexual intercourse, and that consent was irrevocable. As the presumption of consent was irrebuttable, Mr P could not be tried for the rape of his wife. This common law rule was traceable to the writing of Sir Matthew Hale. In fact Bennett suggested that in 1963, Australia was a pre-Enlightenment country as far as women's rights were concerned, as was probably the rest of the world. The Australian public service required women to resign their positions upon marriage. (We have seen the thoughts on women issued by the Trade Commissioner in just this year, and this is precisely how Bennett characterised the social and legal attitude to women.) Anti-discrimination legislation had yet to be passed in 1963. Men ruled the public sphere.

---

[41] Wendy Larcombe and Mary Heath, 'Case Note: Developing the Common Law and Rewriting the History of Rape in Marriage in Australia: *PGA v The Queen*' (2012) 34 *Sydney Law Review* 599, 602.

[42] *R v P, GA* [2010] SASCFC 81, (2010) 109 SASR 1. And for a lively account of the South Australian Court of Appeal and High Court judgments, see Richard Sletvold, 'PGA v The Queen: Do Laws Just Disappear?' (2012) 33 *Adelaide Law Review* 573. See also Kellie Toole, 'Marital Rape: Retrospectivity and the Common Law' (2015) 39 *Criminal Law Journal* 286.

Counsel for the Crown, Mr Hinton, argued the opposite: that South Australia was a progressive state in a progressive nation and that it had not supported the husband's immunity from rape prosecution. This was far more palatable to the Court: the (male) law makers and judges of Australia were portrayed as progressive and egalitarian in their previous attitudes to women. Mr P could therefore be tried for wife rape.[43]

The High Court was asked to determine who was right: whether wife rape was a crime known to law in the 1960s (though a law almost never used) when the alleged offences occurred. It decided that it was a crime known to the common law at least as far back as 1935 when the relevant South Australian law was enacted. Remarkably, the High Court declared that wife rape had in fact been a crime in Australia, at least since the 1930s, and maybe even earlier, thus wiping away a good deal of British criminal law's unlovely past in a major colony and thereby challenging and rejecting the declaration of Lord Hale, of 1736, that by act of marriage, the wife gave her perpetual consent to her husband.

The High Court warmed to the task of exalting its record regarding the excellent legal treatment of Australian women. By 1930, women in Australia had capacity to act in commercial and professional life, to vote, act judicially, own property and sue and be sued in their own right.[44] There was a progressive modernisation of the lives of Australian women in which the immunity came to make little sense. Australia had escaped from its Imperial past. Thus:

> By the time of the enactment in 1935 of the [Criminal Law Consolidation] Act, if not earlier ... in Australia local statute law had removed any basis for continued acceptance of Hale's proposition as part of the English common law received in the Australian colonies. Thus, at all times relevant to this appeal, and contrary to Hale's proposition, at common law a husband could be guilty of a rape committed by him upon his lawful wife. Lawful marriage to a complainant provided neither a defence to, nor an immunity from, a prosecution for rape.[45]

In essence, the High Court, in its majority judgment, declared that the husband's rape immunity was not part of the received law of Australia. In this view, Australian men were probably never permitted to rape their wives. Australia was different from the less enlightened centre of Empire. Unlike the United Kingdom, Australia had responded appropriately to legal changes in women's status early in the century – and indeed Australia, and especially South Australia, was a world leader. Mr Bennett was sent packing. Australia was not to be regarded as a backward country in its treatment of women by men.

To the Australian Court, the marital rape immunity was an 'ancient and perhaps partially forgotten principle' and 'the tooth of time' had gradually eaten

---

[43] This is a trimmed down account of the argument, but contains its essence.
[44] *PGA v The Queen* [2012] HCA 21, para 62, (2012) 245 CLR 355 at 384, para 63, quoting Isaacs J in *Wright v Cedzich* [1930] HCA 4, (1930) 43 CLR 493 at 505.
[45] *PGA v The Queen* [2012] HCA 21, para 63, (2012) 245 CLR 355 at 384, para 64.

away at this 'ancient precedent'. Australian law had become 'animated by a different spirit' and the old rule had 'become obsolete and inoperative'.[46] Thus, inattention to the rule – and the absence of case law – allowed the rule to wither away naturally and the law to change in accordance with more Enlightened Australian thinking about the status of women. The rule died away as the legal reasons for it died away, as the law spontaneously became infused with more modern thinking about women and their rights.

Again the focus was on the changing legal nature of women as the Court rolled back the rights of men, to women. Again there was a failure to dwell on the sad plight of the husband now stripped of his sex rights to his wife, rights which had once been thought fundamental for men, essential to their virility and their masculinity. The sexual master and the little monarch were despatched with almost no reflection about the implications for men. In the Australian case, such male mastery was simply denied.

The fact that Australian husbands were never charged with the rape of their wives did not raise concern about the failures of law to be used. The Court made little of the non-enforcement, the non-prosecution, of husbands for wife rape which it insisted had been a crime in Australia for much of the twentieth century – just never finding its way into the courts. It turned a blind eye to decades of state inaction against husbands who raped their wives. Clearly the crime, which was said to have existed, was tolerated; the absence of prosecutions made this plain.

The dissenting judges, Heydon and Bell JJ, who said that wife rape was not a crime in 1963, told a less heroic tale of Australian law which was frankly more convincing, in view of the non-prosecution of husbands for rape. And yet neither was discombobulated by the misogynist past, though both recognised it, but not as a fundamental failure of principle which should be condemned outright; rather as different mores for different times. Indeed the dissenting judges seemed more concerned to defend the reputations of the great jurists of the past, and to insure against what was viewed as a more abhorrent departure from principle, which was retrospective lawmaking.

Heydon J openly rejected the revisionist history of the majority. In his view, there was legal inattention to the rape of wives because it was so utterly accepted that wife rape was not a crime.

> Even nowadays … ethical and tactical considerations prevent counsel from arguing what they perceive to be unarguable. There are some propositions which seem too clear to the profession to be contradicted by argument. Propositions of that kind are widely accepted as good law.[47]

In effect, the husband's use of sexual force within a marriage was fully tolerated by the men of law and it was lawful. There was no need for the men of law to talk

---

[46] Here the Court is making use of the words of Sir John Salmond about ancient precedents and quoting them approvingly: ibid para 24, 371, para 24.
[47] Ibid para 81, 388, para 82.

about it. There was no need for legal officials to attend to it. And wives got the message. They understood that they could not complain of rape.

The other dissenting judge, Bell J, made much of the long line of distinguished (male) scholars supporting the immunity, starting with Lord Hale whom she portrayed as one of the greatest jurists. Justice Bell provided a frank and plausible history of the husband's immunity and insisted that it had been still firmly in place in 1963, described by Bennett, for the defence, as the pre-Enlightenment period for the married woman. Over the course of her judgment, she built an incremental case for the effective non-personhood of the wife and the amplified powers of the husband. And she did so with little wincing. This is really quite a chilling judgment, but it has a bracing honesty.

There has never been an official apology to married women for the permissive, even justifying, role of criminal law in wife rape and in the force needed for a husband to achieve sex with a wife. One however was offered in the Feminist High Court judgment in 2014, but it is a counterfactual judgment written by feminist judges as part of the Feminist Judgment Project – a project of legal counterfactuals, what could have happened, had the law pursued another trajectory, one driven by feminists.[48]

Mary Heath and Wendy Larcombe, as fictional judges, also offer a dissenting judgment: they determine that the rape of a wife by a husband was *not* a crime known to law in 1963 and so Mr P could not be prosecuted for the rape of his wife. But from the outset, they distinguish their position by acknowledging the deep wrong to women and offering an unqualified apology.

Our feminist judges arrive at their determination after a close analysis of the available case law. They concede that explicit judicial recognition of the immunity is hard to find, but that the immunity could be inferred from a variety of charging and prosecution practices: husbands were charged as accessories but not as principals; wives who left their husbands, supported by a court order, were taken to have revoked consent; and husbands were sometimes charged with false imprisonment and indecent assault of a wife, but not with her rape. These cases show an erosion of the immunity, but not its demise by 1963.[49]

V. Concluding Thoughts

What is most striking about the cases which abolished the immunity is their lopsided analysis of the law, its history and its context. Consistently the talk was of

---

[48] See Mary Heath and Wendy Larcombe (as High Court justices), 'PGA v The Queen' in Heather Douglas et al (eds), *Australian Feminist Judgments: Righting and Re-writing Law* (Oxford, Hart, 2014).

[49] They concur with Heydon J, also in dissent, that a catalyst for reform of the law was second-wave feminism of the 1970s and its demand for the equal treatment of women. And they point out that it was not until 1976 that South Australia partially removed the immunity. This reform, they say, makes little sense if the immunity had already ceased to be law. The partial decriminalisation of the immunity necessarily assumed the existence of the immunity.

the modernisation of the lives of women over the course of the twentieth century, which apparently triggered the abolition of the husband's right to rape (rarely called this). But this was not accompanied by a complementary analysis of the correlative changes in men's lives and their implications for the now modern man.

With the legal focus on women, and the transformations in their lives and legal personality, the idea was that somehow, through the natural evolutionary processes of modernisation, women alone emerged out of status (that is from their reduced legal status), perhaps from some strange primeval female slime. Little was said by the men of law about what these laws meant for men themselves and their correlative rights and duties, both before and after the change: for past and present models of masculinity.

In the dominant legal discourse, men did not have a delimiting legal status: they were not thought to be defined and, in their case, empowered by their sex. And as they entered the modern world, men just slid naturally into the role of individuals. After all, what distinguished the liberal individual, in criminal law theory, was their capacity to make decisions and this was what men had had all along. The changing lives of men, their changing codes of conduct, did not warrant close inspection. Little was said about the changing character of men, and their shifting civil standards, about the human rights abuses condoned by the old law, and now condemned. And yet the changes in men's formal rights and duties, if not in their actual lives, were dramatic.

Hale and Blackstone had declared the wife not to be a legal person. At marriage the husband became a sort of double creature, absorbing the wife into his person. Hale was the seventeenth century source of the immunity whose authority was sustained right up to the 1990s. Blackstone, in the eighteenth century, spelled out the law of coverture and almost absolute male right, with complete confidence in its appropriateness and accuracy. The husband's right to be master of his domestic domain, and to rape, was sustained in the Victorian period by Stephen J, especially in *Clarence*.

The unsuitability of criminal law as a mode of regulating men and their sexual appetites in the home was declared repeatedly by leading scholars of criminal law, through to the final quarter of the twentieth century. Then things changed rather quickly and the husband's right to rape was removed. But where was the deep reflection and analysis? This did not happen. Instead there was a distancing of this law of male sex right; there was a diminution of its significance; and there was even a denial that it had been so in Australia.

The husband's rape immunity was implicitly isolated from the rest of criminal jurisprudence, in the prevailing analysis. It was treated as an incongruity, which could be corrected simply; or as a bit of ancient lore that had served its time and now could be easily dispensed with. By necessary implication, the abolition of the immunity did not have any significant flow-on effects for the rest of criminal law, and especially for the other serious offences against the person.

However in the scholarly analyses of central criminal law we encountered in the first chapter, rape and murder *were* endowed with great moral significance for the discipline. The crime of rape was central, not peripheral. Moreover rape and murder were linked together, as twin horror crimes, which any civilised society must outlaw. (And indeed the implication was that they were thus comprehensively criminalised.) These scholarly treatments of rape and murder, as crimes which had a great bearing on the discipline and its civil credentials, would suggest that significant changes to the scope of either offence would call for a major rethinking of central criminal law. But this was not how reform was achieved, nor interpreted.

There was little sense, within these legal decisions and their analysis, of the broader implications of these now-expanded rape laws for men as a sex, nor for central criminal law and the serious offences against the person. These so-called 'reforms' of rape law were, at least formally, effecting a major change to the scope of the crime of rape, by greatly expanding the population of men who could be charged. They were adding men, in their capacity as husbands, to the population of men who could be held responsible for the crime of rape. These 'reforms' were therefore changing the moral and legal character of one of the most serious offences against the person. They were changing the very landscape of criminal law; but this was not the impression conveyed.

Some years later (as we will see in Chapter 10), the UK legislature would see fit to change the scope of the crime of murder, again in a manner which would effectively make husbands more accountable for their violence, by declaring that a person (man) driven to homicidal anger by news of infidelity (his unfaithful wife) could no longer have his crime downgraded to manslaughter, by the new defence of loss of control.[50] He would remain a murderer. The removal of the husband's legal immunity from rape prosecution was probably the necessary precondition for laws making men more fully responsible for murder, when killing a wife out of rage.[51] It seems likely that the criminal laws of rape and murder, with their changing codes of conduct for men, are thus linked. However the brief and muted treatment of the rape immunity and its removal (as an anomaly corrected or a mere updating of the law), obscured these important cultural shifts occurring within central criminal law. It also kept married men out of the spotlight: as the 'favourites' of criminal law (to borrow a term from Blackstone), once so favoured that the law of rape could not touch them and even the law of murder could be kept at bay.

Married men were treated preferentially within the crimes of rape and murder; both crimes implicitly recognised their controlling interests in women. Thus central criminal law limited men's criminal responsibility for the most serious of crimes, but still it was not seen to have a bearing on male civility in general, nor on the civility of core criminal law. Instead, when their sex rights were removed, men were ushered into the modern period in almost deafening silence, as if they had been good person-respecting types all along. The men of law looked the other way.

---

[50] Coroners and Justice Act 2009, s 54 (UK) Partial defence to murder: loss of control.

[51] The UK did not specify 'men' or 'husbands', when it limited the uses of the new defence of loss of control (which replaced the defence of provocation), but men were effectively the reason for the limitations. See also David Plater, Lucy Line and Kate Fitz-Gibbon, *The Provoking Operation of Provocation: Stage 1* (South Australian Law Reform Institute, Adelaide, 2017) 10.

8

The Invisible Men: Why the Men of Law Cannot See the Men of Law

Over the course of this chapter and the next I consider how the men of criminal law fade from view, as the subjects and objects of knowledge, as the knowers and the known, and who, if anyone, emerges in their place. Changes in men, masculinity and men's legal lives are not part of the orthodox story of the modernisation of criminal law, and its attitudes to sexual and other male violence. This requires some explaining, precisely because men were once so conspicuous as the authoritative experts.

Throughout the book we have encountered influential men of law, speaking authoritatively, often about other men and sometimes interceding on their behalf. With Hale, Blackstone, Stephen and Williams, there was no mistaking their sex and that it influenced how they thought about criminal law. But by the modern period, these assertive masculine legal men, these all-knowing experts, have all but disappeared as explicit legal characters. After so many years of men of influence automatically thinking of criminal law, quite openly, in terms of the male regulation of male life, men have become almost invisible both as the subjects and objects of regulation.

The disappearing modern man of law, the legal expert, who assumes the speaking position for his discipline, is unlike the legal men who ushered in the twentieth century, the likes of Montague and Lush, who were highly conscious of the legal benefits of their sex (you can almost see them rubbing their hands in glee at the sheer luck of having been born a man, given the benighted legal history of the women they survey). Instead the modern legal analyst speaks more drily without a sex as he no longer ostensibly has sexed interests or a sexed outlook or even a deep voice or a man's life. A woman now can also adopt the male speaking position.[1]

This chapter is about the experts of criminal law, the speakers for the discipline, who have formed it, deciding what is central, what is not, what are its organising principles. These are the new men of criminal law, the legal authorities who are making sense of their discipline, who are finding and defining its wrongs and harms, deciding on what is good and bad law. My interest here is in the point of

---

[1] As we saw with Justice Mitchell of the South Australian Mitchell Committee and Justice Heilbron of the UK Heilbron Committee.

view of the discipline and who stands for the discipline, and how these people see their task. These legal experts have been my concern all along, but now I look more closely at why they think as they do, especially in the modern law and scholarship, which aspires to slough off its gendered past and its gendered characters. I consider their thought processes, their biases and their blindness. The one who is perhaps most difficult to discern is the one doing the analysis (the man of law), the knower, especially when he is trying to get himself out of the picture.

I. The Knower and the Known

The effects of the knower on what is known, or thought to be known, have been noted across a range of disciplines. Repeatedly the view expressed is that the expert interpreter or explainer of a given subject comes to their task of interpretation or explanation with a body of assumptions, maybe an orthodoxy, which necessarily has a great bearing on what is found and interpreted, on what is even brought into being. The perspective and set of interpretive conventions held to by the observer affects what is and can be observed. Viewer and viewed are intimately linked. This is as true of the legal analyst as it is for any other expert within a discipline.

In 1961, the English historian EH Carr disputed 'the common sense view of history': that there was 'a corpus of ascertained facts' for the trained historian to locate in 'documents, inscriptions and so on'.[2] In a memorable extended simile, he described the conventional view of historical facts as things that could be handled 'like fish on the fishmonger's slab', taken home and cooked and served up by the historian.[3] But this was not how history really was made. Historical facts did not 'speak for themselves' according to Carr. Rather '[t]he facts speak only when historians call on them: it is he who decides to which facts to give the floor, and in what order or context'.[4] This was a highly selective process. And so 'The belief in a hard core of historical facts existing objectively and independently of the interpretation of the historian is a preposterous fallacy'.[5] What we have come to know as history is a function of the selections and interpretations of the historian.

Carr was reminding us of the need to look at the expert historian to work out the sort of history that we were getting. The producer of the expert knowledge mattered. More recently John Tosh observed about the historian and the idea of historical objectivity that

> nobody actually approaches the sources with a completely open mind ... Even if no specific questions have been formulated, the researcher will study the sources with certain assumptions that are only too likely to be an unthinking reflection of current

---

[2] EH Carr, *What is History?* (New York, Random House, 1961) 6.
[3] Ibid.
[4] Ibid 9.
[5] Ibid 10.

orthodoxy, and the result will be merely a clarification of detail or a modification of emphasis within the prevailing framework of interpretation.[6]

As the philosopher-psychiatrist Iain McGilchrist has expressed it: 'The kind of attention we pay actually alters the world: we are, literally, partners in creation'.[7] To the influential art analyst Ernst Gombrich 'The form of a representation cannot be divorced from its purpose and the requirements of the society in which the given visual language gains currency'.[8] Or as another student of aesthetics, Rudolph Arnheim, put it, 'all observation is also invention'.[9] To invoke again the historian John Tosh,

> The common sense idea (and the central tenet of positivism) that historians efface themselves in front of the facts 'out there' is ... an illusion. The facts are not given, they are selected. Despite appearances they are never left to speak for themselves.[10]

But this selective and creative process may be all but invisible to the creators, who may be utterly convinced that they are simply digging up the facts or explaining what there is. Ignorance of working convictions, and their effects on perception, will only be strengthened when the person perceiving is an expert speaking from the position of influential orthodoxy. Power and authority add force to what is said to be the case, silencing opposition. And this has been especially true of our men of legal authority. As Rheinstein observed,

> the climate of a society's legal system is ultimately determined by the kind of people by whom it is dominated ... It makes a difference whether a legal system is dominated, as that of classical Rome, by gentlemen of leisure and high-ranking administrators, or, as the Islamic, by theologians, or, as the classical Chinese, by philosopher-bureaucrats.[11]

Feminists from a variety of disciplines have also made this epistemological point, giving it an even sharper edge. The superior political and social powers of men, they say, have not only served to silence women, but have impeded the passage of vital information to the more powerful sex. What it is like to experience a world more designed for the other sex than for one's own, a world in which just to be one's sex is to have lesser value, is critical information for those responsible for the design of a fair and civil society (men).

When the political and legal designers have all been men, it is likely that they have experienced a knowledge deficit of which they have been unaware

---

[6] John Tosh with Sean Lang, *The Pursuit of History*, 4th edn (Great Britain, Pearson Education, 2006) 182.

[7] Iain McGilchrist, *The Master and his Emissary: The Divided Brain and the Making of the Western World* (New Haven, Yale University Press, 2009) 5.

[8] Ernst Gombrich, *Art and Illusion: A Study in the Psychology of Pictorial Representation*, 5th edn (Oxford, Phaidon Press, 1977) 78.

[9] Rudolph Arnheim, *Art and Visual Perception: A Psychology of the Creative Eye* (Berkeley, University of California Press, 1974) 6.

[10] Tosh and Lang, above n 6 at 180–181.

[11] M Rheinstein, 'Legal Systems' in David Sills (ed), *International Encyclopaedia of the Social Sciences*, vol IX (New York, Macmillan-Free Press, 1968) 208, quoted in Horst Lucke, 'Good Faith and Contractual Performance' in PD Finn (ed), *Essays on Contract* (Sydney, Law Book Co, 1987) 170.

(an unknown unknown).[12] These are the knowledge limitations that come with political advantage. Having never experienced a world in which to be one's sex is, in itself, to experience inferiority, with little incentive to find out what such an unpleasant experience is like, and indeed with a positive investment in that state of affairs continuing, the limitations and biases of male perception, when all the expert perceivers are male, can be all but invisible. As Sandra Harding has observed, 'Thinking from the perspective of women's lives makes strange what had appeared familiar, which is the beginning of any scientific inquiry'.[13]

Much more than their forebears, modern criminal legal experts have taken themselves out of the problems and concerns they examine and explain, implicitly styling themselves as disinterested and uninvolved observers. This is perverse, perhaps, given that across the hard and soft sciences and even the art world, the contribution of the analyst or observer to what is analysed or observed has become the conventional wisdom. With the analyst of modern criminal legal theory, his male genealogy is of little account. His particular physicality is also of slight interest, though it was once critical, as Stephen made plain. But we need to understand all this if we are to appreciate the effects of the legal knower on the legal known.

II. The Disappearing Expert

When James Fitzjames Stephen was writing, the task of characterising the authoritative men of law was in some ways easier. As we saw in Chapter 4, Stephen understood himself to be a man and a man of legal authority (a man of law), offering an impartial and accurate account of the social and legal world which was the purview of criminal law, and he saw that law as utterly gendered. He moved effortlessly between roles: scholarly analytical writer, legal historian, judge and member of the polity, sometimes even imagining himself as offender and, perhaps less so, as offended against. When he was writing about marriage, he was writing as a male jurist and as husband. He was certainly not writing, in his mind's eye, *as* a wife though he was writing *about* women and wives. Stephen's sex and his intellectual and legal authority were explicit and all sat comfortably together, on show, all supposedly augmenting each other. To think clearly was to think as a man, which was why men exercised such complete legal power, and why women were unfit for public office and all that unattractive knitting of brows.

---

[12] The terms known knowns and unknown unknowns were coined by Donald Rumsfeld and entered the title of his autobiography, *Known and Unknown: A Memoir* (New York, Sentinel, 2011).

[13] Sandra Harding, *Whose Science? Whose Knowledge?* (Ithaca, New York, Cornell University Press, 1991) 150. See also Nancy Hartsock, 'The Feminist Standpoint: Developing the Ground for a Specifically Feminist Historical Materialism' in Sandra Harding and Merrill B Hintikka (eds), *Discovering Reality* (Dordrecht, D Reidel, 1983) and Terri Elliott, 'Making Strange What Had Appeared Familiar' (1994) 77 *Monist* 424. And for a recent discussion of feminist standpoint epistemology and its significance for law and legal theory see Margaret Davies, *Asking the Law Question*, 4th edn (Pyrmont, Thomson Reuters, 2017) ch 6.

The men of law who rang in the twentieth century at Lincoln's Inn were also of this mind. A legal thinker was quite naturally a man, and not a woman, which is why they were seriously surprised that women had in other respects made such legal progress over the course of the nineteenth century. There was no question that men's complete monopoly of legal power had in any way hampered their own capacity to think objectively and impartially and from every point of view that mattered to a legal reasoner.

By the latter part of the twentieth century, the legal expert speaking position, the position of the expert, had lost its explicit sex, though it had been considered vital to have one in the recent past, for the legal thinker had always been a man, which was of course necessary for the acquisition of a law degree. In this chapter we learn more about the mindset of the modern criminal law scholar. My particular concern is how he conceives of his own position and his task in light of the immediate insalubrious past of criminal law, which has been so profoundly gendered.

III. Modern Criminal Law Scholars Adopting the Olympian Stance

The modern criminal legal thinker has partly dealt with this problem of unsavoury forebears, or sent it packing, by detaching himself from his own particular history or genealogy, from his long line of forefathers, and casting himself as a neutral thinking being, expert and theorist: as an anyone; not even an anyman. As a consequence, there is evidence in the modern legal scholarship of the sort of epistemology identified by EH Carr and called 'common sense history'. Carr would call it an historically naïve approach in that the expert takes himself out of his intellectual history. The necessary and unfortunate implication is that he does not have a bearing on his subject and that nor did his forebears.

Some of the most influential contemporary theorists of criminal law neglect the contingencies of history in their theories of crime (perhaps unless they are feminists). They seek to develop universal norms of criminal law, with which any civilised person could agree; and so they adopt the sort of Olympian stance identified and decried by Carr, Tosh, Gombrich and Arnheim. For example, in *Answering for Crime*, Duff declares that 'it is *hard to imagine* a respect [between members of the polity] that is robust enough to underpin the requisite procedures which would not also preclude murdering, raping or subjecting to other central *mala in se* those whom I respect'[14] (emphasis added). Here Duff conjures up a criminal legal world comprising a polity, potential offenders and victims but there is also a more obscure character, the individual who finds it 'hard to imagine'.

---

[14] RA Duff, *Answering for Crime: Responsibility and Liability in the Criminal Law* (Oxford, Hart, 2007) 87.

Whose imagination is this? It is the invisible *speaker* for the discipline, who is Duff here, and we are being invited into this imaginative world. If he and we can't imagine such a polity, then that is definitive. To Duff, 'Some wrongs it would be *hard to imagine* not being criminal in any legal system ... such wrongs as murder and ... rape ... constitute serious violations of *any polity's core values* ... They are wrongs against which *any polity* must protect its members'[15] (emphasis added). But as we know from the foregoing analysis, the men of law of only a generation before found wife rape to be lawful, acceptable and sometimes even desirable. It was well within their imagining.

In his treatise on the moral limits of criminal law, Joel Feinberg issued the same invitation to step into the one civilised world of shared legal agreement.

> About the propriety of one class of crimes *there can be no controversy.* Wilful homicide, forcible rape, [are crimes] ... everywhere in the civilized world, and *no reasonable person* could advocate their 'decriminalisation'.[16] (emphasis added)

Here 'the reasonable person' is someone in and of the polity having an influence on law making. But perhaps more interesting still is the idea of the individual for whom 'there can be no controversy'? This is the most invisible and most influential position – it is the place and community of assumed authoritative intellectual agreement. Again, in this imagined zone of consensus, where there is no controversy, the authoritative thinking of the reasonable men of law who supported the enlarged domestic powers of men, including the use of force, is not in contemplation. Nor is there mention of the reduction of murder to manslaughter, when an enraged husband discovered his wife's infidelity.

Feinberg theorises about such crimes, which entail 'the direct production of serious harm to individual persons and groups'. These are, he says, '*the clearest cases* of legitimate or proper criminalization'[17] (emphasis added). The clearest cases to whom?

The position of the scholar writing is treated as both critical and as a non-position, a neutral expert but invisible witness. The scholar witnessing, after all, in classical analytical thinking, is simply expert: who he is and his particular position is not having a bearing on anything. He is the expert but neutral observer.

For one more illustration of the assumption of the Olympian stance within modern criminal law theory we have Stanton-Ife again advancing the conventional wisdom that rape is a 'horrific crime' and so 'the *easiest of easy cases* for the best known theory of criminalization, based on the harm principle' and in

---

[15] Ibid 143.
[16] Joel Feinberg, *The Moral Limits of Criminal Law: Volume 1 Harm to Others* (Oxford, Oxford University Press, 1984) 10–11.
[17] Ibid.

this regard 'banal from a *theoretical point of view*'[18] (emphasis added). Again one is prompted to ask: whose is the theoretical point of view, for one is necessarily assumed and invoked?

In these accounts of central criminal law, our modern legal experts have shed their sex (perhaps in many ways a good thing) but also the sexed nature and history of their discipline, allowing it to fall away from their analysis. Our modern expert professes to see law as any reasonable or civilised person would do. And for the modern universal legal thinker, certain things have been found to be self-evident – every reasonable (universal) thinker or person would see things thus. They would condemn outright rape and murder.

Each of these claims about the shared objective assessment of the absolute unqualified unacceptability of the central crimes of rape and also murder – these claims that *any* reasonable person in *any* civilised society would see them thus – invoke and rely on an invisible sage inevitably coming to this view. In their invocation of the sage, they foreclose historical discussion of the specificity of the crimes themselves, as well as technical analysis of their formal legal elements, the sort of discussion which is bread and butter to the criminal lawyer. The wrongs and harms of rape and murder are treated as absolutely, intrinsically and enduringly so. But this is simply not the case.

IV. The Problems of the Olympian Stance

The trouble is that the 'self-evident', often linked to the word 'wrong' or 'harm', has been declared in precisely that area of human conduct that legal men of only a previous generation found to be otherwise. Indeed what is self-evidently wrong to the new wave of thinkers was self-evidently right to the old wave. This discontinuity in thinking is itself evidence of historical neglect and evidence of the costs of neglect of history.

What is also disconcerting about these assertions about the universal nature of so-called central criminal law, made up of the wrongs of rape and murder, is that both rape and murder are qualified and conditional, relative and dependent legal concepts. We have spent some time looking at the concept of rape and found it to possess just these characteristics. Rape's meaning and seriousness, indeed its very legal existence, has depended on the sex of the alleged offender and the sex of the alleged victim. It is therefore not a universal wrong, though treated implicitly so in the above claims. Rape's criminality has also depended on the marital status of the alleged offender and the victim. It has depended on the degree of violence used and the reasons for that violence (as with the husband seeking lawful sexual access

[18] John Stanton-Ife, 'Horrific Crime' in RA Duff et al (eds), *The Boundaries of the Criminal Law* (Oxford, Oxford University Press, 2010) 139.

to his wife). Its meaning remains highly variable across jurisdictions, so that in some parts of Australia a woman can now be a rapist[19] but in England this person still must be a man, though now he can rape a man.[20]

Rape has been, and is still, highly sensitive to its context and its characters. Its meaning is not stable and does not emanate from some essential character of the offence. Its meaning is extrinsic rather than intrinsic. It is endowed by law; it is not indwelling. Rape's meaning is therefore not amenable to clear and universal labelling, as an intrinsic horror wrong, by a universal sage.[21] (Plucked out of its changing social and legal contexts, declared as a universal horror crime, the crime of rape goes on holiday.)[22]

There have been great shifts in legal thinking about what makes a rape a rape and then what makes it wrong. As we have seen, distinguished men of law actively defended the husband's sex rights and in the most public legal fora. Their views were hardly sidelined or regarded as the views of mad men. How do these old misogynists relate to the new universal legal sage and indeed to modern criminal legal thought?

What is also curious about these assertions about the nature of rape and murder is that the criminal law scholars know all this. I am stating the legally obvious about the legal character of these offences: the scholars theorise about it, they teach about it, they engage in element analysis of the offences and, as we saw in the first chapter, they have done this extensively to the crime of rape, which has been a favourite offence for moral and legal analysis. It would seem that social and historical and legal amnesia is permitting sudden and unacknowledged jumps in legal thought.

There is a lot to cut through before getting to the modern assertion that rape is a general horror crime or, as Gardner and Shute have dubbed it, 'the central case' of the 'sheer use' of a human being,[23] the treatment of the human as a thing, rather than a person.[24] And indeed if a real effort were made to take account of this history, the statement that rape is a universal horror crime or the central case of 'sheer use' would probably not be made as it would be found to be historically

---

[19] In South Australia for example the defendant and the victim are both called persons, and a penis is not needed to achieve sexual penetration, thus criminalising rape by women.

[20] This is true of the crime of rape in the UK. However, in the UK a woman can be responsible for the offence of 'assault by penetration'. See the Sexual Offences Act 2003, s 2 (UK). This offence is formally gender neutral.

[21] See James Chalmers and Fiona Leverick, 'Fair Labelling in Criminal Law' (2008) 71 *Modern Law Review* 217.

[22] This is how Wittgenstein referred to the fate of words plucked out of their context and usages: Ludwig Wittgenstein, GEM Anscombe (trans), *Philosophical Investigations*, 1st edn (Oxford, Basil Blackwell, 1953).

[23] John Gardner and Stephen Shute, 'The Wrongness of Rape' in J Horder (ed), *Oxford Essays in Jurisprudence* (Oxford, Oxford University Press, 2000) 205.

[24] This is a view of rape sustained by John Gardner in 'The Opposite of Rape' (2018) 38 *Oxford Journal of Legal Studies* 48. There he reaffirms his view that 'Rape is a timeless ritual of humiliation, degradation, dehumanization'.

inaccurate. In which case, rape could not serve its modern purpose of acting as a central plank (or core principle) of criminal law – a clear case of criminalisation. The plank would be missing and then perhaps others planks would seem less sturdy.

This is not to reject the cautionary advice of historian John Morrill to the critics of the past: that one should 'try to let the past speak on its own terms and to enter into the mental world of the past and to grant it its own integrity'.[25] And certainly one should avoid presentism – the filtering of the past through the lens of the present. But to let the past speak, as Morrill insists, that mental world of people of former times must be entered. What we are seeing in the modern scholarship is an implicit denial that the serious offences against the person have a history and that the men of law have themselves changed their thinking and hence these laws in fundamental ways. The 'theoretical point of view' of the discipline is not singular; the men of law of former times thought very differently; the authoritative point of view has therefore undergone a major transformation. In fact one could even speak of incommensurable old and new world views.

V. Fudging the Past and Cognitive Dissonance

It is difficult to work out the relationship between past and present criminal legal thinkers and their thoughts, descriptively and normatively: what the relationship actually was and how it should be. The Olympian Stance implicitly denies the historical change in criminal legal thinking, because it invokes an enduring civilised polity where reasonable men see law and the wrongs it condemns in an enduringly reasonable way. However, legal men of former times did not think like the modern men of criminal law. Instead they positively counselled the use of force, when it was considered necessary for the assertion of a husband's authority. The former men of law accepted the propriety of certain forms of male to female violence, which ran deep within criminal law.

What we have observed so far could be called a *fudged* approach to this legal past. It entails a failure to come to terms with an ugly criminal law that was not committed to universal personal security, though it was said to be. The ugly past has been ignored, or it has been downplayed, or its illiberal features have been treated as anomalous. And so it has been treated as implicitly continuous with modern criminal law, but not a real problem for modern criminal jurisprudence. But there is a problem here. In view of modern liberal commitments to the autonomy and security of all, there is a pressing need to make serious sense of the old ways, alert to their horrors.

---

[25] Interview with John Morrill for the series 'Making History: The Changing Face of the Profession in Britain', The Institute of Historical Research 2008.

There is also something puzzling here. Why is there not a greater felt need among modern scholars to make sense of former ways of thinking which were antithetical to values now thought of as essential and eternal? Why fudge the past?

The concepts of coherence and cognitive dissonance, and the associated research, may help here. There is now broadly-accepted evidence from cognitive psychology and moral philosophy that a desire for coherence is a central feature of ordinary human reasoning.[26] People naturally and intuitively seek to be coherent; they want their reasons and justifications for actions to be consistent; they want their guiding principles to hang together as a whole. As Leon Festinger observed, 'The individual strives towards consistency within himself'.[27] If people find that the principles they hold dear do not cohere, if they are perceived by the person in question not to be congruent, that person may experience what is known as 'cognitive dissonance': a sense of internal conflict, or mental unease, caused by the fact that their values or principles are contradictory. This sense of dissonance is then likely to prompt an endeavour to bring principles into alignment, one way or another.

Law makers and interpreters are especially committed to reasoning and justifications which hang together. They seek to be consistent, principled and coherent in their reasons and their explanations.[28] Conflicting values should therefore set up such cognitive tensions in criminal legal thought. We should expect them to generate cognitive dissonance, which should in turn generate efforts to reconcile the principles that are in conflict, to find reasons for the holding of basic but opposing legal principles.[29] And indeed we have observed just this: the employment of techniques designed to achieve reconciliation of principles in tension such as suppression of anomaly, denial of anomaly, diminution of the conflict or an assertion that the problem has been fixed and a quick moving on.

We have witnessed a fudging of the past, with talk of benign modernisation and reform. In the last chapter we saw the senior judiciary of Scotland, England and Australia extending the scope of the crime of rape to all husbands by producing this simple story of female (rather than male) modernisation. This was hardly probing analysis. These landmark cases, which effected such great legal transformation, relied on the thinnest accounts of social change: there were casual references to changing social mores, perhaps a maturing of women and a maturing of law. There was the implication that the immunity was fit and proper for former conditions. There was the distancing of a law and society which supported the immunity, suggesting that it operated in a vastly different era – a long time

---

[26] Antony Storr, *The Integrity of the Personality* (New York, Atheneum, 1961).

[27] Leon Festinger, *Theory of Cognitive Dissonance* (Stanford, Stanford University Press, 1962). See also Gerben A van Kleef et al, 'Power, Distress and Compassion: Turning a Blind Eye to the Suffering of Others' (2008) 19 *Psychological Science* 1315; Michael Kraus, Stephane Cote and Dacher Keltner, 'Social Class, Contextualism and Empathic Accuracy' (2010) 21 *Psychological Science* 1716.

[28] Ronald Dworkin, *Law's Empire* (Cambridge, Harvard University Press, 1986).

[29] A Amaya, *The Tapestry of Reason* (Oxford, Hart, 2015).

ago – which was simply not true. There was also the implication that it was a quaint curiosity which did not speak of the law as a whole. It was a glitch, something 'odd'. Ashworth and Horder, for example, called the removal of the immunity 'the rectification of an anomaly'.[30] Male sex right was not symptomatic of criminal law generally, in their view.

Or social and legal change have been treated as linear and progressive, leading ultimately to a modern egalitarian society for men and women. None of this speaks of deep or incisive inquiry, which is unusual in thinkers more associated with probing and considered analysis. There has been little reflection on the breadth and depth of the problem of institutionalised, domesticated, state-sanctioned forcible sex by men against women: few demonstrations of concern that it might raise broad and serious questions of principle that call for close inspection.

Along with the too-ready acceptance of the modernisation story, there has been a failure to reflect on the almost total male monopoly of legal power up to the middle of the twentieth century, as well as the tight demography of those all-male holders of power. Criminal law has been steered and made by a small group of powerful men who have not in truth been committed to the general preservation of the personal sovereignty of all. Such a concentration of power has hardly made for broad or representative or impartial legal thinking. And yet this is the intellectual platform upon which modern criminal law has been built. It calls for scrutiny. We need to consider the effects of the knowers on the known.

VI. The Closed Community of Thinkers

In modern criminal law theory, you still get little sense of just how small and unrepresentative and powerful was the community of criminal law thinkers who represent the immediate history and history makers of modern criminal law. This was a narrow band of brothers and they went to considerable effort to maintain their monopoly. It didn't just happen naturally.[31]

The influential persons of criminal law, the lawmakers and legal analysts, were until quite recently all men of a certain privileged class and education, often they knew each other well, and they were exclusively in charge of the making and interpretation of criminal law. They actively excluded the other sex from the places of learning and influence. The earlier generations of legal men acted in their own interests and kept women out of their intellectual community, so women could not effectively point out male partiality, or do much about it. Still revered British jurist AV Dicey, for one, thought that women were intellectually and morally

---

[30] Andrew Ashworth and Jeremy Horder, *Principles of Criminal Law* (Oxford, Oxford University Press, 2013) 39.

[31] According to Lady Hale, the British judiciary is 'not only mainly male, overwhelmingly white, but also largely the product of a limited range of educational institutions and social backgrounds' in Clare Dyer 'The Guardian Profile: Lady Brenda Hale' *The Guardian* (London, 10 January 2004).

inferior to men and so should not get the vote and he made sure that his views were well publicised.[32] Such men of law were male-focused; they discussed the social and antisocial proclivities and activities of men; they analysed male behavioural patterns; they decided what public and intimate male behaviour, including strong force and sexual intrusion, should be criminal and what should fall outside the scope of criminal law. And they met and conferred only with men.

James Fitzjames Stephen for example, our leading man of the Victorian period, was the son of Sir James Stephen who had been Colonial Under-Secretary. The younger James was educated at Eton and then King's College London and Cambridge where he became a member of the Cambridge Apostles. 'His proposer was the young Henry Maine, recently appointed regius professor of civil law, and thereafter a lifelong close friend of Stephen.'[33] Each of these institutions excluded women. Stephen went on to become a Queen's Counsel, and a legal member of the Council of India, successor to Henry Maine, and also a High Court judge. His three sons became lawyers. 'The eldest, Herbert Stephen who succeeded to the baronetcy, was an authority on criminal law and practice. Harry Lushington Stephen the third son, was judge of the high court of Calcutta and was knighted in 1913.'[34]

In Gerald Postema's history of legal philosophy in the common law world we are given useful extended portraits of some of the most influential members of the community of philosopher-lawyers.[35] Postema depicts a demographically constricted intellectual world populated by a small culturally homogeneous group of men,[36] a male elite of rule makers and rule interpreters, located within intellectual families of influence, often actively guarding its terrain,[37] and delivering its opinions to the like-minded. This was a small circle of socially-homogeneous men of great influence who, for most of the time were talking almost exclusively

---

[32] In 'Letters to a Friend on Votes for Woman' (London, John Murray, 1909), Dicey explained that 'women of pre-eminent goodness are often lacking in the virtues, such as active courage, firmness of judgment, self-control, steadiness of conduct, and, above all, a certain sense of justice maintained even in the heat of party conflict, which are often to be found in Englishmen, even of an ordinary type'. *The Spectator* agreed that 'If Englishmen at such a time as this should consent to the experiment of woman suffrage, they would be taking a risk which, in our opinion, no patriotic man has a right to take in the name of his country. They would be playing fast and loose with our security in the world': 'Professor Dicey's Letters on Woman Suffrage' *The Spectator* (London 19 June 1909) archive.spectator.co.uk/article/19th-june-1909/23/professor-diceys-letters-on-woman-suffrage.

[33] KJM Smith, 'Stephen, Sir James Fitzjames, first baronet (1829–1894)' in *Oxford Dictionary of National Biography* (OUP, 2004).

[34] Ibid.

[35] Gerald Postema, *Legal Philosophy in the Twentieth Century: The Common Law World* (London, Springer, 2012).

[36] As Postema explains: 'Oliver Wendell Holmes Jr ... [was] born on March 8, 1841 to a family at the center of Boston's elite legal and literary society ... an aristocrat's overwhelming sense of duty was woven deep in his character' (ibid 45). By 1897 he was 'a prominent Boston lawyer and judge of the Massachusetts Supreme Court – soon to begin a brilliant career as Justice of the United States Supreme Court' (ibid 43). Roscoe Pound (1870) was 'Dean of Harvard Law School from 1916 to 1937, [and] dean of American jurisprudence for more than a generation at the beginning of the century'. John Chipman Gray (1839–1915) 'was a friend and colleague of the younger Holmes. A fellow Bostonian from a very successful legal family (his half-brother was a Justice of the US Supreme Court)' (ibid 84).

[37] As we saw, such legal luminaries as AV Dicey opposed the female franchise.

to each other, while striving and purporting to be writing about the general nature of persons and the law in an objective manner, one which transcended their small place in the world.

A deep male self-interest went into the engineering of law's basic concepts: 'the person', 'man', 'woman', 'the public' and 'the private'. Men of legal influence were deeply invested in the idea of women as the satisfiers of male sexual need, as reproducers, but also as companions of modest intellect. Stephen made this quite clear. And the men of law used criminal law for their male purposes. As we have seen, men of legal influence advanced their interests, through law, openly and unapologetically and then through euphemism. This was a lop-sided legal community producing lop-sided law and this matters for modern criminal law.

The tight demography of the men of law, especially up to the third quarter of the twentieth century, is still not a matter of close inspection. It is as if it does not have a bearing on the character or impartiality of legal thought. Such cultural homogeneity and male exclusiveness is likely to cause strictures in thinking and a failure to reflect on the intellectual effects of a monopoly of public power. It speaks of vested interests and is likely to generate views and understandings which are highly compatible with these interests, such as the view that the legal power of men over women was best for both sexes. In fact, throughout we have observed the intellectual and moral effects on men of their great power: the enhancement of their own rights coupled with the belief that this was the correct and natural distribution of authority through law.

VII. Power and Inattention

Power has corrosive effects on perception and judgement. Our men of law wilfully sustained an almost complete monopoly on legal power (women had virtually none) and so they explained and regulated both themselves and the powerless with supreme intellectual confidence, but with little sense of the limitations of their understanding, and with little chance of being told they were wrong and being held to account. These men so thoroughly removed the powerless (that is women) from their potential role as public commentators, as public critics, as definers of men, that they spoke pretty well only for and to themselves. The powerless (women) were excluded from positions of legal authority and so they were denied the ability to know back, to answer back, to function as authoritative other minds and to say 'You are only looking there. Now look here'. As Naomi Scheman has said about the difficulties of achieving a sound understanding of a problem, when sources of information are heavily constrained, 'Not only do we have to learn from diversely located subjects, but we have to recognize when our own locations are distinctively limiting, when what we say is especially problematically partial'.[38]

---

[38] Naomi Scheman, 'Forms of Life: Mapping the Rough Ground' in Hans Sluga and David G Stern (eds), *The Cambridge Companion to Wittgenstein* (Cambridge, Cambridge University Press, 1996) 391.

Psychologist Daniel Goleman has investigated the claim that power can have morally and intellectually corrosive effects on perception, drawing on extensive psychological research on the nature of attention and inattention. Thus he has sought to demonstrate and explain what feminists have been observing for many years.[39] This is that the powerful (here legal men of influence) can be inattentive, and even blind, to the experiences and understandings of the powerless, especially if those experiences, when noted and registered, would serve as a moral criticism of the powerful and so offer a moral curb on power.

Goleman reports, for example, that in a study from the Netherlands, 'strangers told each other about distressing episodes in their lives, ranging from the death of a loved one or divorce to loss of a love ... Again the more powerful person in the pairs tended to be more indifferent: to feel less of the other person's pain – to be less empathic, let alone compassionate'.[40] Another study

> found similar attention gaps just by comparing high-ranking people in an organization with those at the lower tiers on their skill at reading emotions from facial expression. In any interaction the more high-power person tends to focus his or her gaze on the other person less than others, and is more likely to interrupt and to monopolize the conversation – all signifying a lack of attention.[41]

This failure to attend is of great concern when the powerful are setting the terms of lawful physical relations between the powerful (men) and the powerless (women).

The intellectual and moral effects of power on the perceptions of men of law should concern us all. For those effects can include an impaired capacity to self-reflect, to reason, to operate as moral beings capable of treating others as moral beings, to draw up a fair society, a fair social contract and a fair law, to make truth claims and to make moral claims, to reason dispassionately, to treat the powerless (which they have brought into being) fairly.

Powerful story tellers, those in positions of authority, who are here our men of law, may believe that they see the world as it is, that they are describing their subjects in a neutral manner, and yet be blind to their bias. They may be blind to the limitations of their point of view; to the fact that they lack information. They may be blind to the fact that they have interests and that the way they tell the story of criminal law conceals those interests; and that there are others who could tell a different story about the law, had they sufficient power and authority to do so.

Immense power, a tight social demography and self-interest are poor ingredients for fair and impartial judgement. They have led to what might be called the self-ignorance of the influential. This link between self-interest and ignorance goes beyond wilful blindness. It goes beyond selective attention.[42] It extends to a

---

[39] Daniel Goleman, *Focus: The Hidden Driver of Excellence* (London, Bloomsbury, 2013).
[40] Ibid 124.
[41] Ibid 125.
[42] The remarkable extent to which broad attention can be destroyed when research subjects are given a narrow selective focus is demonstrated by Simons and Chabris in the now famous gorilla experiment. See Daniel J Simons and Christopher F Chabris, 'Gorillas in our Midst: Sustained Inattentional Blindness for Dynamic Events' (1999) 28 *Perception* 1059.

broadly-based existential way of seeing, and mode of being, a world view, according to a set of interests, which has been characteristic of those engaged in the formation of criminal law as a body of principle.

As Dan Kahan and associates have established in their psychological investigations into what they term 'cultural cognition', there is a powerful 'disposition to form perceptions of fact congenial to one's values'.[43] There is an 'unconscious influence of individuals' group commitments' on perception.[44] How others in our social cohort tend to perceive, we also tend to perceive. Their experiments have demonstrated convincingly the operation of value perception: the manner in which cultural values and interests exert a dramatic effect on perception and reasoning, while leaving the perceiver fully ignorant of this fact and convinced of their utter neutrality and perceptual accuracy. Kahan has called this 'cognitive illiberalism'.[45] Despite a genuine conviction that facts are being viewed impartially, simply read off the situation observed, and despite even a genuine endeavour to be impartial, tested observers have been shown to make their assessment of what they are seeing 'along cultural lines'.[46]

The imputed features of women and of men (and the person), and the regulation of their relations within criminal law, need to be seen as a function of power. The moral and legal character of the person, and of men and women, has depended on who has been permitted to define them, to observe them, to posit them, and the powers and interests of those persons with the power to define: what they were attending to, what they wanted to achieve, what they attributed to others. The result has been law in the interests of the powerful, which has not been perceived as such.

We have observed in our men of criminal law a sustained and intriguing absence of concern not only about the effects of self-interest (and the strong possibilities of consequent male bias) on the making of criminal legal rules about men's relations with women – about status conditions, justifications, exemptions etc – but also a lack of concern about the appearance of bias. The judicial principle of recusal, that a judge should not judge their own cause, has not entered criminal legal thinking, but it should have. This gives rise to concerns about good and fair criminal law making. The assertion of male power has operated to the moral detriment, and to the quality of judgement, of legal men and of a principled criminal law and in a manner in which the men of law have found difficult to perceive.

---

[43] Dan M Kahan et al, "'They Saw a Protest": Cognitive Illiberalism and the Speech-Conduct Distinction (2012) 64 *Stanford Law Review* 851, 901.

[44] Ibid 851.

[45] Ibid.

[46] Ibid 860. This point is developed by Dan Kahan and Donald Braman in 'The Self-Defence Cognition of Self Defence' (2008) 45 *American Criminal Law Review* 1.

VIII. Disqualification of the Naysayers: Excluding Women as Experts and Epistemic Injustice

Intellectual isolationism and solipsism have characterised the criminal legal past. With women disbarred from public life and severely constrained within the private, there has been no one to correct legal men's thinking about men and their social and antisocial proclivities. There has been almost no one who was not a man permitted to offer information and criticism. Because women have been thoroughly removed from the story of the persons of criminal law, and this includes as critical commentators on the story, as the anthropologists of men, men have extinguished the points of view of those who could function as informative critics and interlocutors.

As a consequence, the men of law have hampered themselves in their self-defining role as objective, impartial and well-informed legal experts. They have perpetrated what the epistemologist Miranda Fricker has called 'testimonial injustice'.[47] As Fricker explains, such injustice takes place 'when prejudice causes a hearer to give a deflated level of credibility to a speaker's words'.[48] Consistently we have seen and heard the men of law dismissing women as credible, reliable and intelligent persons. And they have done so without justification, explanation or supporting evidence. This has created a problem for the legal experts themselves because prejudice can lead to ignorance, of which, almost by definition, the experts are unaware.

As Fricker puts it, 'the hearer's prejudice' can provide 'an obstacle to truth'.[49] It can not only cause the hearer 'to miss out on a piece of knowledge'[50] but it can block the free 'circulation of critical ideas'.[51] This in turn can limit the nature and scope of knowledge in the public domain. Hence Fricker characterises testimonial injustice as 'a serious form of unfreedom in our collective speech situation'.[52] For freedom of public speaking, in the sense of the ability to contribute one's knowledge to the body of collective knowledge, 'is fundamental to the authority of the polity, even to the authority of reason itself'.[53] When substantial parts of the population have been systematically excluded as credible knowers and speakers, the polity as a civic institution has suffered to this degree.

Throughout we have been observing an in-group talking to themselves, excluding from the discussion those who are unlike them, who might offer a different and

---

[47] Mirander Fricker, *Epistemic Injustice: Power and the Ethics of Knowing* (Oxford, Oxford University Press, 2007) 1.

[48] Ibid.

[49] Ibid 43.

[50] Ibid.

[51] Ibid.

[52] Ibid.

[53] Ibid.

critical point of view. Wives have been missing from this group of discussants.[54] For most of the period of this study, women have been almost entirely excluded from the criminal legal community of perception and judgement. In criminal law, indeed in law generally, we have observed a sustained cultural effort to stop men becoming the objects of women's knowledge. There has been, and remains, remarkably little interest in what women think of men.

If no robust and respected counter point of view is permitted, the influential way of seeing things will just look right and normal and the less influential and different views will seem to be misguided chatterings. Our men of law will be least knowledgeable about their own character as men as they have neutralised the person who is their counter term, who is perhaps best equipped to evaluate them, who might look back at them and say 'this is what you are'.

What we need is open reflection on the moral and intellectual effects on the discipline of criminal law of the simple fact that men have occupied all the positions of influence. Men have been the judges, law-makers, academics, the theorists of the state, the colonial administrators and they have actively preserved their terrain. They have also been the authority figures in the home and actively asserted that authority through law. They have actively excluded women from any position that they wanted for themselves. They have engineered the rules of civilised society according to their own priorities. Our legal knowers have had strong sectional interests in the content and contours of the legal known.

IX. Acknowledging the Past: Recognising the Scale of the Problem

What we could and should have instead of this fudging of principles is a *faithful* approach to the legal past and its implications for modern criminal law. We should have a developed interest in past law and its makers, a desire to know more of its defining features, and then an intellectual and moral decision about what to do about them: what stance to adopt? Should the former men of law and the laws they endorsed be accepted as continuous with modern criminal law, and its makers, thereby contaminating the present and perhaps generating reason for legal apology, given their egregious failings to so many? Or should past misogynist law and past misogynists be regarded as discontinuous with the present; as evidence of a failed and immoral state, which has failed to deliver security to its citizens, and rejected, and perhaps a new criminal law declared? Either way, there should be serious reflection about the intellectual, political, moral and legal obligations

---

[54] The exclusion of the story of the revolt of the first wave feminists has been documented by Jill Elaine Hasday, 'Contest and Consent: A Legal History of Marital Rape' (2000) 88 *California Law Review* 1373.

accruing from such a monopoly of power. The first step, perhaps, would be to register concern about its likely effects on the quality of reasoning.

To keep faith with the past – to acknowledge the interested point of view of the former men of law and the laws they endorsed – we would need also to widen the analysis of criminal law and consider how its rules have operated as incursions into the lives of so many, in cruel and intimate ways and in a manner entirely antithetical to the foundation principle of bodily integrity. The men of law positively licensed male intrusion into the bodies of unwilling women. Positive male self-interest went into the crafting of the laws of rape, as well as associated criminal laws controlling the lives of women in the interests of men. This is the distant and immediate history of criminal law examined in this book which does not feature in modern criminal law theory. It should.

The history of a number of other criminal laws tells a similar story. Criminal law and its makers have, in significant ways, positively undermined, rather than protected, the personal sexual sovereignty of women, as Nicola Lacey has well demonstrated in her legal and literary history of female crime.[55] Past and present laws relating to prostitution and abortion are antithetical to the principle of the self-government of women.

Criminal laws associated with prostitution have punished women for selling their sexual services (rather than giving them away). As Lacey informs us, 'the largest single group of women offenders already known to the police in the second half of the [nineteenth] century (when reliable statistics for the purposes of gender comparisons became available) were prostitutes'.[56] The criminality of their commercial sexual activity exposed women to violent crime, for which they still have little comeback because their own behaviour has been criminal.[57] Criminal law and the state have a continuing interest in women's uses of their own bodies. Criminal laws associated with abortion are necessarily an assertion of the most intimate state control over women during pregnancy and have exposed women to cruel and illicit activity (the backyard abortion as well as blackmail).[58]

Criminal law has also undermined the personal sovereignty of millions of homosexual men. Until 1967 in England homosexual men were committing

---

[55] Nicola Lacey, *Women, Crime and Character: From Moll Flanders to Tess of the d'Urbervilles* (Oxford, Oxford University Press, 2008).

[56] Ibid 111.

[57] See MJ Frug, 'A Postmodern Feminist Legal Manifesto' (1992) 105 *Harvard Law Review* 1045 and Rosemary J Owens 'Working in the Sex Market' in Ngaire Naffine and Rosemary J Owens (eds), *Sexing the Subject of Law* (Pyrmont, Law book Co, 1997) 119.

[58] In the author's home state of South Australia, which is relatively liberal in its laws in this area, the law governing abortion nevertheless still resides within the criminal law. According to s 81 of the Criminal Law Consolidation Act 1935 (SA): 'Any woman who, being with child, with intent to procure her own miscarriage, unlawfully administers to herself any poison or other noxious thing, or unlawfully uses any instrument or other means whatsoever with the like intent, shall be guilty of an offence and liable to be imprisoned for life'. A type of necessity defence then makes it lawful for a doctor to perform an abortion if there is medical agreement that a woman's mental or physical health is endangered by continuation of the pregnancy.

serious crime (gross indecency) by having a sexual life. Criminal law ensured their persecution and implicitly approved it. The extent of the persecution of homosexual men and the role of the criminal law in inciting and sustaining that persecution was finally recognised in 2009 by then Prime Minister Gordon Brown in his apology to the distinguished scientist Alan Turing (who took his life 55 years before) and to the gay men of England, prosecuted and convicted under gross indecency laws. In the words of Brown 'Alan and the many thousands of other gay men who were convicted as he was convicted under homophobic laws were treated terribly. Over the years millions more lived in fear of conviction'.[59] The bold declaration of personal sovereignty made by Mill and his successors, to the present day, simply did not apply to most women nor to many men.

If we turn to the law of murder, there is further clear and compelling evidence of criminal legal principles imbued with misogyny and homophobia. The partial defence to murder of provocation was developed and sustained by such bigotry. As noted in the last chapter, the classic use of the defence was by a husband who was homicidally enraged by the discovery of his wife's infidelity.[60] The other well-known use of the defence was by men who said that they had been provoked into killing by a homosexual advance. (Women did not use the defence in this manner in reply to either heterosexual or homosexual advance and criminal law did not anticipate that they would.)[61] And lest this be thought of as antique law, the Australian High Court recently countenanced just this use of the defence.[62]

Criminal legal attitudes to wife rape were themselves highly compatible with a range of satellite laws, as we have seen: the laws of marital coercion, marital conspiracy and of course the marital unity principle itself – the idea that husbands and wives were to be seen as a legal package, with the husband representing the collective legal person. All of these laws speak of a systematic pattern of legal thought.

So to see that the criminalisation of wife rape is not an 'anomaly' corrected within an otherwise wholesome body of (central) criminal law, but rather one reforming move within a much broader system of highly suspect thought about the limits of personal sovereignty, it is important for modern criminal law scholars to take a closer look at the central institutions of criminal law and their former

---

[59] Caroline Davies, 'PM's Apology to Codebreaker Alan Turing' *The Guardian* (London 11 September 2009) www.theguardian.com/world/2009/sep/11/pm-apology-to-alan-turing. See also the extensive writings of Matthew Weait on the treatment of the gay man by criminal law and especially his *Intimacy and Responsibility* (Oxford, Routledge-Cavendish, 2007).

[60] On the misogynist uses of the defence see Victorian Law Reform Commission, 'Defences to Homicide Final Report' (Victorian Law Reform Commission, 2004); V Nourse, 'Passion's Progress' (1997) 106 *Yale Law Journal* 1331; M Burton, 'Intimate Homicide and the Provocation Defence – Endangering Women? *R v Smith*' (2001) 9 *Feminist Legal Studies* 247.

[61] On the homophobic uses of the provocation defence see A Howe, '*Green v The Queen* – The Provocation Defence: Finally Provoking its Own Demise' (1998) 22 *Melbourne University Law Review* 466; and also the Victorian Law Reform Commission, 'Defences to Homicide Final Report' (Victorian Law Reform Commission, 2004).

[62] See *Lindsay v The Queen* [2015] HCA 16, (2015) 255 CLR 272.

representatives. This inspection of the gendered history of criminal law would quickly undermine the more palatable reform story. And criminal law and its makers would be seen to be implicated in other forms of state-sanctioned cruelty and persecution. This is not a body of law which inspires pride. It is a shameful heritage.

If we think of the South African laws of apartheid, close scrutiny of that country's recent utterly racist legal history was considered critical to the understanding and workings of a modern non-apartheid South African law.[63] Can a modern English criminal law afford not to take account of its former exclusion of women from circles of legal influence and its licensing of the sexual uses of women? What does the failure to do so mean for the integrity of modern criminal law?

The legal men of the past have been let off lightly. There has been a failure to call them to account. This has a direct bearing on the character and quality of modern criminal law and its scholarship. It creates a false impression of steady moral and intellectual development; of linear progress towards an increasingly fair and egalitarian society, with an ironing out of some minor glitches along the way. Anomalies are seen to be corrected, rather than entrenched inequality and misogyny and homophobia positively recognised. It is also consistent with a good deal of reverence for past generations of legal men. They are still portrayed as towering intellectual figures and as fair-minded men, even though they believed in witchcraft or endorsed the rape of wives.[64]

To correct this too-favourable impression of the institutions of criminal law and its representatives, it is necessary to bring into sharper focus not only misogynist law but also misogynist lawyers: the community of legal men who controlled criminal law up to the modern period. This reveals a small intellectual community of the very powerful, which operated with a closed circuit of ideas and disqualified its potential critics (the other sex). This monopoly of power has had intellectually limiting effects and it is vital for modern scholars to recognise them. A small community of men has given form to the very nature of the legal individual, law's central character, who inhabits central criminal law, as we will see in the next chapter.

---

[63] See Richard L Abel, *Politics by Other Means: Law in the Struggle Against Apartheid, 1980–1994* (New York, Routledge, 1995).

[64] In the Australian High Court case of *PGA v The Queen* [2012] HCA 21, 245 CLR 355, members of that Court referred to Hale as a great and revered figure, still, while also recognising him as the source of the marital immunity. According to Bell J, he was thought to be 'the first of our great modern common lawyers', citing Holdsworth for this view (at para 205; 429, para 206). It is difficult to make sense of this bundle of ideas.

9

The Modern Individual of Criminal Law

As with any legal discipline, criminal law takes a view of the people it regulates. In the course of instructing its people how not to behave, it endows them with needs and preferences, as well as physical and mental capacities. Criminal law thus brings its characters into being, by ascribing to them certain personalities and proclivities, as well as certain ways of living.

Men, leading men's lives, were once, quite openly, these central characters of criminal law. And as we have seen, men benefited from illiberal powers conferred by criminal law, especially over women. Men's sexual violence was often condoned, even though criminal law was thought of as an institution which condemned violence.

Then, over the centuries, criminal law underwent a slow 'modernisation' and women were blended in to the story of the discipline. It follows, necessarily, that a modern subject of criminal regulation has come into being, sometime and somehow in this process, one who is supposedly no longer sexed one way or another, or even at all. But this has happened without the necessary accompanying philosophical reflection on the nature of our legal individual's necessary sexual transformation, as women have become notional equals.

In this chapter I examine the individual who has emerged from these historical processes as the subject of regulation. This is the character of modern criminal law, who is now ostensibly without a sex, though once this person's sex was critical.

I. The Abstracted Individual

With the abolition of the spousal immunity, and the other legal privileges of the husband, an ahistorical, conceptually-thin individual was permitted to emerge as the central legal character, with barely a nod to the unseemly and illiberal past of criminal law, to its gendered history. This modern autonomous liberal individual was now constructed as someone fully equipped to exclude all others from his person and equally obliged to keep his hands off all others, now under clear instruction from the criminal law.[1] This person was plucked out of his history,

---

[1] Lindsay Farmer in *Making the Modern Criminal Law* (Oxford, Oxford University Press, 2016) conjures up such a character in his analysis of modern rape law. In Chapter 1 he declares that the crime

which is a history of male power (to control the law), male interests (in sexually controlling women and in having licence to use manly violence in approved circumstances, with other men) and male rights (to control and touch women). He is now quite abstractly conceived as an anyone and as everyone: a character with few defining attributes or qualities.

The language of the individual, of persons, now prevails, the language which invokes anyone. In some of the most influential modern scholarship in criminal law today there is a concerted endeavour to find the wrong or harm of the most serious offences in a manner which removes the need to talk about men and women and their very different histories in criminal law. Similarly theories of criminal responsibility are developed at a high level of abstraction. There is talk of harm by and to 'persons', wrongs by and to 'individuals' or 'citizens', and there is hardly a man or woman in sight. The two sexes are generally dispensed with in these understandings and portrayals of the subjects of criminal law.[2]

These posited artificial legal subjects are poorly defined. They lack the basic attributes of real individuals such as a sex, a race, an age or even a social context. They are universalised rather than particularised. With this legal focus on 'an ideal individual living in an ideal world', as Alan Norrie has observed, 'juridical man' becomes a thin abstraction from real life.[3] Wells and Quick have been similarly exercised by the abstract nature of this individual who inhabits criminal law. In their account, 'the legal subject is constructed as a genderless, raceless, classless individual abstracted from its social situation'.[4]

Such abstraction serves an important practical legal purpose, for it allows the legal individual to be considered analytically on their own, as a centre of rights and duties. It allows for methodological individualism: for the treatment of each as a basic unit of legal analysis and attribution of blame.[5] Removal of detail enables this unit to be treated, at least in theory, in much the same way as the next unit and hence ensures at least formal equality of treatment. It is asserted, by fiat, that we are all reasoning decision-makers – sex and other distinguishing features are all irrelevant – and hence we can all be treated as such.

In that it takes its meaning from a small number of human characteristics, and allows them to stand for all, this postulated human agent of criminal law is

---

of rape 'is now conceived of as an offence against sexual autonomy – the choice of the individual to decide when and with whom to have sexual intercourse ... it is the wrong against sexual autonomy which is central rather than the gender or status of the victim': at 31.

[2] For example, in his theorising about criminal law and its subjects, Duff refers variously to 'members' of a polity, 'citizens' and 'individuals'. See RA Duff, *Answering for Crime: Responsibility and Liability in the Criminal Law* (Oxford, Hart, 2007) 143.

[3] Alan Norrie, *Crime, Reason and History: A Critical Introduction to Criminal Law*, 3rd edn (Cambridge, Cambridge University Press, 2014) 26.

[4] Celia Wells and Oliver Quick, *Lacey, Wells and Quick, Reconstructing Criminal Law: Text and Materials*, 4th edn (Cambridge, Cambridge University Press, 2010) 95.

[5] See Steven Lukes, 'Methodological Individualism Reconsidered' (1969) 19 *British Journal of Sociology* 119; Steven Lukes, *Individualism* (Oxford, Basil Blackwell, 1973); Geoffrey Hodgson, 'Meanings of Methodological Individualism' (2007) 14 *Journal of Economic Methodology* 211.

what Hans Vaihinger has called a conscious 'neglective' abstractive fiction.[6] It is a legal invention which consists of a thinned-out model of a person. Many aspects of real persons are deliberately removed from consideration, for the purposes of this invention.

Modernisation has thus ushered in this new supposedly gender-neutral character: the rational responsible choosing person, now meant to encompass both men and women, without fear or favour, who is required to respect the rights of all other such individuals, especially the right not to be touched, and who is also a bearer of such rights. The person who decides to touch another in the knowledge that they do not have that other person's consent therefore breaches their defining duty not to touch and breaches the right of the victim not to be touched. In the modern period, we are all declared to be choosing individuals. The male monopoly of criminal law, and its implications for the priorities, the principles and persons of criminal law, is put to the side. So too is the gendered history of criminal law where the most fundamental choices were compromised.

But how has this been achieved? How has the profoundly gendered past of criminal law been shaken off so easily and men permitted to become simply persons and individuals, and apparently women too? Essentially it has been achieved by fiat. Women have been deemed to have joined the category of legal individual, as they were once deemed not to be individuals. The individual of criminal law is now said to be inclusive, and women can even stand in for the male case, leaving the gendered past of core criminal law unquestioned.[7] Men do not need to be deemed to be individuals, because they have been thought of as individuals all along. But in an important sense, men have become more individualised. They are more liberally conceived because some of their most basic and illiberal powers of bodily extension and intrusion have been removed. Their beings, or to be more precise their penises, have been reined in. They must now confine themselves to themselves.

II. The Responsible Individual Defendant as Rational Agent and the Disappearing Man

So who is this neutral abstracted legal individual invoked by the criminal law experts as the new modern subject of regulation? After all, criminal law has more than one character in mind: there is the defendant, there is the victim, there is the state or prosecution, and there is even the public (whose interests are notionally being protected, for criminal law is a variety of public law, a thing often overlooked).

---

[6] Hans Vaihinger, *The Philosophy of 'As If'* (London, Kegan Paul, 1924) 201–202.
[7] See the discussion of this peculiar practice in Chapter 10.

The primary concern of criminal law scholars has been, and remains, the conditions of criminal responsibility. The interest is in who can be held to account for criminal wrongdoing and how and why. The central characters of interest are therefore those accused of crime, and their rights as human agents, as moral persons, and as potentially criminally responsible persons. As George Fletcher put it, criminal law's 'central question is justifying the use of the state's coercive power against free and autonomous persons'.[8] These responsible agents are respected as persons precisely by being treated as rational choosing thinking beings who can be addressed directly by the criminal law, informed of their rights and duties, told directly what is permissible, and then held to account for their final decision.

To American criminal legal theorist Michael Moore, the law 'presupposes a view of man that allows us to view his behaviour as the rational product of his autonomous choices'.[9] To the Australian criminal law scholars Waller and Williams, 'almost the whole of our system of substantive criminal law is based upon the view that a human being is a rational creature, free to choose how to act, and deserving of punishment if she or he chooses to act immorally or wickedly'.[10] Or as Antony Duff has expressed this understanding of criminal law and its purpose:

> The underlying assumption here is that criminal liability should, in principle, be ascribed in accordance with moral responsibility. A defendant should be criminally liable only for conduct for which she [sic] can properly be held morally responsible or culpable; and the extent of her criminal liability (the seriousness of the offence for which she is convicted) should match the degree of her moral responsibility or culpability. That is why *mens rea* should be required for criminal liability, and why intention should be the most serious kind of criminal fault.[11]

Moreover, 'ascriptions of criminal liability ought to reflect justified ascriptions of culpable responsibility'.[12] (Please note the gender of the legal subject invoked here, with no mention of his implicit sex change.)

A theory of mind therefore guides modern criminal legal thought. It presupposes that the accused person has the capacity to think and reason, to decide and choose, and then that the court has the ability to establish these cogitations. As Lacey explains, this approach to criminal legal responsibility presupposes a certain

---

[8] George Fletcher, *Rethinking Criminal Law* (Boston, Little, Brown, 1978) xix.

[9] Michael Moore, 'The Relevance of Philosophy to Law and Psychiatry' (1984) 6 *International Journal of Law and Psychiatry* 177, 179. Though writing here of law generally, Moore has propounded this position about criminal law in particular, especially in Michael Moore, *Placing Blame: A General Theory of the Criminal Law* (Oxford, Oxford University Press, 1987).

[10] L Waller and CR Williams, *Criminal Law Text and Cases*, 9th edn (Chatswood, Butterworths, 2001) 258.

[11] RA Duff, *Intention, Agency and Criminal Liability* (Oxford, Basil Blackwell, 1990) 103.

[12] Ibid.

type of 'modern self',[13] a being with a stable unified interior life,[14] whose rational inner thought processes, their decisions and their choices, are known to the individual subject and are also capable of inspection by a court of law. There is an assumed sovereignty over the self: over thought and decision-making. This makes possible the legal determination of subjective intention which is treated as the classic mental element or species of fault – as in 'the intention to kill' of the crime of murder, or 'the intention to have intercourse without consent' of the crime of rape (the very thing of concern in *DPP v Morgan*, and its surrounding debates, as we saw in Chapter 1).

This modern view of the criminal legal subject relies on a 'capacity' theory of responsibility.[15] The idea is that we are thinking agents endowed with the capacity of free will, with cognition and volition, and also with self-control. Because we have agency, we can be held responsible for our chosen actions. Indeed for criminal law to respect our human agency, so the theory goes, criminal law must speak to us as choice-makers, capable of obeying the law.[16]

HLA Hart gave authoritative expression to this characterisation of the individual of criminal law. For Hart, criminal law was an institution that offered choice to a choice maker. Thus, the criminal law should not be treated 'as a system of stimuli goading the individual by its threats to conformity'. Instead it should be thought of as 'a choosing system, in which individuals can find out ... the costs they have to pay if they act in certain ways'.[17] Hart was convinced that a condition of just punishment was that 'the agent "could have helped" doing what he did'.[18]

To modern criminal law scholars, human agency makes it right to hold people accountable for their actions. The person, as rational chooser, of full capacity, must be addressed by criminal law, must have a chance to reply, and their chosen prohibited actions must only be criminalised when they have fair opportunity to avoid them – and all this must be established by a court of law.[19] This model of the criminal agent, deliberating on his criminal actions, represents an important limit to criminalisation and a basis for criticising laws which are thought to punish in the absence of such freely-chosen harmful actions. A vital and highly defensible feature and purpose of this aspirational person is to act as a brake on the actions of the state. We must all be treated as responsible thinkers and choosers: as centres of moral choice. This is a dignifying theory of persons, engaged in an exchange with criminal legal officials, who will be held to account for their chosen actions.

---

[13] Nicola Lacey, *In Search of Criminal Responsibility* (Oxford, Oxford University Press, 2016) 50.

[14] Ibid 51.

[15] Rather than the character theory of responsibility, in which the purpose of the criminal law is to establish the bad character of the person.

[16] Lacey, above n 13 at 27.

[17] HLA Hart, *Punishment and Responsibility* (Oxford, Clarendon Press, 1968) 44.

[18] Ibid 39.

[19] This complex set of communication requirements has been examined by RA Duff in a number of his works including *Punishment, Communication and Community* (Oxford, Oxford University Press, 2001).

Human agency, and so human choice, is implicit in the legal presumption of competence and voluntariness and indeed in all the mental state offences and defences. But more significantly, it is a presupposition running through the entire system of criminal law and justice, which employs a moral language of blame-worthiness and culpability and punishment. As Vaihinger declared, 'the idea of freedom ... is the foundation of criminal law. Without this assumption punish-ment inflicted for any act would, from an ethical standpoint, be unthinkable'.[20]

If we peruse the criminal legal scholarship, we find a strong preoccupation with just this idea of criminal agency and criminal responsibility and how to ascribe it fairly and appropriately.[21] The locus of concern is therefore the potential defendant, the individual who is notionally addressed by criminal law, informed about its norms, who is thus warned not to offend, but still given the positive choice whether to offend or not to offend, and who can be called to account if the decision he makes is to offend. After all, the choice was his. This person can rightly and fairly be held responsible, according to the new men of law, when he has been put in the picture about what he can or cannot do, has been given a real informed choice whether to offend or not, which means that his will has not been crippled nor his opportunities to avoid offending too constrained.[22] He is the responsible subject of criminal law, who is subjected to law: who is imagined as an interlocutor in a conversation with the law, and even with the legal writers.

Nicola Lacey has written extensively about this idea of the person in criminal law, the person with the capacity to exercise choice (to offend or not to offend). Her new history of the concept of responsibility in criminal law documents the changing fortunes of this person. As she explains, 'most contemporary philo-sophical analyses of responsibility are grounded in notions of human agency that emerged ... [in] the Enlightenment ... of the self-determining moral agent, equipped with distinctive cognitive and volitional capacities of understanding and self-control and of a universal human personhood'.[23] This is an 'essentially modern understanding of human being', one 'assumed to transcend place and time'.[24]

The modern criminal legal concern, I suggest, is therefore with the individ-ual as defendant, the person addressed by the criminal law, who can be held to account, for certain actions, for certain reasons, with certain thoughts.[25] It is the

---

[20] Vaihinger, above n 6 at 43.

[21] The titles of two influential books show clearly this preoccupation. They are Duff's *Answering for Crime*, above n 2, and Michael Moore's *Placing Blame*, above n 9.

[22] See James Chalmers and Fiona Leverick, 'Fair Labelling in Criminal Law' (2008) 71 *Modern Law Review* 217, and the work of Andrew Ashworth, given broad treatment in Lucia Zedner and Julian V Roberts (eds), *Principles and Values in Criminal Law and Justice: Essays in Honour of Andrew Ashworth* (Oxford, Oxford University Press, 2012), and see especially the chapter by Victor Tadros: 'Fair Labelling and Social Solidarity'.

[23] Lacey, above n 13 at 5.

[24] Ibid 5–6.

[25] For a critical analysis of Duff's imaginary addressee of criminal law, 'disput[ing] at every available point the right of the polity to call him, or her, to account', see Ian Leader-Elliott, 'A Critical Reading of Duff Answering for Crime' (2010) 31 *Adelaide Law Review* 47.

defendant, rather than the victim or the community, who supplies the subject of analytical interest: the defendant's thoughts and actions, their rationalisations, excuses and justifications. And it is here, in this characterisation of the defendant, that the assiduous gender neutrality of the terms 'person' or 'individual' or 'citizen', deployed by criminal law scholars, and sometimes its feminisation through the unremarked use of female pronouns (witness the quotation of Duff above), becomes a misleading fiction. It is misleading because the criminal norms governing the most serious crimes which are the crimes of violence – the prohibited violent conduct and violent intentions – are, in a practical sense, still mainly directed at men who remain the vast majority of serious offenders. The apparent modernisation of women (and men) has not changed the character of crime.[26]

The fact that the female pronoun is now often used by criminal scholars to refer to, and theorise about, criminals and criminality drives home the point that now women can cover the male case – gender neutrality and hence abstraction is thus accentuated. But in a discipline seeking to define, punish and explain criminality, this is hardly a compliment to women who are not the more criminal sex. And of course this interchangeability of pronouns ignores the actual social and legal history of criminal law and its persons and it ignores the current facts of crime, especially violent crime, which is still, to a large extent, men hurting men and men also being violent to women.

The choice-maker of criminal law, who is of most interest to law makers and to scholars is, in truth, still, the man in the process of deciding whether to commit a crime. And of particular concern is the man contemplating a serious offence against the person: whether to proceed or desist, supposedly mindful of the criminality of his intended behaviour. The preoccupation of criminal law scholars is with this man (oddly described as the responsible rational adult) who is deciding whether or not to flex his muscles, or any other body part, or to control his urges. He is 'responsible' in the sense that he can be held responsible or accountable for his decision. He may or may not be responsible in the ordinary everyday use of the term. Whether he is responsible in a legal sense will depend on the elements of the offence directed at his behaviour and its legal exemptions and defences and how these all apply to his thoughts and actions at the legally-relevant moment.

III. The Critical Legal Moment of Decision-Making

The legal moment that is of greatest interest to the criminal jurist is that of the prohibited act (say the killing or the punching or the forced penetration), at which time our legal individual must have the requisite guilty mind. He must decide to

---

[26] This will be confirmed by a perusal of the latest crime statistics from the Office of National Statistics, though it will also soon become clear that mainly the reporting fails to reveal the sex of offenders, again an institutional blindness to the man problem.

do that act. If intentions are formed too soon and abandoned, or acquired only after the act has been performed, they may not be sufficient to hold him responsible. The rule of contemporaneity, with some exceptions, demands that prohibited thought and prohibited action occur at the same time, for liability to be established. This decision is then understood in a particular criminal-legal way. Much will be removed from our criminal decision-maker for the purposes of the determination of his criminal responsibility – most of his history, his context, his sex (unless the charge is rape and being brought in the UK, in which case he must be a man), and his social conditions. These will be relevant later for the purposes of sentencing, but not strictly speaking for the determination of criminal liability.[27]

The critical moment of decision making is therefore one with which any teacher of criminal law will be familiar, as will the criminal prosecution. It is the imagined moment at which a decision is being made by a legally competent and hence sufficiently rational individual about whether to heed or breach one of the criminal law rules of conduct. If he is angry, should he punch or kick or restrain himself? If he wants sex should he hold the woman down and penetrate her or walk away? When he does the prohibited act, what is he thinking and what law guides him? At this notional moment in time, at the moment of criminal choice, the principle of legality demands that our choice-maker has been (notionally) informed of the law, which must exist at the time of the decision to offend, and the individual is therefore in a position to decide whether to heed it or not. Once properly notified that what he has in mind is criminally proscribed, then it is up to the individual to decide how to proceed. He will be responsible, in the sense that the choice lies with him, and he will face the legal consequences for the wrong choice.[28] Logically, then, the legal interest is in the moment of criminal choice – to offend or not to offend.

In *Answering for Crime*, Duff proclaims that criminal law must give the person at the moment of criminal decision-making 'fair notice of what would make them liable, and a fair opportunity to avoid liability'.[29] His concern is with this person at the moment of decision-making. Has he been warned of the existence of the offence and given a fair chance to avoid committing it?

The glib answer might be, in the case of a rape prosecution, that he could 'avoid liability' by simply asking his prospective victim whether he has her consent. But the complications of rape law before the husband's immunity was finally and fully abolished meant that absence of consent was not the final determinant of legality. The man who was married to his victim might not have had 'fair notice of what would make [him] liable' because the criminal law was issuing complex instructions. It was saying that absence of consent did not make his 'rape'

---

[27] They may supply evidence of intention, but the intention itself is the main thing.

[28] The male pronoun is used here on the basis of the statistical likelihood that the offender will be a man.

[29] Duff, *Answering for Crime*, above n 2 at 43.

a criminal rape; rather it was the associated violence, and this needed to be thought about and calibrated carefully.

IV. The Choice of the Choice-Maker: To Rape or Not to Rape, that is the Question

So the would-be offender's choice that we are considering for the purposes of rape law is – to put it bluntly – should I rape ('have' intercourse knowing that I do not have consent) and in the course of these imagined cogitations, what will make it a rape? Perhaps also: How can I get away with it? The choice, the decision, for the man to make,[30] implicitly guided by or at least informed by the law, is whether or not to rape. In criminal legal analysis, he has this choice. He makes this decision, with his eye notionally on the law, which is telling him not to do it, or when the husband's immunity held good, saying that he could if his victim were his wife. But just what the husband could and could not do was not entirely clear. Our benighted husband was receiving a number of warning signals from criminal law, news of a number of offences against the person, from some of which he was immune. As we have seen, this set of mixed messages slightly worried the criminal lawyers, especially as it was the most serious offence which carried the immunity – the rape – while the assaults associated with the rape could still be criminal.

Still the criminal legal focus, then and now, is on this moment of choice, and the choice is necessarily whether to offend or not, in the knowledge of what is criminal. If our legal individual ever arrives at a court of law, the questions will be: what was he thinking and why at that very moment of offending, or perhaps just before it? In the case of a rape charge, what was he thinking as he proceeded with forced sexual penetration (given the rule of contemporaneity)? How did he arrive at this decision; was he duly warned?[31] What was the internal conversation of the accused, including the implicit conversation with the state who is warning him not to do it? (We can think of Soames Forsyte, here, as he goes through both imaginary dialogues about the propriety of the rape of his wife; he converses with himself and then with the other men of law.) And then there is a second focus on the interaction or conversation between the accused and the court, as this decision is inspected by the court at trial.

In *PGA* the particular concern of the Court was retrospectivity: of punishing the defendant for something that was not a crime at the time that he did it. Was he given fair warning? In the Court of Appeal, the South Australian Chief Justice Doyle briefly conjured up an image of the state warning the defendant at

---

[30] And for the purposes of English rape law 'he' must be a man; by contrast in Australian rape laws, the offence is not gender specific.

[31] The importance of warning is fundamental to the principle that law should not be retrospective.

the moment he was deciding whether to rape. To rape or not to rape, that was the question. The Chief Justice mused that a husband in 1963 would not have thought that he had a right to rape his wife. Or in judicial language: 'Nor can it be said that people would have ordered their affairs or made decisions based on the earlier state of the common law'.[32] Here Doyle CJ is imagining husbands ('people') deciding whether to rape and casting their thoughts to the governing law. The judge cuts off his speculations about the musings of the defendant at this point. The decision whether or not to proceed with sex without consent is described as an 'ordering of affairs', an unfortunate legal description of a decision about a violent rape.

Doyle CJ concedes that there is a judicial horror of retrospective law making. To clarify, he cites Toohey J in the High Court in the war crimes case of *Polyukhovich*[33] who explained the reasons for the 'general abhorrence of retroactive criminal law' in terms of

> the desire to ensure that individuals are reasonably free to maintain control of their lives by choosing to avoid conduct which will attract criminal sanction ... for every individual is, by principle, assured that no future retribution by society can occur except by reference to rules presently known.[34]

In *G v G* the court was clear that current law permitted the husband to proceed lawfully with the rape of his wife. It even admonished him for not getting on with it, as other men would, so sorting out his marriage. The court took the view that he should thus have ordered his affairs, with the implicit knowledge that he had a legal right to do so.

V. Is this Legal Deconstruction of such an Unpleasant and Unsavoury Decision Implausible? Is this Really How Criminal Lawyers Think?

There is something implausible and unpleasant about this imagined legal moment, with the law on the sidelines saying to the about-to-be offender, 'you can do this' but 'you cannot do that'; and also, perhaps, saying 'you have to decide how bad you are going to be'. This act, which you are told you must not do, is worse than that act which you must not do. There is imagined a kind of riffling through the law books, with the man deciding: 'well I am willing to do something *this* bad, but not *that* bad; and here I am allowed to do this. Ah I see I have a legal immunity

---

[32] *R v P, GA* [2010] SASCFC 81, para 81, (2010) 109 SASR 1, 17, para 81.
[33] *Polyukhovich v Commonwealth* [1991] HCA 32, (1991) 172 CLR 501. This was a case about an amendment to the War Crimes Act which would 'make the commission of a "War crime" at an earlier time an indictable offence under the Commonwealth Law': at 16, para 80.
[34] Ibid 688–689.

here, even though I am not allowed to do that (assault for assault's sake) which will probably be necessary to achieve this thing that I am allowed to do. I can rape her but I cannot assault her, or perhaps I can assault her as long as I am not too violent'.

It is as if the legal individual, who forms the focus of the criminal law scholars, were facing a rather tricky criminal law exam, replete with obstacles and tricks; indeed faced with laws that do not cohere. The moral and intellectual puzzles he is set might be acceptable, and plausible, when they take the form of the often gothic criminal law problems of the exam room, when the characters are inventions designed to test student knowledge.[35] But they become more disturbing when the legal individual is thought of as a real man about to rape.

If we place before our would-be offender the South Australian law of rape, at the time when only aggravated rape was criminal for a husband (the 1970s and early 80s), we have an especially perplexing set of rules and decisions. Just what was this husband being warned not to do? Reading his notional rule book, the husband reasons that I can rape her in a manner which is not grossly indecent etc. Mmmmm, just what am I allowed to do here? These implicit communications from law to the husband are frankly grotesque. And yet Colin Howard, in his textbook of criminal law, put the law student, and the imaginary defendant, through his paces in just this way. Recall that Howard instructed the student:

> Logically, since rape is an aggravated assault by the fact of intercourse, it follows that if V cannot withhold her consent to intercourse she cannot withhold her consent to an assault made for the purpose of accomplishing intercourse; so that the law of assault cannot reach a husband who attacks his wife unless the attack is not for the purpose of overcoming her resistance to sexual relations.[36]

Here Howard blended motive (normally legally irrelevant) and intention (legally relevant). If the husband's purpose were to assert his marital rights, then he could use as much force as he needed to have his way. But no more. It was only if the husband employed 'unjustifiable brutality' (an oxymoron?) that he might be convicted of assault 'whatever his object may have been'.[37] So the husband was imagined in the process of working out at which point his 'brutality' became legally 'justifiable'.

If this notional conversation between the officers of the law and the man deciding whether to rape seems farfetched or preposterous (perhaps just an unfortunate habit of the textbook writer wishing to enliven a criminal law class) it was in fact one openly and recently considered by the Chief Justice of the Australian High Court at the hearing of *PGA*. When Mr Bennett, Counsel for the defence,

---

[35] I am grateful to Ian Leader-Elliott for drawing my attention to this ethos of criminal law teaching.
[36] Colin Howard, *Australian Criminal Law*, 4th edn (Sydney, Law Book Co, 1982) 163.
[37] Ibid.

explained to the Bench his view of rape law (that the wife's implied consent to the rape would not apply to any associated assault),[38] French CJ interjected:

> I am just wondering about the coherence of the common law rule which you propound … with the law relating to assault. Can the husband who has non-consensual intercourse with his wife be charged with assault and battery?[39]

Bennett replied: 'Certainly, if it is accompanied by violence, yes'. French CJ then asked: 'What is the lowest threshold for non-consensual physical contact before it becomes violence in relation to intercourse?' In other words, oddly enough, and appreciating the oddness, he wanted to know when did the lawful rape become criminal assault? French CJ persisted, now indeed addressing the imaginary defendant deciding how to proceed:

> I mean, if one says, 'Look, you can have intercourse with your wife without her consent because she is deemed to have given her consent' … but do you say you can still be charged with assault or that you cannot because it is covered by the consent?[40]

Although the Chief Justice's primary purpose, no doubt, was to tease out the argument of defence counsel, and in a manner which would expose the incoherent nature of criminal law as Bennett characterised it (which would for the one act, make assault criminal, but rape lawful), the judge nevertheless used the imagined address to the would-be rapist to work out how the law operated. He was thinking like a classic criminal lawyer, for whom his character of concern was the potential criminal at the point of decision-making. And he saw the criminal law as a form of communication to the would-be rapist, ideally with consistency and clarity, so the potential rapist could decide what he could and could not do and, I suppose, what he was willing to do. This parsing of the law – this discrimination between the lawful rape and the criminal assault – proved equivocal, both morally and as a matter of legal logic, as Williams and Howard found before him.

VI. The Legal Individual as a Physical Being (Without a Sex)

To recapitulate, modern criminal law relies on an abstraction of a person, someone who can be legally accused and found responsible for crime; and he is thought to possess a set of cognitive capacities, as a mental being. As Lacey has explained, this is often called 'capacity responsibility' because it hinges on the assumed mental

---

[38] *PGA v The Queen* [2011] HCA Trans 267 (27 September 2011).
[39] Ibid 16.
[40] Ibid.

capacities of the individual (interestingly not on their physical capacities).[41] The responsible individual is in effect understood *as* a set of cognitive abilities – to know, to think, to choose – to work out whether to offend or not, and to know his own mind. With this conception of the legal individual, he has no legally relevant sex. He has been neutered. He is almost exclusively a Cartesian thinking thing: *cogito ergo sum*.

But modern criminal law also brings into being a human form, a human creature, with human strengths, physical abilities, and human needs and vulnerabilities. This physical being performs the prohibited criminal conduct (or is sometimes at the receiving end of it.) The bounded self, the self-owner, the being with so-called bodily integrity, is an influential characterisation of the physical person in criminal law (as we saw in Chapter 2). There is the physical being who must keep his body to himself and the physical being who must not be intruded upon, in the wrong way.

The legal person as physical being is also a highly abstracted idea of a person. This embodied being is needed to commit the conduct element of offences – physically to hit, to penetrate another with a penis, to kill. These actions are then evaluated for their criminality (eg is the person who hits guilty of assault?) and this will depend on whether the actor had the necessary accompanying mental state. This physicality is also needed in the victims in order for them to have the necessary bodily integrity (as it is typically understood) to be the physical victims of crime. Was their integrity violated? So an idea of physical integrity informs the legal understanding of the physical legal being. But after this, there is not much detail. The mind is an abstraction and so too is the body.

With the legal individual understood as a set of mental capacities and then also as a physical acting being, we have a division of the person into mind and body, each understood in a particular way, quite abstractly, and no longer sexed. In standard criminal law analysis, the mental and physical elements can thus be sharply divided. Necessarily they conjure up either two beings or two aspects of a being. The analytical priority given to the cognitive capacities of the person suggests that the primary being is a mental being and that only secondarily, though necessarily, are they embodied – they punch, kick, stab, rape. And the imagined victim is also embodied. After all they are punched, or kicked, or stabbed or raped. And yet sex is mainly treated as extraneous to analysis. The once extended bodies of men and diminished (invaded) bodies of women are consigned to history.

These oddly neutered mental and physical abstractions of the individual are to be found in the current UK law of rape and to remarkable effect.[42] The removal of the history and the implicit deeming of modernism create some strange characters. The current formulation of rape law in the UK has a highly abstracted

---

[41] Lacey, above n 13 at 27.
[42] See Sexual Offences Act 2003 (UK).

potential offender, A (as mental and physical being) and also an abstracted potential victim, B (also as mental and physical being). To wit:

1 Rape

(1)   A person (A) commits an offence if—
- (a) he intentionally penetrates the vagina, anus or mouth of another person (B) with his penis,
- (b) B does not consent to the penetration, and
- (c) A does not reasonably believe that B consents.

UK rape law addresses a man, not called a man, (A) (a person given the pronoun 'he' who possesses a penis) and the weapon is the penis and until recently it addressed a man who was not the husband. (So two legal statuses once limited, set the contours, of the offence and the individuals referred to therein.)

Though the offence is staunchly gender-neutral, it does not in fact say to women, 'do not rape'. There is no criminal law conception here of women having the capacity to do so.[43] Formerly, it did not say to men, 'do not rape your wife'. And nor did it say to men 'do not rape a man' until 1994.[44] So the individual addressed is not an anyone, though the form of the law, deceptively, suggests otherwise. Women are not addressed by this law. They were and are still not perceived as the criminal problem of rape, as rapists, as the persons posing the threat; nor until quite recently were husbands.

Who is the B that law is implicitly addressing when it says (to B) 'you are protected by rape law; you can complain; you have a right not to be entered without your consent'? Now, in the UK, B is anyone. Men can be raped, but only by a man. Before the abolition of the husband's immunity, B was the non-wife. Before the Criminal Justice and Public Order Act (1994) B was a woman. Sex, sexuality and physicality all matter, in the law, and yet there is also a resolute commitment to abstraction: to As and Bs, not embodied men and women.

For another illustration of modern legal abstraction we can take New Zealand rape law. Here the governing legislation also tries to get men and women out of the picture. For example, the New Zealand offence of 'sexual violation', which includes the crime of rape, uses the following abstracted language: 'Person A rapes person B if person A has sexual connection with person B, effected by the penetration of person B's genitalia by person A's penis'.[45] One assumes that Person A who has the penis is meant to be a man but the term is studiously avoided.

---

[43] And yet the offence of 'assault by penetration' does in fact anticipate a female offender: Sexual Offences Act 2003, s 2 (UK). The more expressive term 'rape' is therefore reserved for the male offender engaged in a forceful act of penetration with his genitalia.

[44] Criminal Justice and Public Order Act 1994 (UK).

[45] Crimes Act 1961, s 128 (NZ): 'Sexual Violation Defined'.

South Australia has taken neutrality further. Under s 48 of the Criminal Law Consolidation Act, which states the crime of 'rape':

> A person (the 'offender') is guilty of the offence of rape if he or she engages, or contin-
> ues to engage, in sexual intercourse with another person who – (a) does not consent to
> engaging in the sexual intercourse; or (b) has withdrawn consent to the sexual inter-
> course, and the offender knows, or is recklessly indifferent to, the fact that the other
> person does not so consent or has so withdrawn consent (as the case may be).

The definition of intercourse then ensures that a penis is not needed to commit the offence: other parts of the body or objects can serve as a weapon. These various criminal laws are all neutral in form and yet they contain different echoes of the past about the gender of the legal individual and of his victim.

VII. And the Deeming of Women

With the shift from explicitly male individualism to modern abstract individual-ism, women are now said to be individuals too, but without the necessary reflection on traditional (that is male) individualism and its implications for the present and the continuing gendered nature of crime and the discipline. In the modern period, there is a declared inclusion of women in the concept of the responsi-ble person, the potential individual defendant, and men are now (nearly) fully included as potential victims. I say 'nearly' because English rape law does not cast the woman as a rapist and hence it does not cast the man as a victim of female rape. Interchangeability of the sexes is taken only so far. But there has been too little inspection of the contents of the concept of the individual; too little thought given to whether he makes both literal and symbolic sense, in light of his history.

It was once assumed that men (understood in certain ways) would be the makers of law, its subjects, its interpreters, and that men would also be the principal subjects of criminal concern. Men were regarded as physically extended persons and this was vital to their sense of themselves. Women, as wives, were treated, in certain respects, as natural apertures. With the new individualism, women have been simply levered into the concept of the individual, as if their inclusion, after long exclusion, had no bearing on the intellectual and moral integrity of the discipline as a whole. The inclusion of women in the concept of the individual of modern individualism is therefore a deeming rather than a thoughtful and consid-ered transformation. To be a considered inclusion it would need to take account of the social and legal history of the concept of the individual, and the social and legal history of crime.

It is also a deeming that is not perceived as such. It is a deeming in the sense that women are declared to be legal individuals, that this will be legally the case, and it is also deemed that women always have been such individuals, for the new individualism treats the individual as a stable concept over time. Women are treated *as if* they are persons/individuals *and* have always been thus, which makes the female legal individual a legal fiction.[46] But we have a fiction which dies immediately in the sense that its as-ifness, the very thing that characterises the legal fiction, disappears almost at the making of women as individuals. The deeming, the sense of fiction, is killed off.

For the fiction of the female legal individual of criminal law to stay alive, for it to be seen that women have been declared into legal being by an act of legal will, rather than by fundamental social and legal transformation, the deeming of women to be individuals would need to be understood as just that: a legal assertion that women will now count fully as persons *and* that they have always counted thus, and that this is all legal artifice; asserted legal truth rather than actual historical truth. It would need to be conceded that it is analytically useful to have a generic universal person at the centre of general theory, and to select terms which enable it to work linguistically: human, citizen, individual, person. Theory can then proceed, with this abstractive but fictive model of the person in place. And perhaps the unexamined Rawlsian assumption implicit in the modern legal individual would need to be examined: the underlying assumption that persons can be meaningfully analysed knowing almost nothing of their basic distinguishing characteristics.[47] For the enduring individualism of women to be acknowledged as the legal fiction that it is, the legal individual would need to be given a history, thus recognising the extended personhood of men and the contracted personhood of women, and then this gendered history would need to be deemed, by fiat, for legal purposes, to be unnecessary to legal analysis – and reasons given.

The open and considered history of the gender of the person of criminal law, demanded by Lacey, has yet to be achieved, though perhaps this book is a contribution. There has been an intellectual jump to a universal trans-historical modern person – the abstract individual – without acknowledgement of that very jump and of the legal artifice entailed, and without a rethinking or recreation or historicisation of the legal person along the way.

VIII. Abstraction and the Disappearing Man

One can see the attraction of the current mode and level of abstraction of the concept of the person in legal analysis and law making, especially the placement

---

[46] See Lon Fuller, *Legal Fictions* (Palo Alto, Stanford University Press, 1968) on the nature of the legal fiction.

[47] This is essentially Rawls' heuristic device of the veil of ignorance, used to work out the rules of a civilised society. Rawls' concept of the individual, in conjunction with his veil of ignorance, for example, might generate such an impression as it was intended to operate in such a neutral way; it was intended to pare back the person to an individual without qualities. But as feminists and communitarians have shown, this person without qualities did have qualities. See John Rawls, *A Theory of Justice* (Cambridge, Harvard University Press, 1971).

of men and women into a lower level of detail, as if the person made sense without a sex; that sex was only incidental. Because the man-specific questions and the woman-specific questions are made lower order matters, matters of greater specificity, they do not demand general theoretical attention. The practical effect is to put the man and woman questions under the radar. These abstractive decisions, typically neither referred to nor justified, relieve the theorist from any moral or intellectual duty to discuss the deep gendering of the person by law, and all the problems it could generate for modern theory.[48]

However the legal absorption of women into the legal identity of the man, 'the unity principle' of the English common law, most conspicuous upon marriage, and operational in criminal law until the last decade of the twentieth century (in the form of the husband's immunity from rape prosecution) is arguably a matter which goes to the very identity and definition of the concept of the person. So too does the amplification of male personality.

Just consider the scale of the problem. We are talking of the unpersonning of half the population, and the legal denial of their capacity to exercise some of the most fundamental choices in life. Scale alone suggests that gender might be fundamental rather than incidental or secondary to the definition of the person, even as abstraction. It was once a basic condition of personhood, being the right sex. Whether it remains so is simply placed outside the realm of discussion, defence and explanation.

The treatment of sex as a secondary or incidental consideration entails a positive fundamental decision, which calls for inspection. Logically gender can be placed inside or outside the concept of the person as abstraction. It entails a positive decision to collapse the sexes into persons, whether it is acknowledged or not. We could have male and female persons. This might seem to generate a problem of dividing the concept of the person always into two, in which case this calls for consideration. Or in the alternative, there could be a discussion of what would make the concept of the person or individual truly general and inclusive.

The unsexing of the modern legal person, by a simple deeming, should be regarded as suspect as it leaves unexamined the positive uses of male power to advance male interests within criminal law. The history of criminal law, until only decades ago, has been one of legal men drawing together and gathering power to themselves and making laws which benefited themselves to the cost of women. The husband's right to rape was not in the interests of women.

Women as wives have been bounded legal individuals for a short time, after centuries of being thought quite otherwise.[49] The female legal condition has been marked by its openness and availability rather than closure. And for the same period, men as men have been extended beings, with the approval of law, who

---

[48] There is an extensive literature on the gender of the legal person. For an earlier account see Ngaire Naffine, *Law and the Sexes* (Sydney, Allen & Unwin 1990).

[49] And still women are subject to laws of abortion and prostitution which, almost by definition, compromise their personal sovereignty.

derived their very masculinity, their very sense of themselves as men, from this extension into women.

What do these old laws mean for the new man and for women as individuals? We do not know because we have not had the discussion. Until recently, the men of law thought of the legal individual as a man. What had to change for this to change? What did change? This part of the story is also missing. We have had more assertion or deeming than deep reflection. The perfunctory story of modernisation did not do the job.

So with the rise of modern legal individualism in a new abstracted gender-neutral form (we are all now bounded individuals, and women can now even stand for men) there is a turning away from, even a positive denial, of the historical abuses entailed in traditional (male) individualism and a simple assertion that women, as legal individuals, can now be exchanged with men, and are fully equivalent to men. Now all is well. But deeming is not explanation. How much is left of the past? Are we living with its legacy? Does it matter? These are questions to be considered in the next chapter.

10

Men, Women and Civil Society: Male Civility in the Twenty-first Century

In 2016, English artist and public intellectual, Grayson Perry, named the man problem of crime and issued a challenge to women:

> Men commit ninety per cent of violent crime. That statistic alone should motivate a government to put gender at the centre of policy but I am not hearing it. The cost of male crime to the UK Exchequer runs into tens of billions of pounds every year. What if female taxpayers decided they were fed up paying for this?[1]

As Perry's provocation makes plain, men are still vastly more criminally violent than women and so women are necessarily paying disproportionately for the imprisonment of men for their violent behaviour. Women are helping to fund the courts, the police and the prosecutors. This is a new way of thinking about the man problem of crime, especially as it adopts a female point of view. That it is so novel, speaks of the continuing invisibility of men as the problem of crime and criminal law. However all is not lost, though we are living in strange times.

I. The Zeitgeist[2]

As Perry correctly observes, late in the second decade of the twenty-first century, men remain the large majority of violent offenders; men remain the often unexamined problem for criminal law.[3] The problem of men and their antisocial behaviour has not gone away.

And yet in interesting and varied ways, the man problem is being identified and the incivilities of men from all quarters of life, incivilities explicitly directed at women, are being exposed. In 2012 then Australian Prime Minister Julia Gillard delivered what has come to be known as 'the Misogyny Speech'.[4] This sustained

---

[1] Grayson Perry, *The Descent of Man* (Great Britain, Allen Lane, 2016) 74.

[2] I am speaking here mainly of the Zeitgeist in the common law world, in the Anglosphere.

[3] See for example Ministry of Justice, 'Statistics on Women and the Criminal Justice System 2013' (A Ministry of Justice publication under the Criminal Justice Act 1991, s 95, 2014).

[4] See full transcript of the Gillard speech in Julia Gilliard, *The Sydney Morning Herald* (Sydney 10 October 2012), www.smh.com.au/politics/federal/transcript-of-julia-gillards-speech-20121010-27c36.html.

piece of rhetoric against misogyny in the highest places, with the cadences of the 'I have a dream' speech of Dr Martin Luther King,[5] had a broad international audience, speaking to millions of women.[6] In 2017, *The Handmaid's Tale*, Atwood's dystopian account of a misogynist society in which Blackstone's coverture was taken to a new level, became a television series, again with great international reach. Over 30 years after the book's first publication, it was seen to have new currency.

The 'MeToo' campaign of women across the world, exposing powerful men and their sexual misuses of power, is still another example of changing times and, perhaps, a reconfiguration of power relations between men and women. As Nadia Khomami explains, 'The origins of #MeToo can be dated back before the predominance of social media, when activist Tarana Burke created the campaign as a grass-roots movement to reach sexual assault survivors in underprivileged communities'.[7]

But there are also signs of male entitlement being reasserted. In October 2016 the *Washington Post* published a tape which 'sent shockwaves through American politics'.[8] The tape recorded Donald Trump 'boasting about grabbing female genitalia'.[9] Trump is reported to have said: 'when you're a star they let you do it. You can do anything'. 'Although a number of major Republican figures withdrew their support for Trump', as *The Guardian* observed, 'after the tape was published, he managed to overcome the revelations and win the presidency despite losing the popular vote'.[10] It remains difficult for many women (and men) around the world to make sense of this fact.

Perceived loss of sexual entitlement has generated extreme and violent responses by men. In April 2018 a member of the Incel (involuntarily celibate) group[11] drove a van into pedestrians in Toronto, as a protest against women who refused sexual intercourse. He killed ten people, mostly women, and injured many others. James Fitzjames Stephen's implicit warning to women, that if they

[5] The fiftieth anniversary of Martin Luther King's speech was commemorated by then President Obama in 2013. See the *Washington Post* (Washington 28 August 2013) www.washingtonpost.com/politics/transcript-president-obamas-speech-on-the-50th-anniversary-of-the-march-on-washington/2013/08/28/0138e01e-0ffb-11e3-8cdd-bcdc09410972_story.html?noredirect=on&utm_term=.f423606b7402, for the transcript of President Obama's own eloquent speech.

[6] Indeed it prompted a change to the dictionary definition of 'misogyny': see Lizzy Davies, 'Julia Gillard speech prompts dictionary to change "misogyny" definition' *The Guardian: Australian Edition* (Sydney 18 October 2012) www.theguardian.com/world/2012/oct/17/julia-gillard-australia-misogyny-dictionary.

[7] Nadia Khomami, '#MeToo: how a hashtag became a rallying cry against sexual harassment' *The Guardian* (London 21 October 2017) www.theguardian.com/world/2017/oct/20/women-worldwide-use-hashtag-metoo-against-sexual-harassment.

[8] Ben Jacobs, '"Of course he said it": Billy Bush counters Trump's pussy tape claims' *The Guardian* (Washington 4 December 2017) www.theguardian.com/us-news/2017/dec/04/of-course-he-said-it-billy-bush-counters-trumps-pussy-tape-claims.

[9] Ibid.

[10] Ibid.

[11] For a short but authoritative account of the history of the Incel group see Melissa J Gismondi, 'Why are "incels" so angry? The History of the Little Known Ideology Behind the Toronto Killings' *Washington Post* (Washington 27 April 2018) www.washingtonpost.com/news/made-by-history/

came out from under the legal cover of men they would be exposed to rougher types of male incivility, now seems prescient.[12]

II. Recognising the Man Problem in the Special Part of Criminal Law

Meanwhile in the special part of criminal law, there has also been a naming of the man problem which has led to legal change. (Here I am drawing on Glanville Williams' classic division of criminal law into the special part of criminal law – that is the specific offences – and the general part, or general principles).[13]

In 2003, after the passage of nearly 30 years, the *Morgan* 'defence', discussed in the first chapter, was removed from the offence of rape by the Sexual Offences Act (UK).[14] A man could no longer rely on an honest though unreasonable belief in his victim's consent to sexual intercourse to avoid blame. In assessing his liability, the fact finder had to consider whether he had taken reasonable steps to find out what his victim thought. The man's innocence or guilt did not depend entirely on his subjective point of view, and of course on his credibility.[15]

In 2009 the Policing and Crime Act (UK) made it an offence to pay 'for the sexual services of a prostitute' but only if a third party had subjected the prostitute to 'exploitative conduct'.[16] This offence made men criminally responsible for buying sex in some of the worst circumstances for women. The purchase of sex in less abusive circumstances remains lawful. Meanwhile 'loitering' or 'soliciting'

---

wp/2018/04/27/why-are-incels-so-angry-the-history-of-the-little-known-ideology-behind-the-toronto-attack/?utm_term=.adffe3d6e411. It begins with the chilling words 'Men no longer have unfettered access to women's bodies. Not everyone is happy about that'.

[12] See discussion of Stephen in Chapter 4.

[13] The division of criminal law into the special and the general part is generally attributed to Glanville Williams. See his classic work, *Criminal Law: The General Part* (London, Steven & Sons, 1961). For a more recent discussion of the distinction see Peter Cane, 'The General/Special Distinction in Criminal Law, Tort Law and Legal Theory' (2007) 26 *Law and Philosophy* 465.

[14] See Jennifer Temkin and Andrew Ashworth, 'The Sexual Offences Act 2003: (1) Rape, Sexual Assault and the Problems of Consent' (2004) *Criminal Law Review* 328. For a critical feminist analysis of this legislation, and especially its consent provisions, see Vanessa E Munro, 'Shifting Sands? Consent, Context and Vulnerability in Contemporary Sexual Offences Policy in England' (2017) 26 *Social and Legal Studies* 417.

[15] See Sexual Offences Act 2003 (UK) Rape:

'(1) A person (A) commits an offence if—

   (a) he intentionally penetrates the vagina, anus or mouth of another person (B) with his penis,
   (b) *B does not consent* to the penetration, and
   (c) *A does not reasonably believe that B consents.*

(2) *Whether a belief is reasonable is to be determined having regard to all the circumstances, including any steps A has taken to ascertain whether B consents'.* (emphasis added)

[16] See Policing and Crime Act 2009, s 14 (UK). For a critical feminist analysis of this legislation see Munro, above n 14.

for prostitution in a public place is still a criminal offence.[17] Thus the working lives of those who sell (rather than give away) sex attracts state condemnation and criminal convictions[18] and exposes the seller but not the buyer to police surveillance and violence.[19]

In other words the (mainly male) buying of sex remains generally lawful while the (mainly female) soliciting for sex remains criminal.[20] To my knowledge there has never been any question of the English criminalising the words and gestures of men who actively solicit (unpaid) sex from women on a daily basis.[21] Think of the young woman who walks past the building site or down any street where men cluster. American politics at the very highest level is now implicated in this culture of male sexual predation. None of this speaks of a deep-seated respect for the personal sovereignty of women. And yet there are continuing legal efforts to identify and criminalise the man problem: the problem of the uncivil man.

In 2010, also in England, there was an explicit banning of sexual infidelity as a legally-recognised trigger for loss of control in the new partial defence to murder. A man could no longer argue that his wife's adultery had driven him into a homicidal rage, once a classic use of the provocation defence.[22] Some Australian

---

[17] See the Street Offences Act 1959, s 1 (UK).

[18] Convictions for soliciting then blight the lives of women who wish to break free from prostitution or simply to conduct a normal life when they are not working. Though in 2018, former prostitutes finally succeeded in their legal challenge to laws requiring them to reveal such convictions to potential employers. See Holly Watt, 'Former Prostitutes Win Legal Challenge Against UK Government' *The Guardian* (London 2 March 2018) www.theguardian.com/society/2018/mar/02/former-prostitutes-win-legal-challenge-against-uk-government.

[19] On the harrowing experiences of sex workers facing police surveillance and police violence see Melissa Gira Grant, *Playing the Whore: The Work of Sex Work* (London, Verso, 2014). Grant says she has 'stopped asking, "Why have we made prostitution illegal?" Instead I want an explanation for, "How much violence against 'prostitutes' have we made acceptable?"': at 6–7.

[20] In 2015 the purchase of sex was made criminal in Northern Ireland by the Human Trafficking and Exploitation (Further Provisions and Support for Victims) Bill.

[21] However, at the time of writing, the French had just made such a move by the introduction of on-the-spot fines for the sexual harassment of women in public places. See Angelique Chrisafis, 'France plans on-the-spot-fines for sexual harassment in public places' *The Guardian* (London 21 March 2018) www.theguardian.com/world/2018/mar/21/france-plans-on-the-spot-fines-for-sexual-harassment-in-public. See also Kim Willsher, 'Uproar in Paris over Video of Woman Hit by Harasser in Paris Street' *The Guardian* (London 30 July 2018) www.theguardian.com/world/2018/jul/30/uproar-in-france-over-video-of-woman-marie-laguerre-hit-by-harasser-in-paris-street and Kim Willsher, '"They Don't See Us as Human": Women Speak out on France's Harassment Problem' *The Guardian* (London 3 August 2018) www.theguardian.com/world/2018/aug/03/they-just-dont-see-us-as-human-women-speak-out-on-frances-harassment-problem.

[22] Coroners and Justice Act 2009 (UK): s 54 Partial defence to murder: loss of control:

'(1) Where a person ("D") kills or is a party to the killing of another ("V2"), D is not to be convicted of murder if—

    (a) D's acts and omissions in doing or being a party to the killing resulted from D's loss of self-control,

    (b) the loss of self-control had a qualifying trigger, and

    (c) a person of D's sex and age, with a normal degree of tolerance and self-restraint and in the circumstances of D, might have reacted in the same or in a similar way to D ...

(6) In determining whether a loss of self-control had a qualifying trigger – ...

    (c) the fact that a thing done or said constituted sexual infidelity is to be disregarded'.

jurisdictions went further. The defence was completely abolished[23] for much the same reason: to stop male misuses of the defence. In 2015 an offence of coercive and controlling behaviour in intimate relationships was created, again a naming of the man problem.[24]

In May of 2018 a constitutional referendum in the Republic of Ireland resulted in a clear vote in favour of abolishing that section of the Constitution which confers equal rights to life on the 'unborn' and its 'mother',[25] thus paving the way for the legalisation of abortion and Irish recognition of the personal sovereignty of women.[26] This change has the strong support of the (male) Irish Prime Minister Leo Varadkar.[27] Meanwhile in the United States, as *The Telegraph* has observed, 'President Donald Trump has issued a rallying call to opponents of abortion, encouraging them to head to the polls to elect conservative lawmakers'.[28] Atwood's *Handmaid's Tale* has assumed a new significance.

III. Recognising the Man Problem in the General Part of Criminal Law

Where has this left criminal law proper, its general principles, its idea of the responsible choosing gender-neutral person and the discipline's claims to civility? Are the changes to specific criminal laws indicative of a new person for criminal law at large, one who could stand for men and women equally?

Certainly legal changes to the status of women in relation to men, and so men in relation to women, have been dramatic over the period spanned by this book. Consider the legal position of women during the times of Hale and Blackstone

---

[23] For a discussion of the abolition of the defence in Victoria see Kate Fitz-Gibbon and Sharon Pickering, 'Homicide Law Reform in Victoria, Australia: From Provocation to Defensive Homicide and Beyond' (2012) 52 *The British Journal of Criminology* 159.

[24] But not quite. See the Serious Crime Act 2015, s 76: 'Coercive or Controlling Behaviour in an Intimate or Family Relationship'. Though the wording of the offence was to remain gender neutral, the main intent of the offence was to stop such behaviour in men. See the influential work of Evan Stark, especially *Coercive Control: How Men Entrap Women in Personal Life* (Oxford, Oxford University Press, 2007).

[25] Eighth Amendment of the Irish Constitution Act 1983 reads as follows: 'The State acknowledges the right to life of the unborn and, with due regard to the equal right to life of the mother, guarantees in its laws to respect, and, as far as practicable, by its laws to defend and vindicate that right'.

[26] The anticipated changes to the law will make available lawful abortion for specified periods of the pregnancy.

[27] William Booth and Isaac Stanley-Becker, 'Ireland votes to overturn its abortion ban, "Culmination of quiet revolution", Prime Minister says' *Washington Post* (Washington, 26 May 2018) www.washingtonpost.com/world/europe/ireland-votes-to-repeal-its-ban-on-abortion/2018/05/26/fb675fa8-603b-11e8-b656-236c6214ef01_story.html?utm_term=.64898b000399.

[28] Foreign Staff, 'Abortion around world: The countries with most restrictive laws and why debate is back in Spotlight' *The Telegraph* (London 23 May 2018) www.telegraph.co.uk/news/2018/05/23/abortion-around-world-countries-restrictive-laws-debate-back/. On the consequences for women of laws which make abortion a criminal offence see Susheela Singh et al, 'Abortion Worldwide 2017 Uneven Progress and Unequal Access' (Guttmacher Institute, 2018).

and then the position of women in the twenty-first century. As Nicola Lacey has observed, 'one of the most radical changes in the conception of legal personhood viewed in modern perspective [is] the relatively recent acknowledgement of women as legal persons'.[29] And because rights and duties are correlative, these changes in the status of women (which are always vis-à-vis men), have necessarily represented changes to the personhood of men.

But can we say that there has been a general rethinking of criminal law's subject, in view of these changes to women (and to men)? Or as Sharon Cowan has recently posed the gender question for criminal law proper: 'we might ask, not simply what impact have ideas of responsibility had on women, but what impact has the idea of *women*, the idea of gender itself, had on the idea of responsibility?'[30] As Cowan points out, this is not a question which has been of general interest to the discipline.

In the light of the findings of this book, we are bound to say that, despite his profoundly gendered history, the criminal legal subject has yet to be reimagined or remediated for the modern age.[31] Criminal law's male history is still weakly articulated and the man problem has hardly been reckoned with in terms of the development of general principle. The modern liberal legal person does not have liberal antecedents; after all he was designed for a certain type of highly illiberal man, once quite explicitly so. Criminal law once permitted the uses of sexual force in a domestic context and gave a partial excuse to men who killed, if their anger was directed at an infuriating wife. These are poor foundations upon which to build a modern legal model of a person, one who is in service to liberal civic values, even though this is precisely the intended purpose of this model in modern criminal law.

As we have seen, criminal law and criminal law theorists have relied heavily on abstraction as a technique for creating a central character for their discipline, one who can stand for anyone. But this technique has its problems. The technique of abstraction calls for decisions about the characteristics that should be included in the abstraction and a justification of the characteristics selected in, and those selected out, such as gender (and other distinguishing characteristics of persons). When the characteristics selected in, to form the abstraction, are all about autonomy (that is self-government), rational decision making and freely chosen actions and relations, when handed this abstraction, we start seeing a man. After all, these characteristics of the person have all been historically associated with men, not with women. It is very difficult to pluck gender out of the abstraction of the person or to neutralise its effects. It calls for a lot of thought and work, the sort of intellectual work that has not been done.

---

[29] Nicola Lacey, *In Search of Criminal Responsibility* (Oxford, Oxford University Press, 2016) 183.

[30] Sharon Cowan, 'In Search of Connections: Reading between the Lines of Nicola Lacey's *In Search of Criminal Responsibility*' (2017) 4 *Critical Analysis of Law* 211, 217.

[31] The 'idea of women' certainly did once give our legal subject meaning, but in a negative sense; to be a responsible subject was precisely not to be a woman, as woman was understood.

There is the further problem of imagining persons or individuals as discrete independent and exchangeable autonomous units, as legal As and Bs (the language of modern legislation) which the legal abstraction of the person also asks us to do, when in fact we do not and cannot live as discrete units, as isolates. Simply this is not the human way of being. Women have never really been thought of as autonomous units, as bounded individuals. The model was not designed for them. But of course men are not really bounded selves either. Real human beings come into the world and flourish only within, and because of, their relations, and continue to make sense only within them. As John Donne said: 'No man is an island entire of itself'.[32] I will return shortly to this existential human and legal matter of the person conceived as their relations, rather than as discrete units or entities.

There is also the problem of how to think of persons as abstractions at all, and not as real human beings: for the individual of criminal law is still necessarily a thought experiment, an exercise of the imagination, which requires us to think of a person with very few defining qualities and also extracted from their social setting.[33] This is hard intellectual labour not easily sustained. Even when handed an abstraction of a person, and counselled to think of them only in the abstract, the human tendency is to visualise a real person with a real history in a real context.[34] This immediately endows our human abstraction with characteristics, making them concrete and particular, so that abstraction stops being abstract. When the defining characteristics of our abstraction of the legal person have been strongly associated with men, and indeed designed for men, again men quickly come to mind. When the decision of our criminal legal individual that most interests us is the decision to offend, again men become our imaginary legal character.

IV. The Abstraction of the Person and the Problem of Bad (Male) Pedigree

To tease out some of these problems with criminal law's abstraction of the individual, I return to a central purpose of this book, which has been to give the modern individual of modern criminal law, and its theory, a history. To do this I have taken

---

[32] John Donne, *Meditation XVII from Devotions upon Emergent Occasions* (1623).

[33] For a fascinating and highly critical account of such philosophical thought experiments see Kathleen V Wilkes, *Real People: Personal Identity without Thought Experiments* (Oxford, Oxford University Press, 1988).

[34] I consider this problem in Ngaire Naffine, 'Who are Law's Persons?: From Cheshire Cats to Responsible Subjects' (2003) 66 *Modern Law Review* 346, and also in Ngaire Naffine, 'Women and the Cast of Legal Persons' in Jackie Jones et al (eds), *Gender, Sexualities and the Law* (Oxford, Routledge, 2011).

this abstraction of the person back to its sources, which we now know to be highly gendered.

Once historicised, our modern legal individual cannot be regarded as a truly neutral abstraction of a human being, which I suspect is a logical and human impossibility, as well as not a particularly helpful organising idea for the discipline.[35] Rather he has a particular male lineage and that lineage is responsible for the character of the abstraction. Male concerns and interests have given form and meaning to law's person, not women's.

This patrimonial lineage of the abstraction of the person is highly destabilising for the discipline of criminal law because of the discipline's defining commitments to the preservation of the bodily integrity and autonomy of *every* individual, not just men. Mostly this problem of shaky moral commitments has simply been bypassed by an explicit or implicit denial of male lineage, the very thing we observed in the modernisation story, which assiduously kept the focus away from men and their carnal, and other, interests in women.

Denial of lineage assumes almost heroic proportions when, without comment or explanation, our modern legal individual is assigned a female pronoun in the criminal legal literature, as 'she' now often is. But this she-ification of the person carries its own moral and intellectual risks for the discipline, as our newly minted she-person should prompt us to trace our modern legal individual back to the female source of the person. But the female case, historically, was one of diminished personhood, of positive legal subjugation to men, not human agency. As we have seen, throughout, what has been distinctively female about the woman of criminal law has been her inability to decide and to act in law and to choose her own relations freely.

This means that the use of 'she' to denote the modern legal individual is a risky ploy which can backfire on its users. 'She' cannot stand for 'him' or for the abstract 'individual' because if we then consider what it has meant to be legally 'she', we find an historical person with almost no positive legal character and certainly little opportunity for legal agency. So when our modern criminal law theorist invokes a female individual to represent the modern ability to exist and to act in law, to be and to do, to exercise choice, we should be reminded of the jarring historical fact that this is the very antithesis of what once distinguished women, especially once they married. As Carole Pateman observed, what once most characterised women was that they were not individuals.[36]

Indeed the modern use of the female pronoun to refer to the central character of criminal law, the legal individual, is not only jarring but offensive to women. For it carries the implication that criminal law has a woman problem: it suggests

---

[35] Again see Wilkes' critical assessment of the utility of such mental experiments in *Real People*, above n 32.

[36] This is the essential message of her classic work *The Sexual Contract* (Stanford, Stanford University Press, 1988).

that women are the antisocial and violent ones in need of criminal regulation; and so it makes sense to treat woman as the general case of the criminal. This is positively misleading. The woman problem of criminal law has not been one of violent women and fearful men,[37] of the incivilities of women to men. Rather the problem posed by women has been more about their sexual availability to men, and ensuring that criminal law did not impede this access, in view of its formal commitments to bodily integrity.

The individual of modern individualism, with his ability to choose and to act, necessarily has a male legal lineage. For the ability to act in law has been defining of men, not of women. But legal men have not only been characterised by their legally-recognised ability to reason and reflect, but also by their extended and abusive forms of decision-making: for raw male power augmented by law. Until very recently, what helped to define a legal man, to make him distinctive, was his legal ability to control and even harm another. In important ways, central criminal law was used to empower, rather than to restrain and punish, the violent man. Rape was a highly qualified offence, which ensured that the husband as rapist committed no crime. Murder was downgraded to manslaughter, if a wife provoked her husband into a homicidal rage by her infidelity. Both crimes took their natures from male sectional interests. Thus the two crimes which demanded absolute condemnation by criminal law, according to the law scholars themselves, were not in fact absolutely condemned.

With this ugly and unconsidered past, we must now question whether women can be modern legal individuals *and* women, and whether men can be modern civil persons *and* men. This leaves modern criminal law in some difficulty: a discipline without a central character of any repute.

True, attention has been paid to the problems of the old models of men and there have been attempts to renovate and modernise them. The remodelling of aspects of rape and murder laws has tried to incorporate new liberal ideas of men and women. But we have not had a thorough rethinking of the idea of the legal individual. Instead we have a rather crude abstraction, who still plays a central character role in the literature. If the change in the character of the legal individual or person were thoroughgoing, if he truly were a new being for the modern age, then the historical maleness of the person should by now have been brought into sharp relief, by the very presence of women who were not there before. And something should have been done to rectify the lop-sided nature of the concept. Now that law has explicitly recognised the maleness of the historical category of person (as in the persons' cases), there is an inescapable demand on law to do something about its central term.

The problem of the unconsidered or obscured past is as much a problem for men as for women. If men are not seen as men, if their history is unconsidered, they cannot be said to be full modern rational civil individuals, who have changed over

---

[37] This is not to say that this never happens.

time and acquired liberal credentials. They were once both bounded and extended legal persons. What are they now? How have men, and law's understanding of men, changed? And why are men still the majority of officially uncivil individuals – that is offenders? What is the problem with men? These are basic and legitimate questions for criminal law.

Men cannot be regarded as a truly modern and civil sex if they have not been reconceived by society's major civil institutions, and brought into the modern world as new types of men; and the idea of the legal person adjusted, considerably, as a consequence. The modern liberal abstraction of the person – the respecter and exerciser of choice and autonomy – does not seem to suit either sex. Indeed, he is not fit for use.

Before I turn to consider just how we might start to make a modern person, or perhaps modern persons, in the plural, for modern criminal law, I want to consider briefly what has happened to the trinity of men who were once endorsed by the Victorians, who were excused and still encouraged by the men of the twentieth century and who are now poorly acknowledged (having been replaced by the modern abstraction of the individual who ostensibly has no sex, but really does). Have these men of criminal law really been despatched? Have they packed up their bags and gone? What has happened to the man problem?

V. What has Happened to the Bounded Individual, the Little Monarch and the Sexual Master?

Are the dark forces of the past still operating? What, if anything, has been done about the male trinity of persons – the tough 'bounded individual', who was designed to be the exclusive occupier of public space and butt up against other men, but only in particular controlled ways. And what has happened to the 'little monarch' of the home and also the man who was once told to employ sexual mastery in order to keep his little kingdom in order: that is, 'the sexual master'?

We can now view our modern legal characters in light of their history. I suggest that the male trinity is with us still, but poorly considered in terms of the general principles and persons of criminal law. Certain laws have recognised and tried to deal with these different characters. The abolition of the husband's rape immunity has required men to retract themselves. The husband forcing sex on a wife has now been placed in the category of rapist. General rape law reform has also pulled men in: the male point of view is no longer the sole determinant of liability. The flouted husband who loses his self-control and kills is now a murderer; he is no longer partially excused. Changes to the provocation defence to murder have required him to control his anger when confronted with news of infidelity. Offences of controlling and coercive behaviour have also criminalised the little monarch.

The extended male, in his different guises, is now perceived to be a problem. The sexual master and the little monarch are no longer ideals of male personality.

And yet it seems likely that the menace of domestic violence, which is responsible for so much of the harm to women and which is especially associated with the killing of women, still owes much to these nasty models of masculinity.

The only vaguely acceptable model for the modern criminal legal person, supplied by the past, as supplied by our trinity of legal men, one from which we could abstract our modern person, is the bounded individual who can repel all others (generally understood as threatening men) from his person and who looks to criminal law to supply him with that right to say no: to choose those with whom he will make contact. And despite the legacy of our male trinity, despite the problems of abstraction from either the male or female case, this faceless sexless abstract individual, repelling all others from his borders, is indeed to be found in the heart of general theory and in much of criminal law. Think of the offences against 'the person'. This modern neutral individual, not man and not woman, is the official character of modern general theory and doctrine. He is a sort-of man who is no longer meant to be a man, nor seen to be a man, because his distinctive history as a man is denied him, because it is so unacceptable. He is extracted and abstracted out of his history and plonked down with women, who are even less considered as legal individuals. He makes sense as a gender-neutral individual only if his past is quietly forgotten.

However this self-possessing other-excluding individual, who asserts his autonomy rights by setting himself apart from others, and always choosing his points of contact, is far from ideal in other ways. As Jennifer Nedelsky has argued, he is an unconvincing model of the person, for either sex.[38] The bounded or bordered individual was designed with men in mind and men understood in a certain way – as if men always had firm borders and border control, despite the permeability of men too. He was not designed for women and the modern bounded woman remains a legal oddity.[39] In an obvious physical way, women are not designed to be bounded when one considers ordinary acts of consenting heterosexual sex and childbirth. And these physical manifestations of what look like poor border control, and understood precisely as poor border control (not as the healthy flourishing natural female form), are still tied symbolically and historically to a legal past in which women, once married, had no formal right to police their own boundaries and men as husbands had an almost unfettered right of entry.[40]

But it is important to say that men are not actually bounded or bordered persons, and the sense that they ever were depended on their positive placement within public and private legal relations in which they were required to rebuff the sexual advances of other men and in which their sexual relations with their

---

[38] See Jennifer Nedelsky, *Law's Relations: A Relational Theory of Self Autonomy and Law* (Oxford, Oxford University Press, 2011), discussed in Chapter 2.

[39] In fact the laws of prostitution and abortion both say to women that they are not in charge of their own borders.

[40] Again, modern laws of abortion and prostitution continue to deny women full border control and in a manner which has no real equivalent for men.

wives were thought to entail possession of a woman in a manner which preserved their borders, physically and legally.[41] Just a moment thinking about the physical changes in a man before, during and after the act of sex with a woman does not conjure up a firm, stable male border.[42] So too the encouraged forms of male aggression within the manly sports such as boxing or football, and the injuries they inflict on a weekly basis, suggest the crushability of male flesh and bones.

The modern bounded individual, repelling all others at his borders, is thus an incoherent and unconvincing idea of a person for criminal law. Not only does he make poor sense of real people and their forms and their natures but he has an unfortunate pedigree: he bears the legacy of illiberal and unexamined models of the person, which keep shaping his modern status. Men keep trying to be bounded and strong and impermeable; women keep finding that they are thought to lack the basic means of establishing a properly modern bounded nature. The old forms keep asserting themselves.

VI. Persons as Relations

As a relational theorist, Jennifer Nedelsky has offered another way of thinking about the person (as we saw in Chapter 2). In *Law's Relations* her declared purpose was 'to advance a shift of presumption about the self and its core values so that a relational perspective becomes a routine part of theorizing about justice, equality, dignity, security, or autonomy'.[43] Nedelsky explains that her relational theory is not simply a plea for greater community, for closer social relations, for tighter social bonds or connections. It is not even, necessarily, a plea for greater care, what Carol Gilligan called an 'ethic of care'.[44] More interestingly, Nedelsky's relational theory offers an account of how humans come into being and sustain meaning, within and as relations: the mother to the child; the wife to the husband; the employer to the employee; the master to the slave. Each side of the relationship takes its meaning from the other. Our relations may be positive and beneficial, they may promote our autonomy, or they may be oppressive and even cruel. Sometimes an ability to sever certain relations may even mean the difference between life and death.

Nedelsky does not sacrifice choice, agency and autonomy in her move from individualistic to relational thinking. There remains a meaning-maker, someone making sense of the relations that make up their life. Autonomy is enhanced when

---

[41] See Ngaire Naffine, 'Possession: Erotic Love in Law of Rape' (1994) 57 *Modern Law Review* 10.

[42] And see also Ngaire Naffine, 'The Body Bag' in Ngaire Naffine and Rosemary J Owens (eds), *Sexing the Subject of Law* (Sydney, Law Book Co, 1997) 79.

[43] Nedelsky, above n 38 at 9.

[44] Carol Gilligan, *In a Different Voice: Psychological Theory and Women's Development* (Cambridge, Harvard University Press, 1982).

the meaning-maker is alert to the complexity of their life's relations, how they operate, how power influences their operation, and how autonomy depends on constructive relations, not the innate characteristics of the individual (say their maleness or their femaleness). It follows that there is a dynamic creative dimension to the making of a person and the making of a life.

In this view, relations are the person and the person is their relations. It is therefore best not to think of the individual as located or positioned *within* or inside a set of relations, which might suggest a pre-social person of stable character (whom one might try to understand: get their natures right, as Stephen did with his strong masterful men and his submissive women) and then their roles and relations. For the individual and their relations cannot be severed. This is perhaps the most important intellectual, moral and political point of relational theory and the one which is most disconcerting and unsettling. When the scientific or legal spotlight is trained on the human individual, or the man or the woman, it may seem that the analyst can discover his or her attributes and nature by hard thought, by sustained observation. But as soon as one gives this individual social and legal meaning, and a history, which we cannot help but do if he is to be more than a scientific object, then he ceases to be a discrete unit and comes to be defined by his human and legal relations.

This relational view of the person is in fact highly compatible with the way in which law brings persons into being, in that legal rights and duties make the legal person and these are inherently relational. In other words a right (holder) depends on another person with a duty (the duty bearer). A right bearing person comes into existence by dint of a duty bearing person, not because of some essential human, or male, nature.[45] For example the husband's extended powers, including the right to the body of his wife, effectively depended on the wife's correlative duty to submit; or perhaps the neutralisation of her right to refuse. Either way, the legal relation made the man, and the woman.

Legal persons make little sense considered on their own. Instead, to make sense of them, one must attend to the legal relations, the rights and the duties, which are both the making of persons and the materials with which persons make themselves, law permitting.[46] Perhaps our criminal law experts could learn from those whom I have elsewhere called 'the legalists'.[47] Such lawyers are characterised by their more modest view that they have no special insights into the human condition and that it is simply not the law's business to engage in such metaphysical speculation. Rather 'the defining characteristic of law's construct of the person' is 'the formal capacity to bear rights and duties' and these are inherently

---

[45] For some classic legal writing on the correlativity of rights and duties see WN Hohfeld, Walter Wheeler Cook (ed), *Fundamental Legal Conceptions as Applied in Judicial Reasoning, and Other Legal Essays* (New Haven, Yale University Press, 1934).

[46] See Naffine 'Who are Law's Persons?' above n 34.

[47] See Ngaire Naffine, *Law's Meaning of Life* (Oxford, Portland, Hart, 2009) 21.

relational and will in fact depend on circumstance and history.[48] To understand a person, socially and legally, you need to see how they are present within relations and for this you need to give them a context and a history. Bold statements about the essential nature of the human will not do the job.[49]

VII. Effecting Change

But to give persons that context and history we need greater self-reflection from influential men. Criminal lawyers need to study men as both subjects and objects. They need therefore to study men as men and reflect on their history and their legacy. As we saw in Chapter 8, men as legal commentators and law makers have often been blind to the intellectual and moral effects of their own placement within gender relations; and they have been blind to the significance of gender for the men and women they were regulating. They have been insensitive to the harms experienced by those who were subject to these laws. They have permitted and even encouraged legal relations which entailed the extension of themselves into women, by way of the amplification of male right and the amplification of female duty. Thus they have defended the use of force and control, while proclaiming the personal sovereignty of every person. They have advanced and held to deeply incompatible ideas. The men of criminal law and their male subjects still have no considered history because they have not been treated as specific historical figures comprising specific and shifting legal powers exercised in relation to those who were concomitantly denied them.

As a consequence, from Lord Hale to Professor Williams, the understanding of the social and legal natures of both men and women has tended to be static, inflexible, stultifying and caricatured.[50] There has been reliance on bald assertion about the intrinsic natures of men and women, rather than a search for robust empirical evidence. There has been remarkably little interest in the actual lives of women, and what those lives could tell men about themselves. It was once simply assumed that women amounted to no more than the very stifling role assigned to them and so must be excluded from male territory, and law was employed to effect this exclusion. This was such a limited and suffocating role that men sought to get away from women, except for two to three specified purposes: sex, procreation and housekeeping (again, given dystopian expression by Atwood in *The Handmaid's Tale*).

The necessary correlative effect on men of the unpersonning, the de-individuation, of the other sex is still rarely considered. Because men are necessarily defined in

---

[48] Ibid.

[49] The sort of bold statement made by Hart with his reference to the giant land crab (see Chapter 2).

[50] With Williams the characterisation of women admittedly varied with law: women were the beneficiaries in his view of abortion law; they were given very different treatment in rape law.

relation to women, as not-women, the frozen role of women has also frozen the role of men and the frozen role of men is not one of rational liberal agent (the prevailing story) but of controller of space, of naming, of property and of the very person of another.

As the neuroscientist Beau Lotto explains, the static is poorly perceived and interpreted because we tend to make meaning by the observation of difference, change and variation.[51] Perception and meaning are inherently relational and depend on movement and change. The static actually loses its sense and meaning. Women have been permitted little variation, let alone a role in the assessment and evaluation of men.[52] But men too have assigned to themselves a role as men, which is correlatively one of rigid control over another rather than relation and interlocution. This has given men themselves little play in their role. Bishop Berkeley said that 'to be is to be perceived'.[53] Women were once not perceived, but then nor were men, as men (that is, it was difficult for women to give public expression to their views of men).

VIII. Studying Men as a Specific Sex and as a Sectional Interest

So what is to be done? We need to consider openly the workings and effects of power and self-interest on modern men as a section of society. Still missing from the orthodox account of criminal law proper, offered by the new liberals, is a sense of the conflicting and sinister male uses of central criminal law; how law has been deployed to empower men and to permit the abuse of women and to lend it legitimacy, as suitable treatment for a less powerful group. We need concerted efforts to understand the man problem of criminal law in its modern forms, the man problem which still fills up the courts and the prisons and keeps public spaces unsafe for both sexes, but especially for women. In fact we need to reflect on the full impost on women of male misconduct.

Because we still do not have a criminal legal story of men, *as men*, and their changing standards of public behaviour, we do not have an understanding of modern men, as men. The dominance of men as offenders across most types of offending is also not treated as a central intellectual, moral and policy problem of criminal law. Just how does it inform thinking in the general part of criminal law, as well as in the special part?

[51] Beau Lotto, *Deviate: The Science of Seeing Differently* (Great Britain, Weidenfeld & Nicholson, 2017).

[52] See Cordelia Fine, *Delusions of Gender: How Our Minds, Society and Neurosexism Create Difference* (New York, London, WW Norton & Company, 2010).

[53] George Berkeley, *A Treatise Concerning the Principles of Human Knowledge* (Dublin, Aaron Rhames, 1710) also expressed as 'esse est percipi'.

The paradoxical idea of the individual as a non-sex-specific type of human is a critical and continuing problem for criminal law because men's specific propensity to offend, to behave in anti-social ways, the sort of ways which create a need for a social contract, are not inspected as male behaviour. Therefore the central problem of criminal law, the man problem of criminal law, what makes men more criminal than women, why they (men) may need regulating in certain male-specific ways, is not inspected.

We need to look at the big picture, criminal law and justice conceived as a whole. Official concerns about male behaviour in relation to women have tended to be confined to certain laws. This is not enough. There has been a failure to perceive the broad effects of masculinist preconceptions on the production of the criminal legal world. And this can be difficult to see and to realise.

IX. Maintaining Moral Coherence and Avoiding Cognitive Dissonance

As we saw in Chapter 8, cognitive dissonance – the holding of incompatible principles and positions, and the mental unease it creates – is generally avoided and people look for good in what they think and do. It seems likely that the influential men of law now believe that their discipline has become neutral and equal, and perhaps that this was always so, in most respects which matter: that the discipline always protected equally the bodily integrity of men and women, even though the legal powers of men were greater than the legal powers of women. This benign view of criminal law would certainly reconcile internal tensions in criminal legal thought, especially the stated commitment to the personal security of all in the knowledge that criminal law has operated with major exemptions from this principle.

As the bioethicist Carolyn McLeod has observed, 'psychological disunity' is the unpleasant fate of those who violate their deepest moral commitments, who feel that they lack moral coherence.[54] But she observes also that the powerful are better placed to sustain their sense of coherence, even when their values clash, because their self-justifications and rationalisations can draw upon prevailing social norms which they themselves have developed and from which they benefit.[55] This would seem to describe precisely the mindset of the men of law made possible by their almost complete dominance of the legal point of view.

---

[54] Carolyn McLeod, 'Taking a Feminist Relational Perspective on Conscience' in Jocelyn Downie and Jennifer Llewellyn (eds), *Being Relational* (Vancouver, Toronto, UBC Press, 2012) 163.

[55] See Peggy McIntosh on the invisible benefits of whiteness in, 'The Invisible Knapsack of privilege' discussed in Grayson Perry, *The Descent of Man*, above n 1. Perry himself describes the invisible benefits of maleness.

Another way that the men of law have maintained moral coherence has been to see the story of male right and female non-right as a story of benign progress and of steady change: of modernisation; bringing laws up to date; making them more civilised (see Chapter 6). In the case of the serious offences against the person, for example, the prevailing idea is that they have steadily become more inclusive; that there have been strong and sustained efforts to produce fairer laws for men and women; that there has been a concerted effort to develop principles of responsibility which will make the laws work better in the sense that they will bring offenders to justice. The official tale is one of 'reform', of progress, a steady trajectory of improvement, as the social roles of men and women have changed. Indeed the term 'reform' which is typically used to refer to legal change could simply mean re-form but now tends to carry the connotation of improvement.

We have observed a general legal tendency to think of social and legal change (at the perceived centre of criminal law, as opposed to the new expanding boundaries or edges)[56] as linear and progressive, especially when the account of change has been given from the point of view of those who claim responsibility for that change. But often legal change is not reform but simply change. The story of change, and whether it is seen as good or bad, as more or less conducive to justice, will depend on a number of things. Where one starts the story is critical; from whose point of view it is told; what is to count as success and failure within this story; what is progress and regression; what is to be omitted and deleted (it cannot be comprehensive); how editing and editorialisation occurs; what will be the underlying or even explicit moral assumptions. If it is taken to be progress, then one needs a standard by which to judge the movement as progress, as better not worse. So how do we disrupt this story of benign progress and take a closer, more critical, view of the whole edifice?

X. Willingness to Attack One's Own Convictions

The counsel of Thomas Nagel for the analyst who wishes to be more self-critical and so more 'objective' is for that analyst to attend to the set of convictions and understandings that they are bringing to their perception, their understanding, of a problem or object, and to include it as one of the objects of understanding. To Nagel

> we can raise our understanding to a new level only if we examine that relation between the world and ourselves which is responsible for our prior understanding, and form

---

[56] There is perhaps a directly contrasting criminal legal literature. There is the story of progress in rape law and homicide law, particularly as they relate to efforts to equalise the treatment of the sexes, and there is a story of regression, and loss of principle, at the so-called boundaries of criminal law. For example the literature on anti-terrorism legislation and on anti-social behaviour orders is highly critical of the expansion of criminal law.

a new conception that includes a more detached understanding of ourselves, of the world, and of the interaction between them.[57]

This self-assessment, says Nagel, 'requires a habitual readiness to attack one's own convictions'.[58] According to Nagel, 'To acquire a more objective understanding of some aspect of life or the world, we step back from our initial view of it and form a new conception which has that view and its relation to the world as its object'.[59]

Men qua men, as the subjects and objects of criminal law, need to make themselves present and visible and then to examine their sex as a subset of the entire population, a little less than half, one with a set of historical and modern sectional interests. And this includes the experts themselves and their interests and their world view and their genealogy. For this, men need to become aware of the need for such self-analysis – for both a stepping back, from their initial working assumptions, and then a coming forward, as men, as the subjects and objects of knowledge. Men remain remarkably under-defined and un-visualised in criminal law analysis. Positive intellectual effort is required to bring them into view and indeed to want to bring them into view: to think that such an effort is intellectually and morally important.

As John Tosh has said in an essay posing the question 'What Should Historians do with Masculinity?':

> [A] crucial feature of masculinity in most societies that we know about, and certainly modern Western ones [is] … its relative invisibility … Masculinity remained largely out of sight since men as a sex were not confined in this or any other way: as Rousseau bluntly put it, 'The male is only a male at times; the female is a female all her life and can never forget her sex'. … A profound dualism in Western thought has sought to keep the spotlight away from men. In the historical record it is as though masculinity is everywhere but nowhere.[60]

Or as Grayson Perry has recently said of 'default man', his term for the white middle class man of easy power, he is difficult to see because he does not have what is normally thought of as a particular conspicuous identity:

> When we talk of identity, we often think of groups such as black Muslim lesbians in wheelchairs. This is because identity only seems to become an issue when it is challenged or under threat. Our classic Default Man is rarely under existential threat; consequently, his identity remains unexamined. It ambles along blithely, never having to stand up for its rights or to defend its homeland.[61]

---

[57] Thomas Nagel, *The View From Nowhere* (New York, Oxford University Press, 1986) 5.

[58] Ibid 9.

[59] Ibid 4.

[60] John Tosh, 'Essays: What Should Historians do with Masculinity? Reflections on Nineteenth-century Britain' (1994) 38 *History Workshop* 179, 180.

[61] Grayson Perry, 'The rise and fall of Default Man: How did the straight, white, middle-class Default Man take control of our society – and how can he be dethroned?' *The New Statesman* (London 8 October 2014) www.newstatesman.com/culture/2014/10/grayson-perry-rise-and-fall-default-man.

Thus: 'It is difficult to tweezer out the effect of Default Man on our culture, so ingrained is it after centuries of their rules'.[62] Or as Tosh has put it, despite 'the incontrovertible fact of men's social power', 'men have seldom advertised the ways in which authority over women has sustained their sense of themselves as men'.[63]

This book has made a start. It has treated the men of law as members of a culture: the culture of men of power and influence.[64] It has treated men as a specific grouping, with a very particular sex and class demography, a common set of understandings and interests, and such a firm grip on legal power that they have been poorly placed to appreciate the legal operations of those interests and their deleterious effects on the coherence of their principles.[65]

XI. Going Further: Effecting Fundamental Change; Kuhn and the Paradigm Shift

In his influential treatise, *The Structure of Scientific Revolutions*, Thomas Kuhn explained how members of a scientific community, who represent a community of common thinking, rely on shared but tacit conventions, assumptions and beliefs which serve to reinforce their thinking and preserve it. He also observed the great investment in prevailing belief systems and resistance to change and suppression of anomalies – things which show up contradictions and inconsistencies in the system.

To Kuhn, 'Normal science ... often suppresses fundamental novelties [or one could say anomalies] because they are necessarily subversive of its basic commitments'.[66] There can be heavy investments in existing ways of thinking. But 'when ... the profession can no longer evade anomalies that subvert the existing tradition of scientific practice – then begin the extraordinary investigations that lead the profession at last to a new set of commitments'. These 'extraordinary episodes in which that shift of professional commitments occurs are the ones known ... as scientific revolutions. They are the tradition-shattering complements to the tradition-bound activity of normal science'.[67]

Here Kuhn explains the characteristics of a paradigm shift within 'the profession', referring to the scientific profession. Kuhn's paradigm shift entails a thorough change of thought: a rethinking of the foundational propositions. The whole edifice of thought falls down and there is a new start. What was thought before, with all its

---

[62] Ibid.
[63] Tosh, above n 60 at 184.
[64] See Tosh, above n 60 and in *Manliness and Masculinities in Nineteenth-Century Britain: Essays on Family, Gender and Empire* (Harlow, Pearson Education, 2005).
[65] See Ngaire Naffine, 'Postema's Persons' (2016) 8 *Jurisprudence* 588.
[66] Thomas S Kuhn, *The Structure of Scientific Revolutions*, 2nd edn (Chigaco, University of Chicago Press, 1970) 5.
[67] Ibid 6.

interconnecting set of beliefs, is no longer thought. But this requires a shift in 'the network of theory through which it deals with the world'.[68]

Kuhn was writing explicitly about the paradigms of the hard sciences, not those of the humanities and social sciences, which he conceded to have competing communities of thought, and he was not writing about legal ways of thought. He was also writing about the emergence of anomalies which are so profound that the rest of the system of thought, its underlying theories, premises and assumptions, can no longer be sustained. They can no longer be dismissed or ignored as an acceptable degree of error. The system of thought is thus thrown into crisis. And so, the entire system of thought must change and a new scientific explanation formed.

We have yet to observe such a Kuhnian paradigm shift in criminal law and its interpretation. Solutions to the man problem have been sought in piecemeal ways. Failures of the system have been treated as correctible anomalies. Or to borrow the words of Hart: We have not seen 'whole ways of thinking and talking which constitute our present conceptual apparatus, through which we see the world and each other ... lapse'.[69] And yet, to invoke the philosopher Susanne Langer, 'the generative ideas of the seventeenth century ... have served their term. The difficulties inherent in their constitutive concepts balk us now: their paradoxes clog our thinking'.[70]

---

[68] Ibid 7.

[69] HLA Hart, 'Positivism and the Separation of Law and Morals' (1958) 71 *Harvard Law Review* 593, 622.

[70] Susanne K Langer, *Philosophy in a New Key: A Study in the Symbolism of Reason, Rite, and Art*, 3rd edn (Cambridge, Harvard University Press, 1956) 13 and discussed in Mary Warnock (ed), *Women Philosophers* (London, Everyman JM Dent, 1996) 119. Remembering that Hale was a man of the seventeenth century.

Recapitulation

Stated simply, this has been a study of the defects of reasoning of some of the most influential men of criminal law, over generations, over centuries, enabled and sustained by their possession of an almost total monopoly of legal, political, social and economic power, and the effects of that flawed reasoning on the moral and intellectual integrity of the discipline as a whole. My claims have been several.

First, that men have been the only real subjects of concern to criminal law; that men have also been conflated with the entire population of persons of interest. The persons of criminal law, around whom rights and duties have clustered, have been thought of as men.

Second, that although men have been the sex of concern to criminal law, they have not been thought of as a sex, as one of two sexes, as slightly less than half the population. The men of criminal legal influence have had men as their real subjects of concern, but have not thought of their sex as possessing distinctive, differentiating and limiting features. Therefore they have not thought about what makes men men, for criminal legal purposes. For men have been thought of as persons, not as a sex.

Third, that this has created a discipline essentially concerned with one specific sex but without a specific subject or character because men have not been seen as a specific class of persons. Instead they have been seen as the general case. The rights and duties considered essential to a criminal legal person have been those considered necessary to men, albeit different types of men, as men, all called persons, but not understood as a sex.

Fourth, that because women have not been the persons in contemplation of criminal law, it has been acceptable, even normal law, to suspend some of their most fundamental rights as criminal legal subjects. What has been necessary to a male person – firm personal border control and self-sovereignty – has not been required in a woman. And so the removal of women's criminal legal rights by criminal law has not generated concerns for the discipline as a principled institution. Criminal law has played a major role in the unpersonning of women but that unpersonning has not been seen as a basic departure from criminal legal principle.

Fifth, that male interest in the unpersonning of women – the removal of basic criminal legal rights from women, and the neutralisation of their basic protections and the lifting of men's criminal legal obligations – has not been acknowledged by men of legal influence, because women have been seen as the wrong kinds of beings for such personating rights. Not all men of law saw it this way. But some of the most important men of influence did see it this way and they steered and guided the law.

Sixth, that the systematic uses of women by men, aided and counselled by criminal law, have therefore not been acknowledged as systematic in their nature. And correlatively that the brutalisation of men, by those permitted uses of another, has not been acknowledged.

Seventh, that we have therefore been left with a legal discipline without a specific subject or character, because of the *silent* specification of being male as the primary condition of subjecthood, and we have also a vast population, the unpersonned, removed as subjects from that discipline, placed beyond consideration.

Much of what has been going on in criminal law has been unspecified and thus unacknowledged. And yet it has been deeply undermining of the basic claims of the discipline. Foundational assumptions about who is and is not a person have been critical to the entire thinking of the discipline but unarticulated and hence unconsidered. The capacity of men of criminal legal influence to think clearly, critically and usefully about their subjects has therefore been impaired.

This book has endeavoured to expose and explain the inconsistency, incoherence, incompatibility (of ideas) of the thinking of the men of law, their bias and subjectivity (rather than objectivity); the promotion of their own interests while regarding themselves as fair minded; the removal of rights from non-men while asserting that the stripping of rights was in the interests of the non-men; the failure to see this promotion of their own interests; and the invention of the complementary interests of the non-men; the suppression of dissent and hence the generation of an appearance of consensus; the failure to apply good reasoning to their own subject and purpose – to devise rules of conduct for a fair and safe society in the light of what is known about the nature and patterns of conduct of its subjects.

Again, this is not to deny the existence of enlightened and reflective men of law. They have not been forgotten in this book. Throughout there have been sceptical men. There was the legal scholar Edward Christian on William Blackstone; the political theorist John Stuart Mill who provoked James Fitzjames Stephen into writing; there was the criminologist Gilbert Geis on Hale and the social historian John Tosh on the social costs of masculinity. There is the artist and public intellectual Grayson Perry, continuing to speak to a general audience on the social deficiencies of 'default man'. The story continues to unfold.

BIBLIOGRAPHY

Primary Sources

Case Law

Collins v Wilcock [1984] 3 All ER 374, [1984] 1 WLR 1172
DPP v Morgan [1975] UKHL 3, [1976] AC 182
G v G [1924] AC 349
Kaslefsky v Kaslefsky [1950] 2 All ER 398, [1951] P 38
Lindsay v The Queen [2015] HCA 16, (2015) 255 CLR 272
Pallante v Stadiums Pty Ltd [1976] VR 331
PGA v The Queen [2011] HCA Trans 267 (27 September 2011)
PGA v The Queen [2012] HCA 21, 245 CLR 355
Polyukhovich v Commonwealth [1991] HCA 32, (1991) 172 CLR 501
R v Clarence (1888) 22 QBD 23
R v Coney (1882) 8 QBD 534
R v David Norman Johns, Supreme Court of South Australia, No SCCRM/91/452, 26 August 1992
R v Donovan [1934] 2 KB 498
R v Miller [1954] 2 QB 282
R v L [1991] HCA 48, (1991) 174 CLR 379
R v P, GA [2010] SASCFC 81, (2010) 109 SASR 1
R v R [1991] 2 WLR 1065, [1992] 1 AC 599
S v HM Advocate [1989] SLT 469
SW and CR v UK (1996) 21 EHRR 363
Wright v Cedzich [1930] HCA 4, (1930) 43 CLR 493

Legislation and Bills

Abortion Act 1967 (UK)
Anti-Social Behaviour, Crime and Policing Act 2014 (UK)
Coroners and Justice Act 2009 (UK)
Crimes Act 1961 (NZ)
Criminal Justice Act 1925 (UK)
Criminal Justice and Public Order Act 1994 (UK)
Criminal Law Consolidation 1935 Act (SA)
Human Trafficking and Exploitation (Further Provisions and Support for Victims) Bill 2013 (NIA)
Irish Constitution Act 1983
Married Women's Property Act 1882 (UK)
Offences Against the Person Act 1861 (UK)
Policing and Crime Act 2009 (UK)
Serious Crime Act 2015
Sexual Offences Act 2003 (UK)
Street Offences Act 1959 (UK)

Secondary Sources

Abbott, Mary, *Family Affairs: A History of the Family in Twentieth Century England* (London, Routledge, 2003)

Abel, Richard L, *Politics by Other Means: Law in the Struggle against Apartheid, 1980–1994* (New York, Routledge, 1995)

Amaya, A, *The Tapestry of Reason* (Oxford, Hart, 2015)

Arnheim, Rudolph, *Art and Visual Perception: A Psychology of the Creative Eye* (Berkeley, University of California Press, 1974 ed)

Ashworth, Andrew, *Principles of Criminal Law*, 4th edn (Oxford, Oxford University Press, 2003)

Ashworth, Andrew and Jeremy Horder, *Principles of Criminal Law* (Oxford, Oxford University Press, 2013)

Attwood, Margaret, *The Handmaid's Tale* (New York, Anchor Books, 1998)

Beard, Mary, *Women and Power: A Manifesto* (Profile Books, London, 2017)

Bell, Clive, *Civilization* (London, Chatto and Windus, 1928)

Bentham, Jeremy, 'Principles of the Civil Code' in Bowring, J (ed), *The Works of Jeremy Bentham, vol 1* (Edinburgh, William Tait, 1843)

—— 'A Comment on the Commentaries and a Fragment on Government' in Burns, JH and Hart, HLA and Schofield, Philip (eds), (Oxford, Clarendon Press, 1977)

Berkeley, George, *A Treatise Concerning the Principles of Human Knowledge* (Dublin, Aaron Rhames, 1710)

Bibbings, Lois S, *Telling Tales about Men: Conceptions of Conscientious Objectors to Military Service during the First World War* (Manchester, Manchester University Press, 2009)

—— *Binding Men: Stories about Violence and Law in Late Victorian England* (Abingdon, Routledge, 2014)

Bishop, Charlotte, 'Why it's so Hard to Prosecute Cases of Coercive or Controlling Behaviour' *The Conversation* (31 October 2016), theconversation.com/why-its-so-hard-to-prosecute-cases-of-coercive-or-controlling-behaviour-66108

Blackstone, William, *Commentaries on the Laws of England, Book 1: 'The Rights of Persons'*, 14th edn (London, Cadell and Davies, 1803)

—— *Commentaries on the Laws of England, vol 3*, 17th edn (1830)

Booth, William and Isaac Stanley-Becker, 'Ireland Votes to Overturn Its Abortion Ban, "Culmination of Quiet Revolution", Prime Minister Says' *Washington Post* (Washington, 26 May 2018), www.washingtonpost.com/world/europe/ireland-votes-to-repeal-its-ban-on-abortion/2018/05/26/fb675fa8-603b-11e8-b656-236c6214ef01_story.html?utm_term=.64898b000399

Brett, P, Waller, L and Williams, CR, *Criminal Law: Text and Cases*, 6th edn (Sydney, Butterworths, 1989)

Brochmann, Nina and Dahl, Elen Stokken, *The Woman Down Under: A User's Guide to the Vagina* (Great Britain, Yellow Kite, 2018)

Bronitt, Simon, 'Rape and Lack of Consent' (1992) 16 *Criminal Law Journal* 289

Burton, M, 'Intimate Homicide and the Provocation Defence – endangering women? R v Smith' (2001) 9 *Feminist Legal Studies* 247

Cane, Peter, 'The General/Special Distinction in Criminal Law, Tort Law and Legal Theory' (2007) 26 *Law and Philosophy* 465

Carey, John, *The Intellectuals and the Masses: Pride and Prejudice Among the Literary Intelligensia, 1880–1939* (Academy, Chicago, 1992)

Carr, EH, *What is History?* (New York, Random House, 1961)

Chalmers, James and Leverick, Fiona 'Fair Labelling in Criminal Law' (2008) 71 *Modern Law Review* 217

Chrisafis, Angelique, 'France plans on-the-spot-fines for sexual harassment in public places' *The Guardian* (21 March 2018), www.theguardian.com/world/2018/mar/21/france-plans-on-the-spot-fines-for-sexual-harassment-in-public

Christman, John, 'Self-Ownership, Equality and the Structure of Property Rights' (1991) 19 *Political Theory* 28

Cohen, Gerald, 'Self-Ownership, World-Ownership, and Equality' in Lucash, F (ed), *Justice and Equality Here and Now* (Ithaca, New York, Cornell University Press, 1986)

Collier, Richard, *Masculinity, Law and the Family* (London, Routledge, 1995)

—— *Masculinities, Crime and Criminology* (London, SAGE, 1998)

—— 'Masculinities, Law and Personal Life: Towards a New Framework for Understanding Men, Law, and Gender' (2010) 33 *Harvard Journal of Law and Gender* 431

—— 'Review of Lois S Bibbings: Binding Men: Stories About Violence and Law in Late Victorian England' (2015) 42 *Journal of Law and Society* 664

Columbia Law Review Association, 'The Effect of Marriage on the Rules of the Criminal Law' (1961) 61 *Columbia Law Review* 73

Conaghan, Joanne, *Law and Gender* (Oxford, Oxford University Press, 2013)

Coombs, Mary Irene, 'Crime in the Stacks, or a Tale of a Text: A Feminist Response to a Criminal Law Textbook' (1988) 38 *Journal of Legal Education* 117

Council of Legal Education, The *A Century of Law Reform: Twelve Lectures on the Changes in the Law of England During the Nineteenth Century Delivered at the Request of the Council of Legal Education* (London, Macmillan and Co., 1901)

Cowan, Sharon, 'In Search of Connections: Reading between the Lines of Nicola Lacey's In Search of Criminal Responsibility' (2017) 4 *Critical Analysis of Law* 211

Crabbe, Annabel, *The Wife Drought* (Sydney, Ebury Press, 2014)

Criminal Law and Penal Methods Reform Committee of South Australia, 'Special Report: rape and other sexual offences' (1976)

Criminal Law Revision Committee, 15th Report, 'Sexual Offences' (London, HMSO, 1984)

Darnton, Robert, *The Great Cat Massacre and Other Episodes in French Cultural History* (New York, Vintage Books, 1985)

Davenport-Hines, Richard, *Sex, Death and Punishment: Attitudes to Sex and Sexuality in Britain* (London, Collins, 1990)

Davies, Caroline, 'PM's Apology to Codebreaker Alan Turing' *The Guardian* (London 11 September 2009), www.theguardian.com/world/2009/sep/11/pm-apology-to-alan-turing

Davies, Lizzy, 'Julia Gillard speech prompts dictionary to change "misogyny" definition' *The Guardian: Australian Edition* (Sydney 18 October 2012), www.theguardian.com/world/2012/oct/17/julia-gillard-australia-misogyny-dictionary

Davies, Margaret, 'Feminist Appropriations: Law, Property and Personality' (1994) 3 *Social and Legal Studies* 365

—— *Property: Meanings, Histories, Theories* (Oxford, Routledge-Cavendish, 2007)

—— *Law Unlimited: Materialism, Pluralism and Legal Theory* (Oxford, Routledge, 2017)

—— *Asking the Law Question*, 4th edn (Pyrmont, Thomson Reuters, 2017)

Deutsch, H, *The Psychology of Women*, 2 vols (New York, Grune & Stratton, 1944–1945)

Donne, John, *Meditation XVII from Devotions upon Emergent Occasions* (1623)

Duff, RA, *Intention, Agency and Criminal Liability* (Oxford, Basil Blackwell, 1990)

—— *Punishment, Communication and Community* (Oxford, Oxford University Press, 2001)

—— *Answering for Crime: Responsibility and Liability in the Criminal Law* (Oxford, Hart, 2007)

Dworkin, Ronald, *Law's Empire* (Cambridge, Harvard University Press, 1986)

Dyer, Clare, 'The Guardian Profile: Lady Brenda Hale' *The Guardian* (London 10 January 2004), www.theguardian.com/uk/2004/jan/09/lords.women

East, Edward Hyde, *Treatise of the Pleas of the Crown, vol 1* (London, A Strahan, 1803)

Elias, Norbert, *The Civilizing Process: Sociogenetic and Psychogenetic Investigations*, trans Jephcott, Edmund, revised edn edited by Dunning, Eric, Goudsblom, Johan and Mennell, Stephen (Blackwell, Oxford, 2000)

Elliott, Terri, 'Making Strange What Had Appeared Familiar' (1994) 77 *Monist* 424

Erwin, JS, 'Husband and Wife in Criminal Law' (1885) vol xvii, 3 *The Criminal Law Magazine and Reporter* 269

Evans, Richard, 'On Her Majesty's Scholarly Service' 7 February 2013, *Times Higher Education*

Farmer, Lindsay, 'The Modest Ambition of Glanville Williams' in Dubber, Markus, (ed), *Foundational Texts in Modern Criminal Law* (Oxford, Oxford University Press, 2014)

—— *Making the Modern Criminal Law: Criminalization and Civil Order* (Oxford, Oxford University Press, 2016)

—— 'DPP v Morgan', in Mares, Henry, Handler, Phil and Williams, Ian, (eds), *Landmark Cases in Criminal Law* (Oxford, Hart, 2017)

Feinberg, Joel, *The Moral Limits of Criminal Law: Volume 1 Harm to Others* (Oxford, Oxford University Press, 1984)

Festinger, Leon, *Theory of Cognitive Dissonance* (Stanford, Stanford University Press, 1962)

Fine, Cordelia, *Delusions of Gender: How Our Minds, Society and Neurosexism Create Difference* (New York, London, WW Norton & Company, 2010)

Fisse, Brent, *Howard's Criminal Law*, 5th edn (Sydney, Law Book Co, 1990)

Fitz-Gibbon, Kate and Pickering, Sharon 'Homicide Law Reform in Victoria, Australia: From Provocation to Defensive Homicide and Beyond' (2012) 52 *The British Journal of Criminology* 159

Fletcher, George, *Rethinking Criminal Law* (Boston, Little, Brown, 1978)

Foreign Staff, 'Abortion around world: The countries with most restrictive laws and why debate is back in spotlight' *The Telegraph* (London 23 May 2018), www.telegraph.co.uk/news/2018/05/23/abortion-around-world-countries-restrictive-laws-debate-back/

Freeman, Michael, '"But If You Can't Rape Your Wife, Who[m] Can You Rape?": The Marital Rape Exemption Re-examined' (1981) 15 *Family Law Quarterly* 1

Fricker, Mirander, *Epistemic Injustice: Power and the Ethics of Knowing* (Oxford, Oxford University Press, 2007)

Frow, John, 'Elvis' Fame: The Commodity Form and the Form of the Person' (1995) 7 *Cardozo Studies in Law and Literature* 131

Frug, MJ, 'A Postmodern Feminist Legal Manifesto' (1992) 105 *Harvard Law Review* 1045

Fuller, Lon L, *Legal Fictions* (Stanford University Press, 1968)

Galsworthy, John, *The Forsyte Saga: The Man of Property* (William Heinemann, 1906)

—— *The Man of Property* (London, William Heinemann, 1953)

Gardner, John, 'The Opposite of Rape' (2018) 38 *Oxford Journal of Legal Studies* 48

Gardner, John and Shute, Stephen, 'The Wrongness of Rape' in Horder, J, (ed), *Oxford Essays in Jurisprudence* (Oxford, Oxford University Press, 2000)

Geis, Gilbert, 'Lord Hale, Witches and Rape' (1978) 5 *British Journal of Law and Society* 26

Geis, Gilbert and Bunn, Ivan, *A Trial of Witches: A Seventeenth-Century Witchcraft Prosecution* (London and New York, Routledge, 1997)

Gilliard, Julia, 'Transcript of Julia Gillard's speech' *Sydney Morning Herald* (Sydney 10 October 2012), www.smh.com.au/politics/federal/transcript-of-julia-gillards-speech-20121010-27c36.html

Gilligan, Carol, *In a Different Voice: Psychological Theory and Women's Development* (Cambridge, Harvard University Press, 1982)

Gismondi, Melissa J, 'Why are "incels" so angry? The History of the Little Known Ideology Behind the Toronto Killings' *Washington Post* (Washington 27 April 2018), www.washingtonpost.com/news/made-by-history/wp/2018/04/27/why-are-incels-so-angry-the-history-of-the-little-known-ideology-behind-the-toronto-attack/?utm_term=.adffe3d6e411

Gleeson, Kate, 'Brutal at his Best, the Problem of Clarence: James Fitzjames Stephen and the Doctrine of Sexual Inequality' (2005) 14 *Nottingham Law Journal* 1

Goleman, Daniel, *Focus: The Hidden Driver of Excellence* (London, Bloomsbury, 2013)

Gombrich, Ernst, *Art and Illusion: A Study in the Psychology of Pictorial Representation*, 5th edn (Oxford, Phaidon Press, 1977)

Grant, Melissa Gira, *Playing the Whore: The Work of Sex Work* (London, Verso, 2014)

Gray, Kevin, 'Property in Thin Air' (1991) 50 *Cambridge Law Journal* 252

Gray, Kevin and Symes, PD, *Real Property and Real People: Principles of Land Law* (London, Butterworths, 1981)

Great Britain Home Office, 'Report of the Advisory Group on the Law of Rape' (Cmnd No 6352, 1975)

Hale, Sir Matthew, *The History of the Pleas of the Crown, vol 1* (1736)
—— *Historia Placitorum Coronae, vol 1* (London, Professional Books, 1971)
Harding, Sandra, *Whose Science? Whose Knowledge?* (Ithaca, New York, Cornell University Press, 1991)
Hart, HLA, 'Positivism and the Separation of Law from Morals' (1958) 71 *Harvard Law Review* 607
—— *Punishment and Responsibility* (Oxford, Clarendon Press, 1968)
Hartsock, Nancy, 'The Feminist Standpoint: Developing the Ground for a Specifically Feminist Historical Materialism' in Harding, Sandra and Hintikka, Merrill B, (eds), *Discovering Reality* (Dordrecht, D Reidel, 1983)
Hasday, Jill Elaine, 'Contest and Consent: A Legal History of Marital Rape' (2000) 88 *California Law Review* 1373
Heath, Mary and Larcombe, Wendy (as High Court justices), 'PGA v The Queen' in Douglas, Heather, Bartlett, Francesca, Luker, Trish and Hunter, Rosemary, (eds), *Australian Feminist Judgments: Righting and Re-writing Law* (Oxford, Hart Publishing, 2014)
Heuser, Alan, (ed), *Selected Literary Criticism of Louis MacNeice* (Oxford, Oxford University Press, 1987)
Hodgson, Geoffrey, 'Meanings of Methodological Individualism' (2007) 14 *Journal of Economic Methodology* 211
Hohfeld, WN, 'Some Fundamental Legal Conceptions as Applied in Judicial Reasoning' (1913) 23 *Yale Law Journal* 16
—— 'Fundamental Legal Conceptions as Applied in Judicial Reasoning' (1917) 26 *Yale Law Journal* 710
Hohfeld, WN, Cook, Walter Wheeler, (ed), *Fundamental Legal Conceptions as Applied in Judicial Reasoning, and Other Legal Essays* (New Haven, Yale University Press, 1934)
Home Office, 'Coercive or Controlling Behaviour in an Intimate or Family Relationship: Statutory Guidance Framework' (December 2015)
Honoré, Tony, *Sex Law* (London, Duckworth, 1978)
Howard, Colin, *Australian Criminal Law* (Melbourne, The Law Book Company, 1965)
—— *Criminal Law*, 3rd edn (Sydney, Law Book Co, 1977)
—— *Australian Criminal Law*, 4th edn (Law Book Co, 1982)
Howe, A, 'Green v The Queen – The Provocation Defence: Finally Provoking its Own Demise' (1998) 22 *Melbourne University Law Review* 466
'Inquiry into Prostitution', Final Report (Victoria, 1985)
Jacobs, Ben, '"Of course he said it": Billy Bush counters Trump's pussy tape claims' *The Guardian* (Washington 4 December 2017), www.theguardian.com/us-news/2017/dec/04/of-course-he-said-it-billy-bush-counters-trumps-pussy-tape-claims
James, Henry, 'Woman and the Woman's Movement' (1853) 1 *Putnam's Monthly* 285
Kahan, Dan and Braman, Donald, 'The Self-Defence Cognition of Self Defence' (2008) 45 *American Criminal Law Review* 1
Kahan, Dan M, Hoffman, David A, Braman, Donald, Evans, Danieli and Rachlinski, Jeffrey J, '"They Saw a Protest": Cognitive Illiberalism and the Speech-Conduct Distinction' (2012) 64 *Stanford Law Review* 851
Kant, Immanuel, *The Metaphysics of Morals* (Cambridge, Cambridge University Press, 1991)
Keatings, Peter, *Into Unknown England, 1866–1913, Selections from the Social Explorers* (Glasgow, Fontana/Collins, 1976)
Khomami, Nadia, '#MeToo: how a hashtag became a rallying cry against sexual harassment' *The Guardian* (London 21 October 2017), www.theguardian.com/world/2017/oct/20/women-worldwide-use-hashtag-metoo-against-sexual-harassment
Kraus, Michael, Cote, Stephane and Keltner, Dacher, 'Social Class, Contextualism and Empathic Accuracy' (2010) 21 *Psychological Science* 1716
Kuhn, Thomas S, *The Structure of Scientific Revolutions*, 2nd edn (Chigaco, University of Chicago Press, 1970)
Kynaston, David, *Family Britain 1951–57* (London, Bloomsbury, 2009)

Lacey, Nicola, 'General Principles of Criminal Law: A Feminist Perspective' in Nicolson, Donald and Bibbings, Lois, (eds), *Feminist Perspectives on Criminal Law* (London, Routledge-Cavendish, 2000)
—— *Women, Crime and Character: From Moll Flanders to Tess of the d'Urbervilles* (Oxford, Oxford University Press, 2008)
—— *In Search of Criminal Responsibility* (Oxford, Oxford University Press, 2016)
Langer, Susanne K, *Philosophy in a New Key: A Study in the Symbolism of Reason, Rite, and Art* (Cambridge, Harvard University Press, 1956, 3rd ed)
Larcombe, Wendy and Heath, Mary, 'Case Note: Developing the Common Law and Rewriting the History of Rape in Marriage in Australia: PGA v The Queen' (2012) 34 *Sydney Law Review* 599
Law Commission, 'Criminal Law: Rape Within Marriage', Law Com No 205 (London, HMSO, 1992)
Leader-Elliott, Ian, 'A Critical Reading of Duff Answering for Crime' (2010) 31 Adelaide Law Review 47
—— 'The "Subjectivist Bug" in Australian Criminal Law, 1937–1965: A History and Epilogue' paper delivered to the University of South Australia (2016)
Lee, Robert G and Morgan, Derek, 'Regulating Risk Society: Stigmata Cases, Scientific Citizenship and Biomedical Diplomacy' (2001) 23 *Sydney Law Review* 297
Lesses, Kos, 'PGA v The Queen: Marital Rape in Australia: The Role of Repetition' (2014) 37 *Melbourne University Law Review* 786
Levine, Philippa, *Prostitution, Race and Politics: Policing Venereal Disease in the British Empire* (New York & London, Routledge, 2003)
Locke, John, *An Essay Concerning Human Understanding*, Yolton, John (ed) (London, JM Dent & Sons, 1991)
Lotto, Beau, *Deviate: The Science of Seeing Differently* (Great Britain, Weidenfeld & Nicholson, 2017)
Lucke, Horst, 'Good Faith and Contractual Performance' in Finn, PD, (ed), *Essays on Contract* (Sydney, Law Book Co, 1987)
Lukes, Steven, 'Methodological Individualism Reconsidered' (1969) 19 *British Journal of Sociology* 119
—— *Individualism* (Oxford, Basil Blackwell, 1973)
Lush, Montague, 'Changes in the law affecting the rights, status, and liabilities of married women' in *The Council of Legal Education, A Century of Law Reform: Twelve Lectures on the Changes in the Law of England During the Nineteenth Century Delivered at the Request of the Council of Legal Education* (London, Macmillan and Co, 1901)
McCutcheon, Paul J, 'Sports Violence, Consent and the Criminal Law' (1994) 45 *Northern Ireland Legal Quarterly* 267
McGilchrist, Iain, *The Master and his Emissary: The Divided Brain and the Making of the Western World* (New Haven, Yale University Press, 2009)
McLeod, Carolyn, 'Taking a Feminist Relational Perspective on Conscience' in Downie, Jocelyn and Llewellyn, Jennifer, (eds), *Being Relational* (Vancouver, Toronto, UBC Press, 2012)
Menand, Louis, *The Metaphysical Club* (London, Flamingo, 2002)
Mill, John Stuart, *Principles of Political Economy*, 2 vols (London, John W Parker, 1848)
—— *On Liberty*, 2nd edn (London, John W Parker and Son, 1859)
—— *Representative Government* (London, Parker, Son and Bourn, 1861)
—— *On Liberty and Other Writings*, Collini, Stephan (ed) (Cambridge, Cambridge University Press, 1989)
—— *The Subjection of Women* in *On Liberty and Other Essays*, Gray, John (ed) (Oxford, Oxford University Press, 1991)
Ministry of Justice, 'Statistics on Women and the Criminal Justice System 2013' (A Ministry of Justice publication under Section 95 of the Criminal Justice Act 1991, 2014)
Minogue, Kenneth, 'The Concept of Property and its Contemporary Significance' in Pennock, R and Chapman, J, (eds), *Nomos XXII: Property* (New York, New York University Press, 1980)
Moore, Michael, 'The Relevance of Philosophy to Law and Psychiatry' (1984) 6 *International Journal of Law and Psychiatry* 177
—— *Placing Blame: A General Theory of the Criminal Law* (Oxford, Oxford University Press, 1987)

Morrill, John, Interview, 'Making History: The Changing Face of the Profession in Britain', The Institute of Historical Research (2008)

Morris, Norval and Turner, AL, 'Two Problems in the Law of Rape' (1954) 2 *University of Queensland Law Journal* 247

Munro, Vanessa E, 'Shifting Sands? Consent, Context and Vulnerability in Contemporary Sexual Offences Policy in England' (2017) 26 *Social and Legal Studies* 417

Naffine, Ngaire, *Law and the Sexes* (Sydney, Allen & Unwin 1990)

—— 'Possession: Erotic Love in the Law of Rape' (1994) 57 *Modern Law Review* 10

—— *Feminism and Criminology* (Polity Press, Cambridge, 1997)

—— 'The Body Bag' in Naffine, Ngaire and Owens, Rosemary J, (eds), *Sexing the Subject of Law* (Sydney, Law Book Co, 1997)

—— 'Who are Law's Persons?: From Cheshire Cats to Responsible Subjects' (2003) 66 *Modern Law Review* 346

—— *Law's Meaning of Life: Philosophy, Religion, Darwin and the Legal Person* (Oxford, Portland, Hart, 2009)

—— 'Women and the Cast of Legal Persons' in Jones, Jackie, Grear, Anna, Fenton, Rachel Anne and Stevenson, Kim, (eds), *Gender, Sexualities and the Law* (Oxford, Routledge, 2011)

—— 'Postema's Persons' (2016) 8 *Jurisprudence* 588

Nagel, Thomas, *The View From Nowhere* (New York, Oxford University Press, 1986)

Neave, Marcia, 'The Failure of Prostitution Law Reform' (1988) 21 *Australian and New Zealand Journal of Criminology* 202

Nedelsky, Jennifer, 'Reconceiving Autonomy: Sources, Thoughts and Possibilities' (1989) 1 *Yale Journal of Law & Feminism* 7

—— 'Law, Boundaries and the Bounded Self' (1990) 30 *Representations* 162

—— *Private Property and the Limits of American Constitutionalism* (Chicago, University of Chicago Press, 1990)

—— *Law's Relations: A Relational Theory of Self Autonomy and Law* (Oxford, Oxford University Press, 2011)

Nietzsche, Friedrich, Kauffman, Walter, (trs), *The Gay Science* (New York, Random House, 1974)

Norrie, Alan, *Crime, Reason and History: A Critical Introduction to Criminal Law*, 3rd edn (Cambridge, Cambridge University Press, 2014)

Nourse, Victoria, 'Passion's Progress: Modern Law Reform and the Provocation Defense' (1997) 106 *Yale Law Journal* 1331

Obama, Barack, 'Full Transcript: President Obama's speech on the 50th anniversary of the March on Washington' *Washington Post* (Washington 28 August 2013), www.washingtonpost.com/politics/transcript-president-obamas-speech-on-the-50th-anniversary-of-the-march-on-washington/2013/08/28/0138e01e-0ffb-11e3-8cdd-bcdc09410972_story.html?noredirect=on&utm_term=.f423606b7402

Odgers, W Blake, 'Changes In The Common Law And In The Law Of Persons, In The Legal Profession And In Legal Education' in *The Council of Legal Education, A Century of Law Reform: Twelve Lectures on the Changes in the Law of England During the Nineteenth Century Delivered at the Request of the Council of Legal Education* (London, Macmillan and Co, 1901)

Olsen, Frances, 'The Family and the Market: A Study of Ideology and Legal Reform' (1983) 96 *Harvard Law Review* 1497

O'Donovan, Katherine, *Sexual Divisions in Law* (London, Weidenfeld & Nicolson, 1986)

—— *Family Law Matters* (London & Boulder, Colorado, Pluto Press, 1993)

—— 'With Sense, Consent, or Just a Con? Legal Subjects in the Discourses of Autonomy' in Naffine, Ngaire and Owens, Rosemary J, (eds), *Sexing the Subject of Law* (North Ryde, Law Book Company, 1997)

Okin, Susan Moller, *Justice, Gender and the Family* (United States of America, Perseus Books Group, 1989)

Orwell, George, *1984* (London, Arcturus Publishing, 2013)

Owens, Rosemary J, 'Working in the Sex Market' in Naffine, Ngaire and Owens, Rosemary J, (eds), *Sexing the Subject of Law* (North Ryde, Law Book Co, 1997)

Palk, Deirdre, *Gender, Crime and Judicial Discretion 1780–1830* (Woodbridge, Royal Historical Society, 2006)

Parker, Kunal, 'Historicising Blackstone's Commentaries on the Laws of England: Difference and Sameness in Historical Time' in Fernandez, Angela and Dubber, Markus, (eds), *Law Books in Action: Essays on the Anglo-American Treatise* (Oxford, Hart, 2012)

Pateman, Carole, *The Sexual Contract* (Stanford, Stanford University Press, 1988)

Perkins, Rollin M, *Perkins on Criminal Law* (Brooklyn, Foundation Press, 1957)

Perkins, Rollin M and Ronald N Boyce, *Criminal Law*, 3rd edn (Mineola, Foundation Press, 1982)

Perry, Grayson, 'The Rise and Fall of Default Man: How did the straight, white, middle-class Default Man take control of our society – and how can he be dethroned?' *New Statesman* (London, 8 October 2014)

—— *The Descent of Man* (Great Britain, Allen Lane, 2016)

Plater, David, Line, Lucy and Fitz-Gibbon, Kate, *The Provoking Operation of Provocation: Stage 1* (South Australian Law Reform Institute, Adelaide, 2017).

Plater, David, Bleby, David, Lawson, Megan, Line, Lucy, Teakle, Amy, O'Connell, Katherine and Fitz-Gibbon, Kate, *The Provoking Operation of Provocation: Stage 2* (South Australian Law Reform Institute, Adelaide, 2018)

'Professor Dicey's Letters on Woman Suffrage' *The Spectator* (London 19 June 1909) <http://archive. spectator.co.uk/article/19th-june-1909/23/professor-diceys-letters-on-woman-suffrage>

Postema, Gerald, *Legal Philosophy in the Twentieth Century: The Common Law World* (London, Springer, 2012)

Prest, Wilfred, 'Blackstone, Sir William' in the *Oxford Dictionary of National Biography* (Oxford University Press, 2004; online edn, October 2009), www.oxforddnb.com/view/article/2536

—— 'Life' in Prest, Wilfrid, (ed), *Blackstone and His Commentaries* (Hart, Oxford, 2009)

Rawls, John, *A Theory of Justice* (Cambridge, Harvard University Press, 1971)

Report of the Advisory Group on the Law of Rape (London, HMSO, 1975)

Report of the Select Committee of the Legislative Assembly upon Prostitution (New South Wales, 1986)

Rheinstein, M, 'Legal Systems' in Sills, David, (ed), *International Encyclopaedia of the Social Sciences, vol IX* (New York, Macmillan-Free Press, 1968)

Richards, Janette Radcliffe, *Human Nature After Darwin: A Philosophical Introduction* (Oxford, Routledge, 2000)

Richards, Louis, 'The Doctrine of Marital Unity in the Modern Criminal Law' (1891) vol xiii, 3 *The Criminal Law Magazine and Reporter* 325

Rosenberg, David, 'Coverture in Criminal Law: Ancient Defender of Married Women' (1973) 6 *University of California, Davis Law Review* 83

Rumsfeld, Donald, *Known and Unknown: A Memoir* (New York, Sentinel, 2011)

Ryan, Rebecca M, 'The Sex Right: A Legal History of the Marital Rape Exemption' (1995) 20 *Law and Social Inquiry* 941

Sachs, Albie and Wilson, Joan Hoff, *Sexism and the Law: A Study of Male Beliefs and Judicial Bias* (Oxford, Martin Robertson, 1978)

Schama, Simon, *The Face of Britain: A History of the Nation Through its Portraits* (New York, Oxford University Press, 2016)

Scheman, Naomi, 'Forms of Life: Mapping the Rough Ground' in Sluga, Hans and Stern, David G, (eds), *The Cambridge Companion to Wittgenstein* (Cambridge, Cambridge University Press, 1996)

Scutt, Jocelynne A, 'Consent in Rape: The Problem of the Marriage Contract' (1977) 3 *Monash University Law Review* 255

Sheldon, Sally, *Beyond Control: Medical Power and Abortion Law* (London, Pluto, 1997)

Shute, Stephen and Simester, AP, (eds), *Criminal Law Theory: Doctrines of the General Part* (Oxford, Oxford University Press, 2002)

Simester, AP and von Hirsch, Andrew, *Crimes, Harms and Wrongs* (Oxford, Hart, 2011)

Simons, Daniel J and Chabris, Christopher F, 'Gorillas in our Midst: Sustained Inattentional Blindness for Dynamic Events' (1999) 28 *Perception* 1059

Singh, Susheela, Remez, Lisa, Sedgh, Gilda, Kwok, Lorraine and Onda, Tsuyoshi, 'Abortion Worldwide 2017 Uneven Progress and Unequal Access' (Guttmacher Institute, 2018)

Sletvold, Richard, 'PGA v The Queen: Do Laws Just Disappear?' (2012) 33 *Adelaide Law Review* 573

Smart, Carol, *The Ties that Bind: Law, Marriage and the Reproduction of Patriarchal Relations* (London, Routledge & Kegan Paul, 1984)

—— *Regulating Womanhood: Historical Essays on Marriage, Motherhood and Sexuality* (London, Routledge, 1992)

Smith, JC and Hogan, Brian, *Criminal Law* (London, Butterworths, 1965)

Smith, KJM, *James Fitzjames Smith: Portrait of a Victorian Rationalist* (Cambridge, Cambridge University Press, 1988)

—— 'Stephen, Sir James Fitzjames, first baronet (1829–1894)' in *Oxford Dictionary of National Biography* (Oxford University Press, 2004; online edn, Jan 2012), www.oxforddnb.com/view/article/26375

Sokol, Mary, *Bentham, Law and Marriage: A Utilitarian Code of Law in Historical Contexts* (London, Bloomsbury, 2013)

—— 'Blackstone and Bentham on the Law of Marriage' in Prest, Wilfrid, (ed), *Blackstone and his Commentaries* (Oxford, Hart, 2014)

Soloman, RC, and Higgins, KM, (eds), *The Philosophy of (Erotic) Love* (United States of America, University Press of Kansas, 1991)

Spencer, JR, 'Glanville Williams Obituary' (1997) 56 *Cambridge Law Journal* 437

Stanton-Ife, John, 'Horrific Crime' in Duff, RA, Farmer, Lindsay, Marshall, SE, Renzo, Massimo and Tadros, Victor, (eds), *The Boundaries of the Criminal Law* (Oxford, Oxford University Press, 2010)

Stark, Evan, *Coercive Control: How Men Entrap Women in Personal Life* (New York, Oxford University Press, 2007)

Stephen, James Fitzjames, *A General View of the Criminal Laws of England* (London, Macmillan and Co, 1863)

—— *Liberty, Equality and Fraternity* (New York, Holt and Williams, 1873)

—— *A Digest of the Criminal Law*, 4th edn (London, Macmillan and Co, 1877)

—— *A History of the Criminal Law of England, 3 vols* (London, Macmillan and Co, 1883)

—— *Liberty, Equality, Fraternity*, Warner, Stuart D, (ed) (Indianapolis, Liberty Fund, 1993)

Stephen, Leslie, *Life of Sir James Fitzjames Stephen* (London, Smith, Elder & Co, 1895)

Storr, Antony, *The Integrity of the Personality* (New York, Atheneum, 1961)

Stretton, Tim, 'Coverture and Unity of Person in Blackstone's Commentaries' in Prest, Wilfrid, (ed), *Blackstone and His Commentaries* (Oxford, Hart, 2009)

Stretton, Tim and Kesselring, Krista, (eds), *Married Women and the Law: Coverture in England and the Common Law World* (London, McGill-Queens University Press, 2013)

Szreter, Simon and Fisher, Kate, *Sex Before the Sexual Revolution: Intimate Life in England 1918–1963* (Cambridge, Cambridge University Press, 2010)

Tadros, Victor, *Criminal Responsibility* (Oxford, Oxford University Press, 2005)

Taysom, AR, Acting Director of the Trade Commissioner Service, internal memo to the Director, entitled 'Women Trade Commissioners?' under the letterhead of the Commonwealth of Australia (see Australian Archives)

Temkin, Jennifer, 'Towards a Modern Law of Rape' (1982) 45 *Modern Law Review* 399

—— 'The Limits of Reckless Rape' (1983) *Criminal Law Review* 5

—— *Rape and the Legal Process* (London, Street & Maxwell, 1987)

—— *Rape and the Legal Process*, 2nd edn (Oxford, Oxford University Press, 2002)

Temkin, Jennifer and Andrew Ashworth, 'The Sexual Offences Act 2003: (1) Rape, Sexual Assault and the Problems of Consent' (2004) *Criminal Law Review* 328

Toole, Kellie, 'Marital Rape: Retrospectivity and the Common Law' (2015) 39 *Criminal Law Journal* 286

Tosh, John, 'Essays: What Should Historians do with Masculinity? Reflections on Nineteenth-century Britain (1994) 38 *History Workshop Journal* 179

Thompson, EP, *The Making of the English Working Class* (New York, Vintage Books, 1963)

Toner, Barbara, *The Facts of Rape* (London, Hutchinson, 1977)

Tosh, Josh, *Manliness and Masculinities in Nineteenth-Century Britain: Essays on Family, Gender and Empire* (Harlow, Pearson Education, 2005)

Tosh, John with Lang, Sean, *The Pursuit of History*, 4th edn (Great Britain, Pearson Education, 2006)

Vaihinger, Hans, *The Philosophy of 'As If'* (London, Kegan Paul, 1924)

van Kleef, Gerben A, et al, 'Power, Distress and Compassion: Turning a Blind Eye to the Suffering of Others' (2008) 19 *Psychological Science* 1315

Victorian Law Reform Commission, 'Defences to Homicide Final Report' (Victorian Law Reform Commission, 2004)

Walkowitz, Judith R and Walkowitz, Daniel J, '"We Are Not Beasts of the Field": Prostitution and the Poor in Plymouth and Southampton under the Contagious Diseases Acts' (1973) 1 *Feminist Studies* 73

Waller, L and Williams, CR, *Criminal Law Text and Cases*, 9th edn (Chatswood, Butterworths, 2001)

Warnock, Mary, (ed), *Women Philosophers* (London, Everyman JM Dent, 1996)

Watt, Holly, 'Former Prostitutes Win Legal Challenge Against UK Government' *The Guardian* (London 2 March 2018), www.theguardian.com/society/2018/mar/02/former-prostitutes-win-legal-challenge-against-uk-government

Weait, Matthew, *Intimacy and Responsibility* (Oxford, Routledge-Cavendish, 2007)

Wells, Celia, 'Swatting the Subjectivist Bug' (1982) *Criminal Law Review* 209

Wells, Celia, and Quick, Oliver, *Lacey, Wells and Quick, Reconstructing Criminal Law: Text and Materials*, 4th edn (Cambridge, Cambridge University Press, 2010)

Wiener, Martin J, *Men of Blood: Violence, Manliness and Criminal Justice in Victorian England* (Cambridge, Cambridge University Press, 2004)

Wilkes, Kathleen V, *Real People: Personal Identity without Thought Experiments* (Oxford, Oxford University Press, 1988)

Williams, Glanville, 'The Legal Unity of Husband and Wife' (1947) 10 *Modern Law Review* 16

—— *Criminal Law: The General Part* (London, Stevens, 1953)

—— *The Sanctity of Life and the Criminal Law* (London, Faber & Faber, 1958)

—— *Textbook of Criminal Law* (London, Stevens & Sons, 1978)

—— *Textbook of Criminal Law*, 2nd edn (London, Stevens and Sons, 1983)

—— 'Rape is Rape' (1992) 142 *New Law Journal* 11

Willsher, Kim, 'Uproar in Paris over Video of Woman Hit by Harasser on Paris Street' *The Guardian* (30 July 2018), www.theguardian.com/world/2018/jul/30/uproar-in-france-over-video-of-woman-marie-laguerre-hit-by-harasser-in-paris-street

—— '"They Don't See Us as Human": Women Speak out on France's Harassment Problem' *The Guardian* (3 August 2018), www.theguardian.com/world/2018/aug/03/they-just-dont-see-us-as-human-women-speak-out-on-frances-harassment-problem

Wittgenstein, Ludwig, Anscombe, GEM (trans), *Philosophical Investigations*, 1st edn (Oxford, Basil Blackwell, 1953)

Wolff, Robert, 'There's nobody here but us persons' in Gould, Carol and Wartofsky, Marx, (eds), *Women and Philosophy: Toward a Theory of Liberation* (New York, Putnam, 1976)

Wyles, Lilian, *A Woman at Scotland Yard* (London, Faber & Faber, 1952)

Yale, David, 'Matthew Hale', *Encyclopaedia Britannica* online version

Zaher, Claudia, 'When a Woman's Marital Status Determined her Legal Status: A Research Guide on the Common Law Doctrine of Coverture' (2002) 94 *Law Library Journal* 459

Zedner, Lucia and Roberts, Julian V (eds), *Principles and Values in Criminal Law and Justice: Essays in Honour of Andrew Ashworth* (Oxford, Oxford University Press, 2012)

INDEX

www.ingramcontent.com/pod-product-compliance
Lightning Source LLC
Chambersburg PA
CBHW050434280326
41932CB00013BA/2111